Romantic Days and Nights® Series

ROMANTIC

DAYS AND NIGHTS® IN

ATLANTA

ROMANTIC DIVERSIONS
IN AND AROUND THE CITY

by Carol and Dan Thalimer

The
Globe
Pequot
Press

OLD SAYBROOK, CONNECTICUT

ALSO BY CAROL AND DAN THALIMER

Family Adventure Guide: Georgia
Quick Escapes™ Atlanta

Copyright ©1999 by Carol and Dan Thalimer

Cover photo: Terri Froelich/Index Stock Imagery
Cover and text design by Lana Mullen
Illustrations by Maryann Dubé

Romantic Days and Nights is a registered trademark of The Globe Pequot Press.

Library of Congress Cataloging-in-Publication Data
Thalimer, Carol.
    Romantic days and nights in Atlanta : romantic diversions in and around the city / by Carol and Dan Thalimer. — 1st ed.
        p.   cm. — (Romantic days and nights series)
    Includes index.
    ISBN 0-7627-0202-8
    1. Atlanta (Ga.)—Guidebooks.   I. Thalimer, Dan.   II. Title.   III. Series.
F294.A83T46   1998
917.58'2310443—dc21

                                                                        98-46677
                                                                            CIP

Manufactured in the United States of America
First Edition/First Printing

To Laura Strom—
the editor with the patience of a saint

ACKNOWLEDGMENTS

We want to thank the following for their advice about what to include in this book: Brandy O'Quinn of the Atlanta Convention and Visitors Bureau for her extensive help; Chandler Haydon and Barbara Daniell of Georgia Department of Industry, Trade and Tourism for their personal favorites; Maizie Hale, Melissa Libby, and Rafih Benjoullen for their invaluable recommendations concerning restaurants and lodgings: Mr. Atlanta—Franklin Garrett and Pete Bonner for historical advice; Bill Schemmell for guided tours of Decatur, Virginia–Highland, and East Atlanta; director Ned Rifkin, Angela Kingerey, and the curators at the High Museum; the production staff at the Alliance Theater; Hilda Wiggs for information about roses; *Atlanta Magazine* for permission to use several of their "Best of Atlanta" lists; Dan Spinella for his gentle editing; and all our friends, neighbors, acquaintances, and co-workers who shared their romantic fantasies with us.

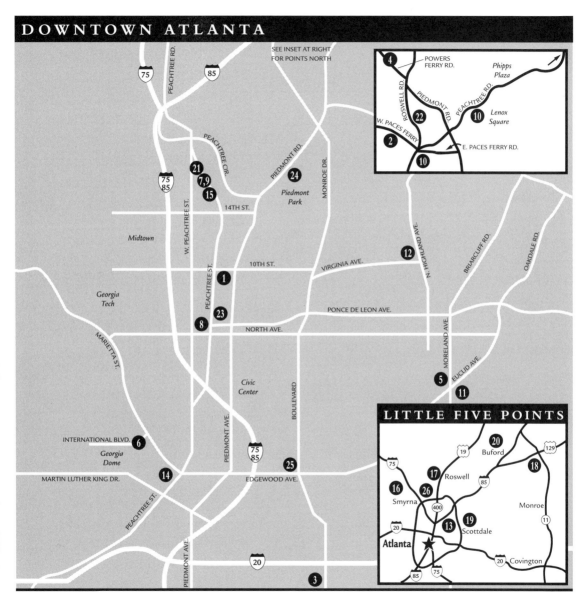

DOWNTOWN ATLANTA

SEE INSET AT RIGHT
FOR POINTS NORTH

POWERS FERRY RD.
Phipps Plaza
ROSWELL RD.
PIEDMONT RD.
PEACHTREE RD.
W. PACES FERRY
Lenox Square
E. PACES FERRY RD.

PEACHTREE RD.
PEACHTREE CIR.
PIEDMONT RD.
MONROE DR.
W. PEACHTREE ST.
PEACHTREE ST.

Piedmont Park

14TH ST.

Midtown

10TH ST.
VIRGINIA AVE.

Georgia Tech

PONCE DE LEON AVE.

NORTH AVE.

MARIETTA ST.

N. HIGHLAND AVE.
BRIARCLIFF RD.
OAKDALE RD.
MORELAND AVE.
EUCLID AVE.

Civic Center

BOULEVARD

INTERNATIONAL BLVD.

Georgia Dome

PIEDMONT AVE.

MARTIN LUTHER KING DR.

EDGEWOOD AVE.

PEACHTREE ST.

PIEDMONT AVE.

LITTLE FIVE POINTS

Buford
Roswell
Smyrna
Monroe
Scottdale
Atlanta
Covington

Numbers on map correspond to itinerary numbers (see Table of Contents).

CONTENTS

[*Contents*]

The prices and rates listed in this guidebook were confirmed at press time. We recommend, however, that you call establishments before traveling to obtain current information.

Help Us Keep This Guide Up to Date

Every effort has been made by the authors and editors to make this guide as accurate and useful as possible. However, many things can change after a guide is published—establishments close, phone numbers change, facilities come under new management, etc.

We would love to hear from you concerning your experiences with this guide and how you feel it could be made better and be kept up to date. While we may not be able to respond to all comments and suggestions, we'll take them to heart and we'll make certain to share them with the authors. Please send your comments and suggestions to the following address:

The Globe Pequot Press
Reader Response/Editorial Department
P.O. Box 833
Old Saybrook, CT 06475

Or you may e-mail us at:

editorial@globe-pequot.com

Thanks for your input, and happy travels!

*I*n Atlanta, every day can be Valentine's Day, your birthday, and anniversaries all rolled into one if you're with the one you love (whether your relationship is newly in bloom or your love is a perennial affair that has lasted fifty years). There's more to romance than champagne, roses, and chocolates—although such accoutrements are welcome accompaniments to any fantasy weekend in Atlanta—so let the city's other attractions draw you in to its excitement.

When it comes to the tender emotions, Atlanta is true to its southern roots, passing up the merely ostentatious for a more subtle, understated flavor. To the very casual observer, the city and its people may appear to be very similar to hundreds of other modern-day cities and their residents. That's because these skeptics haven't bothered or had time to explore beyond the surface glitz of the shiny newness Atlanta radiates as the fastest growing city in the country. (Although the city celebrated its 150th anniversary in 1998, the towering skyline is less than thirty years old.) Because everyone can't be as lucky as we've been to live here for two decades (nearly the entire duration of our relationship) and to participate in Atlanta's love affair with life, we want to share our amorous discoveries with you.

If one takes the time to think about it, how can Atlanta—the city Scarlett and Rhett made so famous with their tempestuous relationship, the city that rose from the ashes to earn the sobriquet "the city too busy to hate"—be anything other than one of the most romantic cities in America? Although the delicious confections of colorful, ruffled hoop skirts, parasols, and picture hats once worn by demure southern belles, and the suave, sophisticated top hats, frock coats, and ivory-handled walking sticks sported by worldly southern gentleman may be long gone, the patina of Old South moonlight and magnolias lingers. Antebellum homes still proudly endure on streets over which canopies of ancient trees meet.

Not by accident is Atlanta known as the Capital of the New South—with its soaring skyscrapers and contemporary sports facilities. The city has managed to retain the charm of the quintessential southern city, where every day and everywhere we turn we find reminders of romance. We refer not only to the love between man and woman, but to the love of ideals: looking forward as well as back, perpetuating the fact (not the myth) of southern hospitality, embracing adventure with exuberance.

Atlanta's exploits have ranged from recovering from devastation few other American cities have experienced (the purposeful burning of the city during the Civil War and an accidental conflagration at the turn of the century) to the quest of continually rebuilding and redefining itself, to being a forerunner in an ongoing worldwide movement (for civil rights), to hosting such world-famous events as the Super Bowl and the 1996 Centennial Olympic Summer Games. In addition, the city has created sophisticated architecture, an internationally renowned symphony orchestra, and many and varied cultural arts organizations.

Atlanta's climate is divine, with mild winters, long springs and falls, and usually much milder summers than one would expect—drawing lovers outside year-round. Flowers bloom throughout the year, adding to the sentimental ambience. In addition to several major parks, deeply shaded and profusely landscaped pocket parks and corporate campuses are delightful oases in a city where it seems that time can stand still or return to the grandeur of a former time—quiet, almost private places where you can lose yourselves in each other. Atlanta provides numerous places where active couples can hike, bike, jog, in-line skate, ride horseback, or play tennis or golf year-round as well.

Water seems to attract the dreamer in all of us, and unfortunately our fair city is one of the few first-class municipalities in the world that is neither on a coast nor a major navigable river—a negative we must admit. But all is not lost! Although we don't have a beautifully romantic shoreline or an active commercial riverfront to focus on, the shallow, languid Chattahoochee River meanders through the metropolitan area, providing endless opportunities for fishing, canoeing, kayaking, and rafting. Trails along the shoreline invite lovers to stroll along the river hand in hand or to enjoy a picnic along its banks. Several restaurants overlook the river and provide secluded places for dinner or drinks.

Atlantans themselves are a mixed bag. Many are transplants, as we are—moved here by their corporations, but then staying (even turning down transfers or changing jobs) because they love the city so much. The population is on the whole young and active, but even the affectionately spoofed "Damn Yankees" (Yankees are northerners who come to visit; Damn Yankees are those who come and won't leave) are caught up in the feelings of gentility the city fosters. The Civil War—also known as the War of Northern Aggression or the Recent Unpleasantness—is not forgotten, but in contrast to the Atlanta of that sad period, this is a boisterous young city that is growing by leaps and bounds. Whether native or transplant, Atlantans are extremely friendly—a trait that was praised worldwide during the Olympics. In fact, the hospitable Ambassador Corps foot patrol developed during the Olympics to aid visitors in getting around downtown was so successful it has become a permanent feature.

In addition to staying in cozy or sophisticated, often historic, bed-and-breakfasts or swanky modern high-rise hotels and touring the city's many attractions, lovers can take a horse-and-carriage ride around downtown; fly a kite in Piedmont Park; soar above the city in a hot-air balloon; drift down the Chattahoochee River in a raft; tickle their toes (or depending on what they're wearing, get their whole bodies) in the Centennial Olympic Park Fountain of Rings; stroll hand in hand through an art museum; gaze into each other's eyes across a candlelit table in a secluded corner of an elegant restaurant; enjoy a jug of wine, a loaf of bread, and each other at a picnic on the banks of a river or lake; and much, much more.

With no natural boundaries—oceans, rivers, or mountains to stem its growth—Atlanta continues to grow unchecked in all directions. The concept of neighborhoods versus nearby towns is extremely blurred as the city grows ever-outward, gobbling up entire towns. In this book, when we talk about Atlanta, we're talking about Greater Atlanta, an eight-county area that extends in a circle with a radius more than 40 miles from downtown. We include such true neighborhoods within the city limits as downtown, Midtown, Buckhead, Little Five

Points, and Virginia-Highland, but also separate municipalities such as Decatur, which is inside the I–285 perimeter highway, and Marietta and Roswell, which are outside the perimeter.

As we've found out from personal experience, Atlanta is a great place to be in love. Every day we're presented with another display of beauty and excitement. You have almost no alternative but to participate in the romance of this great city.

We don't have any preconceived notions that couples who read this book are limited to the young and newly in love, so we've also included senior citizen admission prices to attractions in addition to the regular price of admission. We also don't assume that all romantic couples are heterosexual. In the course of researching the material for this guide, we've talked to couples of all ages, religions, and sexual orientations and have included romantic ideas for all of them.

So read this guide, make your plans and reservations, pack your suitcases, and discover for yourselves the seduction of Atlanta. And when you finally have to drag yourselves away to return home, someone will surely say, "Y'all come back now, hear!"

THE ITINERARIES

Love is found anywhere that two like-minded people share stimulating experiences. We've tried to offer suggestions that are obviously romantic, as well as some that may seem offbeat at first glance, itineraries that are luxurious as well as economical. Each sentimental travel plan is based on some theme, whether it's history, music, art, sports, or a neighborhood. These tender agendas, which are designed for Atlantans in love and out-of-towners seeking romance, are only road maps to passion, so feel free to give your fantasies free reign and personalize these itineraries.

USING THIS BOOK

We've devised most of these itineraries presuming that you'll be getting away for an amorous holiday on a Friday through Sunday or on two of those days. If you're residents with days off during the week, or out-of-towners lucky enough to linger in Atlanta several weekdays before or after a convention or business trip, you may have to make some adjustments in these itineraries, but be aware, most special reduced-rate hotel packages aren't available during the week.

Attractions, restaurants, hotels, nightspots, prices, hours of operation, and other details were correct at press time, but they are always subject to change on a moment's notice. In fact, the old saying that the only thing that's constant is change is particularly accurate in relation to the restaurant, hospitality, and tourism businesses. Be sure to call ahead to verify times and ensure availability.

For those fortunate enough to live in greater Atlanta or able to spend additional days on holiday, almost any of these itineraries can be linked together very nicely. For example, the Midtown itinerary "Atlanta's Cultural Heart" is a natural to combine with the visual arts itinerary, "A Feast for the Eye," as well as the musical arts itinerary, "Let Your Hearts Sing." So before you plan a longer trip, read through this book to find itineraries that make good soulmates.

GETTING HERE AND GETTING AROUND

We assume that most weekend visitors to Atlanta will be driving in from around the state or the Southeast. If, however, you're flying in, Atlanta Hartsfield International Airport brings thousands of visitors to the city every day from all parts of the globe. In fact, the airport is consistently in the top three busiest airports in the country. Five domestic and one international terminal (served by every major U.S. airline and dozens of international airlines) are linked with each other and the main terminal by an efficient subway system. The airport is linked to downtown—only fifteen minutes away via a rapid rail line of the city's fine transit system, the Metropolitan Atlanta Rapid Transit Authority (MARTA), and other parts of the city primarily inside the I–285 perimeter highway. MARTA includes north-south and east-west rail lines and numerous bus routes. One-way bus and rail fares are $1.50 and include transfers. Many downtown and some outlying hotels offer free shuttle services from the airport, or you can take a cab. Unless, however, you're going to remain in a very confined area, such as downtown or Midtown, we recommend that you rent a car. All the major car rental services have counters at the airport.

AMTRAK (168 Peachtree Street, 404–872–7245) has one train arriving at the Brookwood Station, located between Midtown and Buckhead, from Washington, D.C., and cities to the northeast of Atlanta in the evening; another arrives from New Orleans and cities west of Atlanta in the morning. There are no car rental facilities or van services at the station. You'll have to take a cab to your hotel, and since only a few cabs meet the trains, you may have to call for one.

Three interstate highways intersect in downtown Atlanta: I–20, which runs east-west; I–75, which runs northwest-southeast, and I–85, which runs northeast-southwest. Two of them, I–75 and I–85, merge and run together for several miles through downtown. This section of highway is known locally as the I–75/I–85 Connector or simply the Connector. We will refer to it frequently in giving directions to and from downtown.

We've previously referred to Greater Atlanta's immense size. As a result, although some attractions are located close to public transportation, to reach many others you'll need a car— either your own or a rental. Also, because some of these attractions are far flung, if traffic is particularly bad, you may not be able to see all of those we describe in the time allotted. Atlanta seems to have a love affair with the automobile, and her residents are reputed to drive more than the citizens of any other American city (ninety million miles a day and thirty minutes to two hours one way commuting to work or play), so if some of our suggestions seem like a long way to drive to readers who are residents of small towns or more compact cities such as New York or Boston, remember, the time involved is simply a normal part of life to Atlantans. Don't let perceived distance deter you from enjoying many of Atlanta's pleasures.

We give detailed directions to every attraction in every itinerary for those unfamiliar with the city; however, we strongly urge you to get a map of the city. Be fully prepared to make changes in your route in the event of road construction or recently added one-way streets. Atlantans who are enjoying playing hookey in their own backyard can, of course, simply ignore all the directions.

Atlantic area codes: Initially visitors and newcomers may be confused by telephoning in Atlanta. Although none of these calls is long distance, you must dial the complete ten-digit number (even if calling between two numbers in the same area code) no matter where you are within the metro area because there are three area codes—a result of massive growth, fax lines, cellular phones, and the like. In general, but with a few exceptions, the area inside the I–285 perimeter highway, including Atlanta and Decatur, is assigned the 404 area code. A huge area outside I–285 stretching as far south as Newnan and as far north as Lake Lanier uses the 770 area code. However, to make things even more complicated, new numbers in both areas are being assigned the 678 area code. Therefore, it's even possible for two numbers at the same address to have different area codes. Pay phones cost thirty-five cents and often don't give change, so you need to have the correct amount if you want to avoid paying extra for the call.

FOR MORE INFORMATION

The **Atlanta Convention and Visitors Bureau** (233 Peachtree Street, N.E., Suite 100, 800-ATLANTA; Web site: www.acvb.com) operates several **ACVB Information Centers**: **Hartsfield Atlanta International Airport** (5000 North Terminal—PRW—West Cross Over), open Monday–Friday 9:00 A.M.–9:00 P.M., Saturday 9:00 A.M.–6:00 P.M., Sunday 12:30–6:00 P.M.; **Georgia World Congress Center** (285 International Boulevard) operates only during conventions; **Lenox Square Mall** (3393 Peachtree Road), open Tuesday–Sunday 11:00 A.M.–5:00 P.M., Sunday noon–6:00 P.M.; and **Underground Atlanta** (65 Upper Alabama Street; 404–222–6688), open Monday–Saturday 10:00 A.M.–6:00 P.M., Sunday noon–6:00 P.M. The Underground location features an interactive cultural exhibit that lists sixty cultural organizations categorized as theater, dance, music, heritage and history, arts festivals, science and nature, visual arts, community arts centers; it gives a fifteen-second video presentation, a calendar, map locations, and directions.

RESTAURANT GROUPS

We're terribly distressed that we weren't able to include anywhere near all of the wonderful romantic restaurants in Atlanta. If for some reason you aren't able to or don't want to go to a restaurant we've suggested in an itinerary, you can't ever go wrong with any of the eateries from these groups: **Buckhead Life Restaurant Group** (primarily expensive and formal), which includes 103 West, Atlanta Fish Company, Buckhead Bread Company, Buckhead Diner, Chops, Corner Cafe, NAVA, Pano's Food Shop, Pano & Paul's, Pricci, and Veni, Vidi, Vici; **Cartel Restaurants** (moderate, semiformal), which includes Azio, The Lodge Buckhead, Nickiemoto's, Otto's, and Peachtree Cafe; **Metrotainment** (moderate, informal), which includes Cheyenne Grill, Cowtippers, Einstein's, Joe's on Juniper, Martini Club, and Metropoli, A Village Cafe; **Peasants and Mick's Restaurants** (semiformal to formal, moderate to expensive), which include Country Place, Dailey's, Mick's, Peasant, Peasant Uptown, Pleasant Peasant, and the Public House.

SUPER ROMANTIC OR JUST PLAIN FUN RESTAURANTS

American: Bacchanalia, Bone's, Chops and the Lobster Bar, Chow, Coohill's—A Steakhouse and Bar, Encore at the Fox, McArthur's, The Palm, Pano & Paul's, Peachtree Cafe, Winfield's

Continental: 103 West, Carbo's Cafe, Nikolai's Roof, Seeger's

French and French Country: Anis Cafe/Bistro, Brasserie Le Coze, Ciboulette

Seafood: The Atlanta Fish Market, Squid Roe Coastal Cuisine

Southern: Blue Ridge Grill

Southwestern: Georgia Grill

Vegetarian: Cafe Sunflower

THE OLD SOUTH

ITINERARY 1
Three days and two nights

IN SCARLETT'S FOOTSTEPS

MARGARET MITCHELL'S ATLANTA

*M*oonlight and magnolias, hoop skirts and parasols, Greek Revival mansions and grand balls, a fiery war between brothers, and torrid love affairs—these are stereotypes about the Old South, quite often developed from reading the timeless classic *Gone With the Wind* (*GWTW*) by native Atlantan Margaret Mitchell or from seeing the ever-popular movie made from the book. Her fictional account of the Civil War and its effects on Atlanta and the South started people all over the world dreaming about the mystical and romantic Old South—few realizing that true conditions didn't always match those in Mitchell's imagination. Visitors from all over the world come to Atlanta fruitlessly searching for Tara, Twelve Oaks, and other landmarks, not understanding that they never existed.

That doesn't mean, however, that Atlanta doesn't pay homage to the story. You and your loved one can re-create the tempestuous relationship of Scarlett and Rhett during this exciting weekend in Atlanta by visiting many of the sites that inspired Mitchell's fictional Atlanta. Y'all will stay in historic lodgings and dine on innovative New South cuisine served at fine restaurants that preserve the ambience of the Old South.

Practical notes: This chapter involves a bit of travel around the outskirts of Atlanta. Get a good map of the city (from the ACVB; call 800–ATLANTA) and use it—preferably before you start out. Although the old saying goes "real men don't ask directions," be an exception if you have any problems. The Fox Theater is across the street from your hotel, the Georgian Terrace, and when there is an event at the theater, theater-goers park at the hotel's parking deck. Although as a guest of the hotel, you are assured a parking place, you could get tied up in the traffic jam getting in and out, so try to time your arrivals and departures at periods other than the busiest. Finally, if you want Pete Bonner to give you a personalized tour of Jonesboro (see p. 9), make arrangements well ahead of your visit.

Romance at a Glance

♥ *Make a pilgrimage to "The Dump."*

♥ *OD on GWTW memorabilia at the Road to Tara Museum.*

♥ *Search for Tara on Pete Bonner's Historical and Hysterical Tour of Jonesboro.*

♥ *Tread the grounds of Stately Oaks Plantation*

♥ *Rock on Pittypat's Porch with a mint julep.*

♥ *Feast on a plantation dinner at Anthony's.*

DAY ONE: MORNING

What possessed Margaret Mitchell to write her opus about the excesses of the Old South and the tragedy of the Civil War? You and your Scarlett or Rhett will find out when you begin your weekend of *GWTW* immersion at "The Dump," the **Margaret Mitchell House** (990 Peachtree Street; 404–249–7012; admission $6.00; $5.00 for seniors)—Mitchell's small apartment in the turn-of-the-century, three-story, Tudor Revival Crescent Apartments. Historically, Atlanta has continuously risen above adversity. Restoring this house and opening it as a museum dedicated to Mitchell's memory could well be an metaphor for Atlanta's story. Talk about a phoenix rising from the ashes—this house is in its third reincarnation! It was almost completely destroyed by fire (arson?) twice during restoration. Who would want to burn down this historical icon? Could it have been Mitchell herself? When the author died, she directed that her childhood home on Peachtree Street be torn down and all her papers be destroyed because she didn't want a shrine to herself and her work. Perhaps her ghost was displeased that The Dump was being turned into a monument and caused it to self-immolate. Serendipitously, however, both fires failed to reach the Mitchell apartment, and the third effort to revitalize the house was successful, so you can now visit the place where the author labored for several years on her more-than-one-thousand-page epic. In answer to our original question, she started it as a lark when she was bedridden with an ankle injury and arthritis. Her husband, John Marsh, said he was tired of lugging books home from the library for her to read, so he got her a typewriter and suggested she begin a new career.

Mitchell and Marsh lived in this tiny, dark apartment, which today contains original Mitchell pieces and appropriate period furnishings. Among the treasures is the typewriter the author used to transcribe her handwritten manuscript and her 1937 Pulitzer Prize. The remainder of the house and the adjacent visitors center contain exclusive photographs and archival displays about the book, the movie, the author's life, and Atlanta during her lifetime. It also shows a film entitled *It May Not Be Tara*. The museum shop carries a great variety of *Gone With the Wind* memorabilia.

Mitchell was born in 1900 in Atlanta—a seventh-generation Georgian who didn't learn that the South lost the war until she was 10. A saucy tomboy, known to her friends as Peggy, Mitchell led an active life. The similarities between herself and her heroine Scarlett quickly become evident—although Scarlett could be described as the bad twin to Peggy's good twin. (Mitchell claimed that Scarlett was based on her imperious grandmother, Annie Fitzgerald Stephens.) Peggy often visited her grandparents in rural Georgia, near Folsom Road and Tara Road south of the Atlanta. Her grandfather's story and those of his friends and neighbors who suffered and survived the Civil War were told over and over to Peggy, and she was in awe of their "gumption." It was only natural that she situated her novel in this area and drew from people she knew to create her memorable characters. (More about that later.)

Gone With the Wind devotees will want to make a pilgrimage to Margaret Mitchell's grave at **Oakland Cemetery** (248 Oakland Avenue, S.E.; 404–688–2107; free). The author shares a simple headstone with her husband, so look for Marsh rather than Mitchell. The plot is beautifully tended and often ablaze with colorful flowers appropriate to the season. As is a Southern burial custom, cedars are planted at the four corners of the family plot. Visit the Civil War section as well.

Spend as long as you like at the cemetery but leave time to check into your hotel, get settled, freshen up.

DAY ONE: AFTERNOON

Stay where the stars stayed and attended the glittering gala cast party for the 1939 premiere of the movie—the luxuriously restored **Georgian Terrace, a Grand Heritage Hotel** (659 Peachtree Street; 404–897–1991; $88–$323). The hotel's connection with the movie started even earlier. In 1935, Mitchell met Harold Latham of Macmillan Publishing at the hotel to deliver her manuscript, which filled sixty manila envelopes. Until that time, no one but her husband had seen the manuscript.

Built in 1911 and listed on the National Register of Historic Places, the Georgian Terrace consists of the handsome original ten-story building and a new nineteen-story wing connected by a stunning atrium. The hotel features 320 elegant junior, one-, two-, and three-bedroom suites. For this special weekend, the hardest thing you'll have to do is decide which size suite you want. You'll feel as decadent as we always do whenever we stay in a suite. For those couples addicted to exercise, the hotel boasts a large fitness center and a rooftop lap pool. Located at the very southern edge of Midtown, the hotel is extremely convenient to downtown as well. A MARTA rapid rail station is only a block away.

Classic Couples: Margaret Mitchell and John Marsh

Peggy and John were a vivacious, fun-loving couple, and The Dump became an enclave for bohemian Atlanta, a place where swarms of friends gathered constantly for drinks and lively conversation. Not only did Peggy and John sleep in their bedroom, they ate their meals there as well. John did most of the cooking. It is reported that he would fry chicken by shaking it in flour while standing at the edge of the bed, then toss it into the frying pan in the adjacent kitchen—spraying hot oil everywhere. Despite his unorthodox cooking methods, Peggy swore his chicken was the best she had ever tasted. Their perfect union was shattered on August 11, 1949, when she was struck by a car driven by an off-duty cab driver as they crossed Peachtree Street. She died five days later. John died of a heart attack only three years later, and they were reunited at Oakland Cemetery.

In addition to a fully equipped kitchen, every suite contains a large living/dining area, a sizable bathroom, and televisions in the living room and bedroom. Tastefully furnished in traditional style, any one of the suites is a perfect place for a couple to unveil their deepest secrets and fantasies. You surely don't want to do any cooking during your romantic tryst, but you can save some money by picking up some snacks and libations to keep in the refrigerator.

Wander through the historic areas of the Grand Dame of Peachtree Street to admire the marble floors, towering marble and wood columns, Palladian and French windows, spiral staircases, stained-glass skylight, gold-colored sconces, intricate plaster moldings, bas-relief artwork, crystal chandeliers, elegant latticework, and large murals. Don't miss the ornate Grand Ballroom, where the premiere party was held. Remember that Mitchell, Clark Gable, Vivian Leigh, David O. Selznick, and many others partied here ahead of you. You can almost hear their laughter and the clink of fine crystal champagne glasses.

♥ *The book's last chapter was written first; the first chapter, last.*

♥ *GWTW sold one million copies in the first one hundred days.*

♥ *Printed in twenty-four languages, it is the best-selling book of all time after the Bible.*

♥ *Movie rights were purchased for an unprecedented $50,000.*

♥ *Premiered in Atlanta, December 14, 1939.*

♥ *Fifty thousand hardcover and a quarter of a million paperback copies continue to be sold annually.*

♥ *More than four thousand people were involved in making the movie, which cost $4 million to complete.*

♥ *GWTW won ten Academy Awards.*

DAY ONE: EVENING

Dinner

Naturally some Atlanta entrepreneurs capitalize on the *GWTW* obsession, and you're going to spend a pleasant, romantic evening at a restaurant whose inspiration came from the book. Readers and movie fans will remember Scarlett's funny, flighty Aunt Pittypat, with whom Scarlett lived in Atlanta for awhile. The restaurant **Pittypat's Porch** (24 International Boulevard, N.W.; 404–525–8228; expensive; reservations suggested) has been a downtown stop for celebrities for more than thirty years. Step through the unassuming street entrance and be transported to the time before the Civil War.

The restaurant is actually one level down from the street, and the entrance area is designed as an interior, rocker-filled, wraparound balcony, which resembles the porch of

Pittypat's house. Sit a spell in one of the rockers and sip something cold—a mint julep brings the Old South wafting back. After you've imbibed, escort your Scarlett or Rhett downstairs to the newly renovated dining room, where exposed bricks walls, pristine table linens, traditional furnishings, period art, crystal, and china complete the transformation to antebellum Atlanta. The updated menu focuses on regional cuisine, including such dishes as venison, Savannah crab cakes, and Twelve Oaks barbecue. For dessert it's hard to choose between the bread pudding and the peach cobbler, so get one of each and share them.

Nightlife

If you're not ready to turn in yet, walk or drive to the **Hyatt Regency Atlanta** (265 Peachtree Street; 404–577–1234), ride the elevator to the top to the **Polaris Lounge,** a revolving lounge in a blue UFO-like bubble, for drinks and a splendid 365-degree view of modern-day downtown Atlanta. It's a great place to replay your day and make plans for tomorrow and the rest of your lives. After you've had all the Atlanta charm you want for one day, return to the privacy of your suite to create a little amorous ambience of your own.

DAY TWO: MORNING

Breakfast

Emulate your hero and heroine's decadent lifestyle by sleeping in. Enjoy a leisurely breakfast at **Alon's on the Terrace** at the hotel (404–724–0444). If the weather is nice, sit outside and watch the world go by. Then continue your *GWTW* fantasy by driving to the visitors center at the depot in Jonesboro. Mitchell's impressions of Civil War plantation life were heavily influenced by her many trips to Fayette and Clayton Counties just south of the city. You'll retrace her footsteps in historic Jonesboro. Although you have the option of taking a self-guided driving tour using a free brochure or a self-guided tour using an audiotape narrated by historian Pete Bonner ($6), both of which you can pick up from the **Jonesboro Depot Welcome Center** (104 North Main Street; 770–478–4800 or 800–662–STAY), we strongly recommend that you make prior arrangements with Pete to take one of his guided **Historical and Hysterical Tours** (471 Parkwood Way; 770–477–8864; $15). His vast store of trivia about Margaret Mitchell, *GWTW,* the Civil War, and Jonesboro, combined with his infectious earthiness, will add zest to your day.

Before you leave the depot, however, visit the **Road to Tara Museum** (770–210–1017; admission $3.00) located there. Only a small part of one of the largest permanent collections of *Gone With the Wind* memorabilia in the world is displayed. Among the most treasured mementos are signed first editions; foreign editions; a large mural of scenes from the book and movie; reproductions of costumes from the movie, including the famous green outfit made from Tara's velvet draperies and the slinky red dress with feather boa that convinced Scarlett's friends and neighbors that she was indeed a scarlet woman; examples of collectible character dolls produced between 1937 and the present; artifacts from Atlanta battlefields and Civil War soldiers; and the history and maps of 1860 Georgia. In the gift shop you can purchase an astounding array of *GWTW* souvenirs and collectibles.

DAY TWO: AFTERNOON

Lunch

Butch's (192 Highway 54; 770–478–2586; inexpensive) is a good, old-fashioned, down-home eatery where you can get a rib-sticking lunch of Southern comfort foods—fried chicken, chicken and dumplings, greens, cornbread, and sweet tea all for $5.00.

Whether you tour on your own or with Pete, you'll see the following significant Civil War sites and places that inspired *GWTW* in Jonesboro. Visit the **Patrick**

Clebourne Confederate Cemetery (Johnson and McDonough Streets, no phone; free), where the remains of from 600 to 1,000 Confederate soldiers are buried. Immediately after the battle of Jonesboro, they were buried where they fell and only moved to this location in 1872. Symbolically, the unmarked headstones are arrayed in the shape of a Confederate battle flag.

Stately Oaks Plantation (100 Carriage Lane at Jodeco Road, 770–473–0197; $5.00), which was built in 1839 4 miles north of its present location, is one of the oft-mentioned inspirations for Mitchell's work. It was a landmark for both Union and Confederate troops, and Yankee soldiers camped in the fields around the house during the Battle of Jonesboro. Although the stately house does have simple white columns, it is not a stereotypical grandiose Greek Revival. The agricultural acres are long gone, but the house is still surrounded by outbuildings, including its original log kitchen house, Juddy's Country Store, and the Bethel schoolhouse. Learn about life in early 1800s rural Georgia and how genteel Mrs. McCord dressed down Union soldiers who invaded her home.

Surrounded by ancient trees, **Ashley Oaks** (144 College Street; 770–478–8986; $5.00), a redbrick mansion with graceful verandas, was Mitchell's inspirations for *GWTW.* Lovingly restored, the house is elegantly furnished in a style appropriate to the mid-1800s. More than one million handmade bricks were required to build the house in 1879; the exterior walls are twenty-four-inches thick, the interior walls are twelve inches thick, and each of the downstairs rooms rests on its own foundation.

The whole downtown area of Jonesboro appears much as it did before the Civil War because although the town was torched, the brick exteriors of the structures withstood the fire. With their interiors restored, the historic buildings along Main and McDonough Streets house charming shops purveying European and American antiques, *Gone With the Wind* memorabilia, special collectibles, Georgia gifts, and other extraordinary finds. Perhaps you'll find a memento to take home.

Among other important sites in Jonesboro are the **1898 Courthouse** (121 South McDonough Street) where Mitchell spent long hours researching local records while she was writing *Gone With the Wind*. The 1869 jail (125 King Street, 770–473–0197; contribution) houses the **Clayton County Historical Museum.** Through a large display window at the rear of the **Pope Dickson and Son Funeral Home** (168 North McDonough Street), you can see the ornate hearse that in 1883 carried the body of Alexander H. Stephens, vice president of the Confederacy and later governor of Georgia, to his final resting place at his Crawfordville home. (This is the only drive-up museum we know of.)

Sashay around Jonesboro to your hearts' content. When you've had your fill of *GWTW* history, return to your hotel to create some history of your own.

Day Two: Evening

Dinner

For a truly elegant, intimate evening, in an authentic plantation house, dine at **Anthony's Plantation Restaurant** in Buckhead (3109 Piedmont Road, 404–262–7379; expensive). The 1797 plantation house, which was moved to these ample wooded grounds, is a quiet oasis in busy Buckhead. Anthony's manages to pull off a unique combination of Old South elegance and New South flair. Twelve unique dining rooms, many of them with open hearth fireplaces, are exquisitely furnished with beautiful eighteenth-century pieces. Named one of America's "Top Ten Restaurants" by the American Academy of Restaurant Science, Anthony's serves a variety of seafood, game, beef, pork, buffalo, lamb, and duck entrees. The specialties of the house include Veal Anthony, Chef Brant's Antebellum Surf and Turf, Southern Filet Mignon, and chateaubriand for two carved tableside. In addition, the restaurant boasts an excellent wine list and sinfully delicious desserts. Reservations are suggested.

Return to the Georgian Terrace and take the elevator to the rooftop where you'll get one of the best views in town of the Atlanta skyline. Relaxing with a nightcap there as you cuddle under the stars will prolong the magic.

DAY THREE: MORNING

Breakfast

Why not luxuriate by staying in bed late and ordering room service to enjoy in the privacy of your suite while the two of you further investigate each other? Although your suite has a dining area, doesn't breakfast in bed sound divine? You could even bring a bottle of champagne or two to keep in your refrigerator for these occasions and for your rooftop trysts.

If there's any shopping you failed to do yesterday, here's an opportunity to do it. Hint: There's a Road to Tara store at Underground Atlanta downtown, so if you've decided you can't live without some *GWTW* bauble you saw somewhere else, you can probably get it there. Take your time to return to the hustle and bustle of the twentieth century from the slower paced antebellum era because, as Scarlett would say, "fiddle-dee-dee," it's time to go home.

ITINERARY 2
Three days and two nights

THAT PYROMANIAC FROM THE NORTH
WHEN THE CIVIL WAR RAGED

*I*f you are history buffs and are particularly inflamed by the Civil War period, you'll lose yourselves in learning about the battle for Atlanta. Even if all you remember about the Civil War is seeing Atlanta torched in *Gone With the Wind,* you know the city figured prominently in that war, and that Atlanta's downfall meant disaster to the Confederacy. In fact, the loss of the city sealed the South's doom. In today's capital of the New South, where "The War" will never *really* be over, there are countless reminders of that great struggle— museums, restaurants, bed-and-breakfasts, private homes, and cemeteries all reflect the war's effects. Numerous encampments and reenactments during the year bring that fiery period to life. You and your sweetheart will trace the progression of the Battle of Atlanta as Union troops pillaged and burned their way from northern outposts to downtown. The biggest villain in the piece from a Southerner's point of view was Union General William Tecumseh Sherman, whose slash-and-burn policy left much of Georgia a smoking ruin. In a war variously known around the South as the War Between the States, the War of Northern Aggression, the War for Southern Independence, and more decorously the Recent (or Late) Unpleasantness, Sherman is considered the devil incarnate and is unkindly referred to as

"That Pyromaniac from the North." Despite the loss of more than 625,000 Americans and the untold suffering of countless other soldiers and civilians, the Civil War remains a period of intense interest to Americans, and it persists in retaining a romantic aura. Maybe we all want to see ourselves as Scarlett and Rhett. You'll have a chance to ignite your historic and personal passions by staying at a historic bed-and-breakfast and by dining at restaurants in historically significant buildings.

Practical Notes: Bring comfortable shoes because you will be visiting a lot of outdoor sites that require some walking. Pick up a detailed Atlanta map because you'll be exploring hither and yon on this tour as you relive some of the tumult and passion of that era.

Romance at a Glance

♥ *Fire up your imagination at the Atlanta History Center.*

♥ *Envision the cannons blazing at Kennesaw Mountain National Battlefield Park.*

♥ *Let the battle for Atlanta envelop you at the Atlanta Cyclorama and Civil War Museum.*

♥ *Set up headquarters at the Whitlock Inn.*

♥ *Warm up your romance in the Stone Kitchen of the 1848 House.*

DAY ONE: AFTERNOON

Immerse yourselves in this country's most fiery and tragic war while visiting the **Atlanta History Center** (130 West Paces Ferry Road N.W.; 404–814–4000; admission $7 to $10/$5 to $8 for seniors). Situated on thirty-three acres of woods and gardens in a tony residential Buckhead neighborhood, the history center includes a magnificent museum building with permanent and changing displays as well as an 1840s farmstead and a magnificent 1920s in-town mansion. (This chapter concentrates on the gargantuan "Turning Point: The American Civil War" exhibit at the museum. The other permanent displays are described in "Phoenix Rising," "In Scarlett's Footsteps," and "Full Bloom of Love.")

The heart and soul of the permanent Civil War exhibit is the DuBose Civil War Collection, the largest private collection of Civil War memorabilia in the country. More than 5,000 articles were collected by the father-and-son team, Beverly M. DuBose Jr. and Beverly M. DuBose III, and donated to the History Center in the 1980s. Uniforms, weapons, cooking gear, medical instruments, games, and other memorabilia represent the lives of common foot soldiers—both Johnny Rebs and Billy Yanks. Lift a filled backpack and rifle to get an idea of the burden these soldiers struggled under on a daily basis. Just remember though that you aren't hungry, tired, dirty, scared, or homesick. Particularly ponder the poignant love letters soldiers on both sides wrote to their wives and sweethearts. Most of us couldn't express ourselves as well today. The final section deals with the reunited nation's search for meaning in the tragedy and includes memorabilia from old soldiers' homes and battlefield reunions. The entire exhibit may reduce you to tears.

Because you're on the trail of history, we suggest that you stay in a historic bed-and-breakfast. The **Whitlock Inn** (57 Whitlock Avenue, Marietta; 770–428–1495; $85 to $125), although not built until the turn of the century, has the ambience of antebellum days. The owners explain that "here in Marietta we hold onto anything that's old, our houses, our furniture, our recipes, and our accents." Each of the five guest rooms features a private bath, working fireplace, queen- or twin-size beds, phone, TV, and ceiling fan. Check in and freshen up for dinner, but bank the embers of your hot romance until after dinner because you will be having a one-of-a-kind dining experience at one of Atlanta's most fashionable antebellum restaurants.

DAY ONE: EVENING

Dinner

As you and your loved one drive up the long tree-lined driveway to the distant white columns of the **1848 House** (780 South Cobb Drive; 770–428–1848; expensive), the mad modern world seeps away to be replaced by the epitome of grace and beauty of the wealthy pre–Civil War planter class. This gorgeous authentic plantation home, listed on National Register of Historic Places, was the site of a Civil War battle; it survived the war because it served as a Union hospital and because of Sherman's friendship with the owner. In contrast with the ten historically decorated dining rooms in the main house and the Old South formality of its three acres of gardens and grounds, the menu here emphasizes contemporary Southern cuisine.

Dinner this evening will be the ultimate romantic experience. Reserve the intimate Stone Kitchen for a completely private banquet for just the two of you. Located to the rear of the main house, the secluded historic building features a large fireplace and one table—perfect for lovers. Its rustic charm is enhanced by cooking gear and utensils of the period. If it's chilly, a cheerful fire will be roaring in the fireplace, casting just enough light to augment the candlelight and allow you to enjoy your repast and each other in flickering light. One unobtrusive waiter serves only you all evening. This is the perfect opportunity to propose if you aren't already wed or to exchange meaningful anniversary or other special gifts. The exciting menu runs the gamut from quail to venison acommpanied by exotic flourishes. There are a few Old South favorites like grits with the extra flair of smoky cheddar. Begin with the 1848 House signature soup: Charleston She-Crab. Desserts range from the ridiculous (shoo-fly pie) to the sublime (the trio plate of mousses).

After your gastronomic overindulgence, wend your way back to your own personal lovenest. If the weather is cool, light a fire in your fireplace and ignite your passions.

DAY TWO: MORNING

Breakfast

After a good night's sleep, rise and shine—but not too late. Fortify yourselves with the B&B's full Southern breakfast before today's rendezvous with history. Follow the Union's inexorable march toward Atlanta by visiting important sites in what are now the northwest suburbs.

One of the best-preserved battlefields in the country for you and your sweetheart to explore, **Pickett's Mill State Historic Site** in nearby Dallas (2640 Mount Tabor Road, 770–443–7850), was the site of a significant Confederate victory during the Atlanta campaign (actually one of the only victories). The visitors center has an excellent film about the battle and an impressive small museum. Any time you visit, you can choose one or all of the three self-guided loop tours of the battlefield. If you visit during the first or third weekend of the month, costumed reenacters present living history programs.

Your next stop is Kennesaw. In June 1864, after thwarting the Union advance at Pickett's Mill, Confederate General Joseph E. Johnston and his troops entrenched along the ridgetops of Big and Little Kennesaw Mountains north of Atlanta and held off the advance of Sherman's troops for two weeks. **Kennesaw Mountain National Battlefield Park** (900 Kennesaw Mountain Drive; 770–427–4686/7), which safeguards the hallowed grounds, is known for its particularly well-preserved earthworks and trenches. Begin at the visitors center at the foot of the mountain, which features an orientation program, exhibits, and a bookstore. Most folks then choose to hike to the top of the mountain. (The paths are paved although somewhat steep. During some seasons of the year, free shuttle buses offer alternative access to the summit.) Along the way, you'll pass troop movement maps, cannon emplacements, and historical markers. Once you reach the top, depending on the weather, there may be a stunning view of the downtown Atlanta skyline and faraway Stone Mountain. In all there are 16 additional miles of hiking trails. Among these heavily wooded acres are any number of secluded little spots that have beckoned couples throughout the years for a quiet tryst. We've been told that watching the moon rise from the top of the mountain with your sweetie is *the* most romantic thing to do in Atlanta.

Just north of Kennesaw, now incorporated into it, was the small town of Big Shanty from which one of the greatest adventures of the Civil War commenced. It was from here early in the war, when the Confederacy was mounting an attack on Chattanooga, that Union spy James Andrews and Union soldiers disguised in civilian clothes hijacked the train pulled by the locomotive the *General*. Their intent was to flee north to Chattanooga, tearing up track and burning bridges behind them to destroy supply lines to the Confederate army surrounding that city. Quick pursuit by the *General*'s conductor William Fuller using the locomotive *Texas*—running in reverse—foiled their plans, capturing the train after an 87-mile chase. A restored former cotton gin now provides a home for the *General*. Called the **Kennesaw Civil War Museum** (2829 Cherokee Street; 770–427–2117 or 800–742–6897), but known locally as the Big Shanty Museum, the archive also houses exhibits of Civil War artifacts, and you can watch scenes from the Disney movie *The Great Locomotive Chase*.

The quaint historic commercial buildings across the tracks from the museum house antiques shops, such as **By-gone Treasures** (2839 South Main Street; 770–428–2262), and crafts emporiums, such as **Rose Cottage** (3008 Cherokee Street, N.W.; 770–428–9255) and **Country Cottage Pine** (2237 Whitfield Place; 770–427–0076). Surplus items from the Civil War through the present, along with everything from antiques to junk, are waiting for you to paw over at **Wild Man's Civil War Surplus** (2879 South Main Street; 770–422–1785).

DAY TWO: AFTERNOON

Lunch

Fuel your flagging energy level with a casual lunch at **My Country Kitchen** (2740 Summers Street; 770–423–9448; inexpensive) where you can chow down on Southern comfort foods, such as fried chicken, greens, cornbread, and sweet tea. Don't eat too much though. You don't have time to nap before continuing your tour.

After lunch, you'll be exploring your home base of Marietta, which figured in the battle for Atlanta. Marietta was an important railroad town. Holding on to it was crucial if the Confederacy were to keep supplies flowing to its troops in Atlanta. During and after the battle at Kennesaw Mountain, soldiers from both sides were nursed in Marietta. When Sherman departed Marietta, he showed one of his earlier proclivities for being careless with fire, although not as extensively as he was later in Atlanta and south Georgia.

Continue your tour of Civil War hot spots by stopping at the **Marietta/Cobb Welcome Center and Visitors Bureau** located just off the square in the old Western and Atlantic passenger depot (Four Depot Street; 770–429–1115 or 800–835–0445) to pick up the brochure, *Cannonball Tour of Homes,* for a self-guided driving tour past many homes that were commandeered for use as headquarters or hospitals by both sides in the conflict and fortunately were spared Sherman's incendiary tendencies. All, however, are now private homes not open to the public. Several historic churches and a few commercial buildings are on the tour as well.

Before you begin your driving tour, however, go next door to the depot to the second floor of the old Kennesaw House, which was damaged in the war, to visit the **Marietta Museum of History** (One Depot Street, 770–528–0431 or 770–528–0430) where a room is devoted to "those people"—James Andrews and his raiders who stayed there the night before they hijacked the *General.* (For more information about the museum, see the Marietta chapter, "Love Squared.")

Among the places on the driving tour where you'll want to stop with your sweetheart are the **Confederate Cemetery** (Powder Springs Extension at Cemetery Street; no phone; free) and the **National Cemetery** (Washington Avenue at Cole Street). Marietta is one of the few towns in the country that has both. A Confederate Cemetery had been established in 1863 in Marietta for the burial of Southern soldiers. After the war in 1866, Confederate dead were removed from the Chickamauga and Atlanta battle sites and reburied in Marietta. The

Oakland Cemetery Birthday Bash

Have you ever heard of a cemetery that has an annual birthday party? Well, here's one that does and quite a shindig it is. Oakland Cemetery's active historical society sponsors a free birthday celebration every September with tours and storytelling by costumed guides, singing, refreshments, graves and mausoleums decorated in the opulent Victorian manner, birthday cake, and more. The birthday festivity revives the old custom of sharing one's past with loved ones by celebrating ancestors at an outing—usually a picnic—in the cemetery. Even if your weekend in Atlanta doesn't coincide with the birthday party, you can order a picnic from a caterer and have a romantic meal for just the two of you.

cemetery holds the remains of three thousand soldiers from fourteen states, including one thousand unknown dead. The Marietta Confederate Cemetery is the oldest Confederate cemetery in the country and the largest one south of Richmond. Today, the cemetery is a peaceful place where canopies of ancient trees shade simple headstones curving in wide arcs across the gentle slopes. It's a place for a quiet stroll with your honey. Other landmarks in the cemetery include a memorial arch, several state memorials, and the "Little Cannon," which was originally at the Georgia Military Institute in Marietta, taken to war when the cadets from the school enlisted en masse, captured by Union forces in Savannah in 1864, and finally brought to the cemetery in 1910.

The same year the Confederate dead were reburied in Marietta, a National Cemetery was developed on twenty-three acres donated by Henry Cole. Cole had originally tried to donate the land for use as a joint Confederate and National Cemetery in an effort to help heal the rift between the national government and the South. However, his idea of a joint cemetery was refused, so he consented to its use as a National Cemetery. More elegant and ostentatious than the smaller Confederate Cemetery, it is the final resting place of ten thousand Union soldiers of whom three thousand are unknown. Soldiers from all America's subsequent wars are buried there as well.

Continue your pyrotecnic weekend of shared exploration of Atlanta's Civil War history at the **Atlanta Cyclorama and Civil War Museum** in Grant Park (800-C Cherokee Avenue; 404–624–1071 or 404–658–7625; admission $5/$4 for seniors). This fascinating attraction provides a unique way to learn about the Battle of Atlanta. Although the central attraction is a single, gigantic painting, it is so much more than just a illustration. In fact, it is one of the city's most treasured artifacts. Once these gargantuan art works, which are in curved cylinders, were extremely popular around the world, but today only a few survive. Atlanta's one-hundred-year-old, 358-foot (that's longer than a football field) painting in-the-round is the only one we know of where stadium seating revolves within the circle of the painting while narration, lighting, sound effects, and a three-dimensional diorama aid in telling the intense story of the fierce battle that occurred in and around Atlanta on July 22, 1864. You and your sweetie can huddle together for protection as the battle roars around you. Before viewing the painting, however, see the short introductory presentation, *The Atlanta Campaign,* narrated by James Earl Jones. Afterward peruse the Civil War artifacts in the museum and look at the famous steam locomotive, *Texas,* which succeeded in chasing down the hijacked *General,* the train captured by Union spies. The facility also has an excellent gift shop and bookstore where you can purchase books about the Civil War from an extensive collection.

Wind up your day's study of the events leading up to the burning of Atlanta by paying your respects to the brave young men who fell on both sides of the issue at **Oakland Cemetery** (248 Oakland Avenue, S.E.; 404–688–2107; free), the final resting place for twenty-four hundred Confederate and twenty Union soldiers. In fact, this is the only cemetery in the country where the graves are intermixed rather than being in separate sections. These poignant graves are watched over by a magnificent statue of the Confederate lion—you decide whether he's crying or sleeping. Margaret Mitchell, author of the great Civil War opus *Gone with the Wind,* is buried here as well. Guided or self-guided tours of the cemetery are available.

You may want to return to your B&B and freshen up for dinner.

DAY TWO: EVENING

Dinner

After this day of fiery recollections, quench the flames with some home brew at **Max Lager's American Grill and Brewery** (320 Peachtree Street; 404–525–4400; moderate). Wood-fired cuisine and home-brewed beverages are offered in a beautifully renovated turn-of-the-century building in the heart of downtown. Here, the restaurant surrounds the brewery. Watch the menu items being prepared in the exhibition kitchen. The comfortable, casual environment is enhanced by outdoor seating on a patio or deck, although most diners enjoy overseeing the brewing process. The grill has a full menu, including appetizers, salads, sandwiches, pastas, pizza, and entrees. Some unusual items include Caesar salad in a tortilla, Old Chicago prime rib sandwich, and apple max pizza. Five standard beers are always available, as are one or two specialty beers. We hear that the chocolate beer is outstanding. You can order a sampler of four beers, or you can ask to taste any of the beers before you order them. Lager's has an extensive American wine list and brews its own root beer and ginger beer.

If you want to linger after dinner, the bar is open until 1:00 A.M. Otherwise, return to the safe haven of your B&B and snuggle up together to ward off the memories of Atlanta's battle.

DAY THREE: MORNING

Breakfast

Enjoy another hearty meal at the B&B, then pack up and bid farewell to your hosts.

Atlanta has now fallen and Sherman's March to the Sea is about to begin. Travel east of Atlanta to **Georgia's Stone Mountain Park** (US 78; 770–498–5600; $6), a state park specifically developed as a memorial to fallen southern Civil War heroes. The park gets its name from the colossal mountain of granite that is its focal point. In fact, the mountain is the largest exposed mass of granite in the world. Covering three acres of its side, a huge bas-relief sculpture has been carved, the mounted figures of Robert E. Lee, Jefferson Davis, and Stonewall Jackson. In addition, the park contains the Discovering Stone Mountain Museum (770–413–5086) and Confederate Hall.

Located in Memorial Hall, the Discovering Stone Mountain Museum features exhibits, touchable models, full-scale photo murals that orient visitors to the size of the carving, and also Civil War artifacts. The War in Georgia Museum in Confederate Hall uses a room-size, horizontal, three-dimensional map with narration, lighting, and sound effects to describe Sherman's march through Georgia in 1864.

Unfortunately, it's now time for you to go home, and you'll have realized that there is so much more to Atlanta's and the immediately surrounding area's role in the Civil War that you haven't seen. There's one simple solution—you'll just have to come back.

FOR MORE ROMANCE

A significant battle occurred right in downtown Jonesboro, south of Atlanta, over the last Confederate-controlled rail line into Atlanta. During the battle on September 1, 1864, sixty thousand Union soldiers were pitted against only twelve thousand Confederates. However, the Confederates fought so furiously that whole Union companies were reported to have fallen as one man. The battle ended when darkness fell, the Confederates retreated, and the Union took control of the rail lines, sealing Atlanta's doom. The London *Times* reported that "compared with the great battles of the war, the action at Jonesborough is little more than a skirmish, yet it has been more decisive than all the fighting and bloodshed of Grant's campaign." (See "In Scarlett's Footsteps" for other Jonesboro attractions.) You might want to schedule your trip to coincide with one of Jonesboro's special events: a reenactment of the evacuation of civilians from Jonesboro is held on Labor Day weekend; a reenactment of the battle in late October. Call the welcome center for exact dates and details.

PHOENIX RISING
HISTORIC ATLANTA

*A*tlanta is all about rebirth and renewal. Although most people know that the city burned during the Civil War, few of even her own current citizens are aware that the city suffered another devastating fire in 1917. So Atlanta has literally risen from the ashes not once, but twice. No wonder that the fabled phoenix was adopted as a symbol for the burgeoning city. Founded as a railroad hub, the city suffered through the Civil War, led the way during the Civil Rights movement, became a transportation phenomenon, and rose to near greatness. Unfortunately, until recently, the powers that be and the citizenry placed too little value on preservation and much significant historic architecture was lost. Today saving venerable buildings is still a challenge. (In fact, Atlanta's official historian Franklin Garret has said, "In Atlanta, there's nothing they wouldn't tear down to make a parking lot." And "The only thing in the Atlanta area that never has been moved is Stone Mountain.") Few structures survive that are older than the turn of the century, and there are not many of those. Most of the stunning buildings in today's dramatic skyline are less than twenty years old. Therefore, despite the city's antebellum roots, Atlanta looks and feels young and vibrant and is constantly reinventing and reconstructing itself—just as you two keep renewing your relationship.

The city is an easy place to love and in which to be in love. This weekend you and your sweetheart will explore Atlanta's fascinating past: the things, the people, and the places that have helped make it great. You're in for an enlightening weekend exploring Atlanta and being treated like celebrities. You'll be staying in a world-class hotel and dining at some of Atlanta's most-popular restaurants—often frequented by the glitterati.

Romance at a Glance

♥ *Rise above it all at the Westin Peachtree Plaza.*

♥ *See a rousing show at the fabulous, but almost razed, Fox Theater.*

♥ *Heighten your appreciation of our best ex-president at the Carter Center.*

♥ *Raise a glass to your sweetheart at the Sun Dial.*

♥ *Put on the ritz for real at the Ritz-Carlton Buckhead.*

Practical notes: Although most of the sites and activities in this weekend's getaway are downtown or in Buckhead and can be reached by public transportation, it's more convenient to use your car to get from place to place. Use surface streets to go between the two districts rather than the "downtown connector" (I–75/I–85) if you find yourself downtown at rush hour on a weekday; otherwise, the connector boasts the convenience of HOV (high occupancy vehicle) lanes for which you and your honey meet the two-passenger requirement.

DAY ONE: MORNING

Exploring Atlanta's exciting history with the one you love will give you memories to share forever. To get your romantic weekend off to a good start, learn about the city's complexities and intricacies at the **Atlanta History Center** (130 West Paces Ferry Road, 404–814–4000; admission $7 to $10/$5 to $8 for seniors), where you will study mementos from the thousands of triumphant and tragic stories that make Atlanta what it is today. (The museum's fabulous Civil War collection is described in "That Pyromaniac from the North" and the gardens in "Full Bloom of Love.")

Bygone (and Good Riddance) Atlanta

In its early days, when it was still a small, rough-and-ready railroad town, Atlanta had some pretty seedy areas where toughs and scoundrels hung out. Fortunately, the city has risen above this low-life period, and all these nefarious neighborhoods are long gone, but they still make interesting and amusing reading. "Murrel's Row," between Peachtree and Pryor, was a particularly nasty place filled with bandits, gamblers, and hookers and was the scene of constant free-for-alls and illegal gaming events, such as cockfights. Honest citizens who wanted to journey from downtown to Buckhead had to run the gauntlet of outlaws at "Tight Squeeze," a notorious hangout for trouble-makers at today's Peachtree and Tenth Streets. Too many folks were relieved of their money and other valuables at Tight Squeeze. Not so nasty but still vulgar was "Humbug Square," where today's Underground Atlanta now stands. Here the citizenry could be entertained by dancing bears, jugglers, and musicians, or purchase the wares of drummers, snake-oil salesmen, root doctors, and medicine men.

"Metropolitan Frontiers: Atlanta 1835–2000," the primary permanent exhibition, is the largest and most comprehensive examination of urban history in the Southeast. Explore Atlanta's meteoric rise by visiting four period cities: the Rural Region of the early 1800s, the Transportation City of the late 1800s, the Commercial City of the early 1900s, and the Suburban Metropolis (late 1900s). Each period reveals its spellbinding story through large-scale objects, smaller artifacts, period clothing, furniture, photographs, maps, and documents. Videos in transition galleries reveal changes that occurred during the Civil War, at the turn of the century, and during World War II. Try to envision what your love affair would have been like at those heady times. You leave the exhibit with the sense that Atlanta is truly a city without limits— always venturing to new frontiers with almost infinite possibilities, always rising to the challenge.

Spring for a combination admission so you can also visit the two historic houses on the museum's grounds. The contrast between the two illustrates how Atlanta changed from its infancy in the 1840s to the wealth and sophistication of the 1920s. The Tullie Smith Farm, a typical piedmont farm that was moved to the site, features a plantation-plain-style house furnished with simple antiques of the period and several authentic outbuildings. Costumed docents give lively tours filled with little tidbits about rural life in Georgia. Picture the two of you in homespun, working your own little piece of paradise. Visitors learn that this type of farm was much more characteristic of the Southern lifestyle than the grand plantations were. (In fact, Margaret Mitchell's imaginary Tara was much more like this simple farm than it was the mansion in the movie.)

Next visit the Swan House, an elegant Classic Revival mansion designed and built in 1928 by noted architect Philip Trammell Schutze for the wealthy Inman family. Among its outstanding interior features is a stunning spiral staircase in the central hall. You can just envision yourself or your loved one as a bride or debutante sweeping down the staircase to meet your intended. Because most of the lavish furnishings are original to the Inmans, you'll feel as if they could have lived here just yesterday. Better yet, imagine yourselves living here today. Challenge each other to find the swan motifs throughout the house. Then take your sweetie by the hand and stroll through the thirty-three acres of gardens. Stay as long as you like, but although you're feeding your souls, you may need to nourish your bodies as well.

DAY ONE: AFTERNOON

Lunch

There's a simple solution to your hunger problem: Have an elegant lunch at the classy **Swan Coach House** (3130 Sloan Drive, 404–261–0636 or 404–261–4735; moderate), located in the reborn carriage house/garage of the mansion. Although the gracious restaurant is one of *the* places the ladies who lunch gather, couples enjoy the delicious food and an intimate setting that is so conducive to romance. Dine on elegant soups, salads, and sandwiches while you feast on each other.

Continue your search for the phoenix on Peachtree Street. For many years, Peachtree Street was the most fashionable address in Atlanta. Just a short drive south on Peachtree is **Rhodes Hall** (1516 Peachtree Street, N.W.; 404–881–9980; tours $3 unguided, $5 guided). One of the last grand mansions on Peachtree, the heavy Romanesque Revival-style home combines the elements of several Rhineland castles. Completed in 1904 by the Rhodes Furniture family, the mansion showcases such diverse exterior architectural details as a Syrian-style, four-story corner tower, and battlements all around. The interior is equally rich in design and ornamentation and is considered to be Atlanta's finest existing Victorian interior. Among the ornate elements are a winding hand-carved Honduran mahogany staircase, elaborate woodwork and plasterwork, and beautiful fireplaces surrounded by colorful mosaics. The crowning touch, however, is the series of stained-glass windows created as a memorial to the Confederacy. Tours are given Monday through Friday, so don't put off a visit thinking you can take a tour the Saturday or Sunday of your getaway.

Taking this chapter's theme of "rising above it all" to another level, for your amorous weekend assignation, we've chosen a hotel that has risen to unsurpassed heights—the soaring giant glass cylindrical **Westin Peachtree Plaza** (210 Peachtree Street, N.W., 404–659–1400; $109–$1,500). At seventy-five stories from the subbasement to the top floor, it is the tallest hotel in Atlanta . . . and in the entire Western Hemisphere (and the second tallest in the world). Its sleek shape makes it one of the most distinctive structures in the city. Take your relationship to a new high by requesting a bed chamber on one of the lofty upper stories where you can look down on Atlanta, Centennial Olympic Park, and see far into the suburbs—even to Stone Mountain. In fact, we recommend that you choose one of the suites or the premier guest rooms (starting at $250) for your romantic aerie. With upgraded amenities including turn-down service, bathrobes, complimentary use of the fitness center, and complimentary continental breakfast, you'll feel like royalty.

Spend the remainder of the afternoon reveling in the Peachtree Plaza's many amenities. Shape up at the health club, which boasts an all-season lap pool and a sundeck with a retractable roof, strength training circuit, other fitness machines, and saunas. Why not loosen all the kinks from your everyday life with some massage therapy? If you're not feeling active, engage in some people watching while you dally over an espresso in the **Tivoli Coffee Bar** or an international beer, wine, or cocktail from the **International Bar**. Wander through the sixth-level Shopping Gallery where there are several clothing and gifts and sundries shops. Stop at **Buds N' Blooms** to buy a rose or a balloon to give your sweetie's spirit a rise.

DAY ONE: EVENING

Dinner and Nightlife

Shoot up to the zenith of the hotel, the trilevel revolving **Sun Dial** restaurant, bar, and viewing area, for a natural high. On level 72, the hotel's crowning glory **Sun Dial View**—a self-guided, 360-degree walking tour with conveniently placed telescopes—offers Atlanta's best panoramas ($3 for the public, free for guests). From this lofty perch, Atlanta's buildings, cars, and parks look like toys. Here are two extra tips: The view from here can help you learn your way around town, and the telescopes give a bleacher-seat view of Turner Field. When you've completed your tour, pick up a souvenir of your lofty liaison. Then ascend to level 73 for a before-dinner drink at the **Sun Dial Bar.** Top it off by dining high above the twinkling city lights on a sumptuous meal of steak, prime rib, or seafood (expensive) in the upscale steakhouse.

Following your leisurely dinner, retire to the Sun Dial Bar and snuggle up to listen to live jazz while you watch the magically lit nighttime city. The combination is guaranteed to heighten your romantic impulses.

DAY TWO: MORNING

Breakfast

Now it's time to come down to earth. Depending on your gastronomic appetites, take advantage of the continental breakfast in the private lounge on level 45, the American/continental buffet at the **Cafe** in the dramatic atrium lobby, or the fresh-baked pastries in the sidewalk cafelike **Tivoli Coffee Bar** in the garden-style lobby. Then it's off to sample more of Atlanta's history.

Learn more about nineteenth-century Atlanta at the **Georgia Capitol** (206 Washington Street, 404–656–2884; free). Hand-in-hand stroll the shady grounds past numerous historical markers and statues of famous Georgians chronicle the rebuilding of the city after the Civil War. Then marvel at the outside of the imposing structure before you go inside. Built in 1889, the classic edifice is topped by a gleaming dome plated in gold mined in the north Georgia mountains. Inside a historical museum and galleries will elevate your fascination with historical artifacts.

"The city too busy too hate" was in the forefront of adjusting to the changes made by the Civil Rights movement. Although the crusade itself started in Montgomery, Alabama, it's best-known leader was a native Atlantan, Dr. Martin Luther King Jr. His birthplace, Ebenezer Baptist Church where he preached, his tomb, and the Martin Luther King Jr. Center for Nonviolent Social Change make up the **Martin Luther King Jr. National Historic Site** (449 Auburn Avenue, N.E.; 404–524–1956; free). (For more detailed information, see "Roots.")

DAY TWO: AFTERNOON

Lunch

After visiting the King Center, take Freedom Parkway to the **Carter Presidential Center** (One Copenhill, 441 Freedom Parkway; 404–331–3942; admission $5/$4 for seniors) and enjoy a leisurely light lunch at the **Copenhill Cafe** (404–420–5136; inexpensive), located just off the lobby. The casual eatery offers two hot entrees with vegetables each day, as well as fruits, sandwiches, and salads. Best yet, if the weather is chilly, you can get a table by the windows and, if you can take your eyes off each other, gaze at the stunning downtown Atlanta skyline. When the weather is nice eat outside on the terrace overlooking the gorgeous Japanese garden. (Learn more about the garden in "Full Bloom of Love.")

Once you've relaxed over lunch, it's time for the two of you to see the library and museum themselves where a range of exhibits offers an overview of the office of the presidency, important events in the twentieth-century, and the Carter administration. Trace the career of the peanut farmer from Plains who became the leader of the free world. Among the highlights are a replica of the Oval Office, a film on the evolution of the presidency, an interactive video of a Carter Town Hall meeting where you choose the questions you want the president to answer, reproductions of First Lady inaugural gowns, a formal White House dinner setting, memorabilia from the 1976 campaign, and many of the gifts presented to the Carters while in office. The library, open by appointment, is a rich resource for students and scholars of American history.

Return to your love nest on high and "freshen up" for dinner.

DAY TWO: EVENING

Dinner

You're going to share in the grandeur of a performance at the Fox Theater this evening so eat an early dinner near the theater at the **Pleasant Peasant Restaurant** (555 Peachtree Street, N.E.; 404–874–3223; moderate). It's most convenient to park at one of the several parking lots and decks between the two rather than moving your car. Located in a historic former drugstore, the cozy eatery features white tile floors, heavy paneling, and high ceilings and encourages intimacy. Appetizers range from crab cakes to marinated goat cheese and vegetables. Black bean soup is a specialty. Dinner entrees include plum pork, pepper-crusted New York strip or salmon, grilled lamb, duck breast, and pastas.

Nightlife

The reborn fabulous **Fox Theater** (660 Peachtree Street, N.E.; 404–881–2100) is your destination for some outstanding entertainment. The Fox plays host to traveling Broadway shows; the Atlanta Opera, other national and international groups, ranging from the Kirov Ballet to Smashing Pumpkins; and a summer classic movie series—so there's something for every couple's tastes. Check ahead or with your concierge as soon as you check in to see what might be playing so you can get your tickets in advance. Ticket prices can range from $5 to more than $100, depending on the event.

This theater, an architectural treasure Atlanta nearly lost to "progress," is a spectacle in itself. Slated for demolition in the late 1970s to be replaced by a parking deck, the extraordinary theater was saved and restored by the Herculean efforts of the citizenry. The fanciful auditorium, built in 1929 as a combination movie palace and Masonic Hall, is an extravaganza of soaring excess that has to be seen to be believed. Outside mosaic-covered minarets and the opulent arcade give only a hint of the surprises in store inside. The 4,500-seat hall is a flamboyant combination of Moorish, Egyptian, and Art Deco influences combined to resemble the courtyard of a fortress. Get to the theater early enough to take a self-guided tour. See the flamboyant grand lobby, the Spanish Room where refreshments are sold, the priceless antiques, and even the lavish anteroom lounges in the restrooms. We recommend sitting in the loge or first dress circle, but even if your seats are in the orchestra, go upstairs anyway to see the "sky" with its moving clouds and twinkling stars on the vaulted ceiling, as well as the massive sheik's "tent" overhanging the gallery. (Even if you're much too young to remember silent movies, you can still imagine Rudolph Valentino ravishing a beautiful harem girl.) The ambience is sure to heighten your sense of fantasy.

Before movies and some live performances, an organist pounds out rousing tunes on the gargantuan and ornate Mollier organ, which rises magically from beneath the floor. (If you want to see even more of the theater including the Grand Salon, Egyptian Ballroom, behind the scenes, and the sunrise and sunset, formal tours are given year-round by the **Atlanta Preservation Society** (404–876–2041) on Monday and Thursday mornings and twice on Saturday (admission $5/$4 for seniors).

You'll so easily lose yourselves in the enchantment of the performance and your surroundings that it will come as a surprise to you that it's so late when the show ends. Unless you're dedicated night owls, it's time to come down from the clouds and call it a day. Restore yourselves with sweet dreams.

DAY THREE: Morning

Brunch

Be lazy and sleep as late as you like or hop right up to swim or exercise. When it gets to be noonish, check out of your lofty aerie and depart for brunch in another Atlanta building that has had more than one life. **The Mansion** (179 Ponce de Leon Avenue; 404–876–0727; moderate to expensive; reservations suggested), an elegant 1895 Victorian villa, is an Atlanta rarity in that not only has it survived urbanization, but it still retains an entire square block of property shaded by stately old trees, as well as a courtyard, gazebo, fountains, lily pond, and an impressive view of downtown. Inside, thirteen dining rooms each have a different personality, but all are appropriately decorated in the Victorian manner. In addition to regular luncheon choices, you can order eggs Benedict and other traditional brunch items.

Thus nourished both physically and emotionally, your visitation to Atlanta's past and present has come to an end.

FOR MORE ROMANCE

If you're lucky enough to have more time, visit the **Wren's Nest** (1050 Ralph David Abernathy Boulevard, S.W.; 404–753–8535 or 753–7735; admission $6/$4 for seniors), the West End home of Joel Chandler Harris. A well-known turn-of-the-century newspaperman, Harris is best remembered as the chronicler of the Uncle Remus tales he heard as a child near Eatonton, Georgia. This lovely Victorian cottage is furnished with Harris's own things, so the house looks as if he just stepped out for a short walk. Periodically, storytellers put new life into Harris's old tales.

End your journey through Atlanta's past by stopping at **Westview Cemetery** (1680 Westview Drive; 404–755–6611; free). Begun in 1884, during the golden age of the rural cemetery movement, it contains opulent Victorian gravestones, mausoleums, and memorial art. Among the famous Atlantans buried there are Asa G. Candler and Robert W. Woodruff of Coca-Cola, newspapermen Henry Grady and Joel Chandler Harris, former mayor William B. Hartsfield (for whom the airport and Atlanta's famous silverback gorilla are named), as well as philanthropists Henrietta Egleston, Hyatt M. Patterson, Joseph M. High, and Richard B. Rich. The South's most famous shrine, the Westview Mausoleum, contains twenty-seven stained-glass windows depicting milestones in the life of Christ, four paintings of parables, and a mural called *Faith, Hope, and Charity*.

If you have several days instead of just a weekend, some of the attractions in this itinerary of historic sites overlap with those in "In Scarlett's Footsteps," and "That Pyromaniac from the North," so the three are easily combined.

HOLIDAY HIGH JINX

ITINERARY 4
Three days and two nights

ADDING SPARKLE TO YOUR LIFE
FOURTH OF JULY ATLANTA STYLE

*A*s a prelude to sparking your own personal fireworks during this festive getaway celebrating our country's birthday, get a bang out of our favorite July Fourth skyrocket extravaganzas: a rousing outdoor concert performance of the Atlanta Symphony Orchestra at Chastain Park amphitheater, followed by a spectacular fireworks finale. This special weekend is a perfect time to challenge yourselves in the Peachtree Road Race, become kids again at the Salute 2 America Parade, shop till you drop at Fourth of July sales, sample some exquisite restaurants, and dance till dawn at lively nightspots—kindling or rekindling your relationship.

Practical Notes: Any one of the popular Fourth of July holiday activities draws huge crowds, so get there early to ensure a parking or watching place. In addition, make your hotel reservations and purchase your symphony tickets in advance because the event often sells out early. The symphony series at Chastain Park takes place on Wednesday, Friday, and Saturday nights, so the Fourth of July performance may not actually be on the Fourth but the one of those days nearest to it. If the production isn't actually on the Fourth, you can also take in one of Atlanta's many other Independence Day fireworks presentations. Although the concert doesn't begin until 8:30 P.M., if you're driving, do yourself a big favor and get there soon after the gates open at 6:30 P.M. if you want to get a parking place anywhere in the vicinity. We advise parking on Park Road or the Red Lot if possible because they offer the most direct ways to get out after the concert. Our suggestion, however, is to splurge and be delivered and picked up by limo or taxi. One last note: Personal fireworks, even sparklers, are illegal in Georgia.

Romance at a Glance

♥ *Challenge yourselves in the Peachtree Road Race.*

♥ *Cheer to the blare of seventy-six trombones at the Salute 2 America Parade.*

♥ *Shop till you drop at Fourth of July blockbuster sales.*

♥ *Ooh and aah at the rocket's red glare.*

♥ *Boogie till the dawn's early light.*

DAY ONE: AFTERNOON

Arrive in upscale Buckhead, Atlanta's hottest neighborhood, in the late afternoon and check into your weekend way station. To avoid breaking the bank this weekend, make the recently renovated and upgraded **Terrace Garden Inn** (3405 Lenox Road, N.E.; 404–261–9250, moderate), directly across the street from Lenox Square Mall, your holiday headquarters. The inn is convenient to Chastain Park and is only half a block from the MARTA rapid rail station, allowing you to gain easy access to downtown and other areas without worrying about driving and parking. In addition, the hotel makes a perfect vantage point from which to gawk at Lenox's fireworks display without being crushed by the spectators. Ask for a room facing the mall. The intimate hostelry offers every amenity you need for a sizzling getaway weekend—spacious, comfortable guest rooms; restaurant; cozy lounge; outdoor terrace with live entertainment; outdoor pool; and indoor sports facilities, boasting a swimming pool, racquetball court, sauna, steam rooms, and fully equipped Nautilus weight room. A licensed massage therapist is available as well. Wouldn't a massage for two be a sensual addition to your weekend? Revel in the hotel's facilities and each other for the remainder of the afternoon.

DAY ONE: EVENING

Dinner

Celebrate each other and your American heritage by feasting on some traditional American cuisine. **NAVA**'s (3060 Peachtree Road, 404–240–1984, moderate to expensive) indigenous Southern and Southwestern ingredients coupled with fiery Latin and Native American influences explode your tastebuds in "sophisticated Southwestern reinvented" cuisine. A wide array of enchiladas, fritters, quesadillas, tostadas, rellenos, and tacos, using seafood, rabbit, quail, chicken, beef, and pork, give the menu its pizzazz. If your mouth is on fire, douse the flames with NAVA's signature margaritas, Atlanta-brewed beers, or selections from the excellent wine list. Specialty desserts, such as an apple-piñon enchilada or banana quesadilla, are a perfect climax to your meal. The decor is bright and stylish; the atmosphere lively. Reservations are suggested.

Stoke up the fires in your relationship by sampling Buckhead's smorgasbord of nightlife options. In the late evening, the area is practically transformed into a pedestrian mall where couples and groups of friends bounce from one nightspot to another. Your choices will depend on your age, love quotient, and personal tastes in music. Atlantans frequent these favorites: Dancing to music of the seventies and eighties surrounded by seventies nostalgia—such as go-go cages, lava lamps, and Twister games—characterize **Bell Bottoms** (225 Pharr Road, 404–816–9669) where there are three bars. The establishment rocks until 3:00 or 4:00 A.M. An older crowd jitterbugs, shags, and twists at **Johnny's Hideaway** (3771 Roswell Road; 404–233–8026). Popular with the late-30s to 50s crowd, this hole in the wall is where to go for big band and fifties/sixties music. Small, dark, and smoky, nevertheless, it's always standing room only. Plenty of slow songs encourage dancing cheek to cheek. Johnny's smolders until 4:00 A.M. (Saturdays 3:00 A.M.). **Tongue and Groove** (3055 Peachtree Road; 404–261–2325), a cocktail lounge and nightclub with a see-and-be-seen attitude, attracts a predominantly younger crowd. There's a $5.00

cover charge after 10:00 P.M., and the club sparkles until 4:00 A.M. (Saturdays 3:00 A.M.). **Otto's** (265 East Paces Ferry; 404–233–1133) is popular with the 30s-to-40s crowd. Considered sophisticated, the club presents live blues/jazz/contemporary entertainment nightly. There is a dress code and a cover charge. Closing time is 2:00 A.M. weekdays, 4:00 A.M. Fridays, 3:00 A.M. Saturdays.

One of the best aphrodisiacs is laughter. Extend the evening on a mirthful note by laughing through a performance at the **Uptown Comedy Corner** (2140 Peachtree Road; 404–350–6990). The host and a local act or two warm up the crowd for a featured comedian. Shows are performed Friday and Saturday nights. The Comedy Corner serves finger food and has full bar service.

After exploring some of Buckhead's hot spots, make your way back to your hotel to light up life with your own brand of fireworks.

DAY TWO: MORNING

The steamy early, early morning of July Fourth in Atlanta brings worldwide attention to the **Peachtree Road Race** (404–231–9064), which draws fifty thousand racers from all over the world, and tens of thousands of spectators as well. Although running, sweating, gasping for breath, and perhaps collapsing from exhaustion definitely don't bring a romantic spark to our eyes, we know two young ladies and two young men who met each other while participating in the race, paired up afterward, and married a year later, so obviously love is in the eye of the beholder. If you want to run, you must apply for a number well ahead of time. Finishers earn a coveted T-shirt that they wear like a badge of courage or honor, and it seems to make all the effort worth while.

If one or both of you are running the Peachtree Road Race, rise and shine mighty early because the 10K race is run before the heat of the day sets in. Do whatever it is that runners do before a race and good luck.

Breakfast

More sedentary types and even some fitness fanatics may think all this outpouring of energy is totally misplaced and wasted on a romantic getaway, so simply watching the race may be excitement enough. If you and your sweetie are among the latter group, you'll need breakfast and a spot from which to watch the race. We suggest **Huey's** (1816 Peachtree Road, N.E., 404–873–2037; inexpensive), a New Orleans tradition and Atlanta favorite for coffee and crispy hot beignets smothered with powdered sugar. Watch the race from there in air-conditioned comfort.

⸙

Later in the morning, gratify the kid in you by watching the **Salute 2 America Parade** (404–897–7000) up close and personal. Sponsored by WSB-TV Channel 2 (hence the "2" in the parade name), this is the largest July Fourth parade in the country. Bands, drill teams, floats, and celebrities are guaranteed to get your spirits soaring.

DAY TWO: AFTERNOON

Lunch

After the parade, return to the inn and cross the street to Lenox Square Mall for lunch. The food outlets at the mall feature something for every taste and pocketbook from food court fast food joints to moderately priced and expensive restaurants. We suggest **Prime** (3393 Peachtree Road; 404–812–0555, expensive) because it has such a unique concept. Tom Catherall, a longtime star in Atlanta's culinary firmament, married the current interest in sushi with a resurgence in the consumption of beef. The stunning restaurant merges the dramatic theatrical element of the authentic Japanese sushi bar with natural lighting from floor to ceiling windows, lavish colors, and large-scale works of art. Lunch menus offer entrees and sophisticated sandwiches as well as seafood.

⸙

You're already at Lenox Square and the Phipps Plaza shopping mall is within easy walking distance, so take this perfect opportunity to peruse the July Fourth bargains. Both fashionable malls boast valet parking, concierge service, personal shoppers, food courts and high-class dining. **Lenox Square** (3393 Peachtree Road, N.E., 404–233–6767 or 800–344–5222) offers "shopper beepers" so the two of you can keep in touch with each other if you want to shop separately for surprise gifts for each other to make you weekend even racier. Pick up the beepers at the Concierge Center. Lenox Square is anchored by Neiman Marcus, Rich's, and Macy's and spotlights such upscale specialty shops as Louis Vuitton, Brooks Brothers, Polo by Ralph Lauren, Versace Jeans Couture, and Cartier. **Phipps Plaza's** (3500 Peachtree Road, N.E., 404–261–7910) anchors are Saks Fifth Avenue, Lord and Taylor, and Parisian. Its boutiques include A/X Armani Exchange, Abercrombie and Fitch, Gianni Versace, Gucci, and Tiffany & Co. For sports and fitness nuts, Nike Town is an attraction in itself. If you can't discover extravagant keepsakes at these malls, you obviously aren't championship caliber shoppers.

After your shopping spree, return to the inn to cool off with a swim and an icy drink or keep those fires burning in your own unique way.

DAY TWO: EVENING

Dinner and Nightlife

Whether it's the Fourth of July or not, concerts at **Chastain Park** win our vote for being the most romantic thing to do in Atlanta—bar none. The amphitheater is consistently named as one of the country's top ten outdoor venues. Entertainment by a world-class orchestra and/or big name performers is just part of the appeal, but the major allure is the seductive setting and the accoutrements—and your partner makes an evening there absolutely perfect, of course. The horseshoe-shaped natural stone amphitheater was built in the 1940s, but a

America's Couple: Ted Turner and Jane Fonda

Captain Outrageous Meets Hanoi Jane. A decade ago, when various media sources, including Turner's own CNN, reported that the media mogul and America's Team owner (sometimes called the Mouth of the South) was wooing the glamorous movie star, no one in Atlanta thought the love affair would last. After all, their differences seemed so great. How could a self-admitted male chauvinist succeed with an ardent feminist and political activist? Well, it seems they've both mellowed with age and experience. Atlanta's biggest wedding in memory took place right before Christmas 1991 with only a small group of family and friends in attendance at Turner's Avalon ranch near Tallahassee, Florida. The plans were so secret that the actual location of the wedding was changed only a few hours before the ceremony. Originally planned for the tiny chapel on the property, the wedding actually took place in the house— completely foiling the media flock outside the gates and those in a helicopter flying overhead. Former Atlanta Mayor Andrew Young, who has known each of the dynamic duo longer than they've known each other, was quoted as saying he thought Jane was the only person with Ted's energy level, so they should do very well together. Time has certainly proven him correct.

modern state–of-the art stage ensures a superior performance. Magnolias planted around the periphery have grown to epic size and erupt with their own show of creamy white blossoms. (For a schedule of events call TicketMaster at 404–249–6400.)

Local folks create a not-so-typical Independence Day picnic by bringing TV-tray tables, colorful table linens and dinnerware, wine goblets, small or spectacular floral arrangements, simple candles or ornate silver candelabra, and a sumptuous picnic dinners. On the Fourth of July, attendees outdo themselves to concoct the most elaborate red, white, and blue table setting and often dress in patriotic colors as well. Part of the attraction before the concert is people watching and admiring the table settings before it gets dark. As twilight and then night begin to fall, the curving rows of flickering candles can't help but lead you to put your arm around your sweetie as you drink in the music.

For simplicity's sake, skip the table, elaborate settings, and other paraphernalia and let someone else to all the work. Two catering companies: **Affairs to Remember** (680 Ponce de Leon, N.E.; 404–872–7859) and **Proof of the Pudding** with two locations (2033 Monroe Drive, N.E.; 404–892–2359 and 1201 Hammond Drive, N.E.; 770–804–9880) will whip up a simple but elegant dinner if you call ahead. They have a variety of menus and price ranges. You simply pick up your dinners when you arrive at the park. Fresh flowers and candles can be purchased at the amphitheater as well, so you can still create your own little piece of paradise. In addition, wine is sold by the glass and the bottle, and you can purchase mixed drinks, snacks, sandwiches, pizza, ice cream, and other cold drinks if you want to eat a la carte.

Savor your elegant picnic meal, then settle back while you tap your toes in time to a stirring musical program. An Independence Day program traditionally includes a variety of patriotic tunes and works by American composers. A guest artist or two may perform as well. In recent years, a band of Civil War reenactors played instruments and tunes from the Civil War, and a cowboy group entertained with old favorites from the West. The evening ends with a rousing rendition of Tchaikovsky's *1812 Overture*. When the piece reaches its crescendo and the cannon fire explodes, fireworks light up the night sky—accompanied by the appreciative "oohs" and "ahs" of the audience. Pop goes the Fourth if you can time the opening of a bottle of champagne to the cannon's roar. As an added attraction, you can often see the fireworks erupting at Lenox Square in the background.

Keep the embers from going out when you return to the inn.

DAY THREE: Morning

Brunch

Last night was late, so wallow in luxury by sleeping in. When you finally force yourselves out of bed, check out and drive to **Canoe** (4199 Paces Ferry Road; 770–432–2663; moderate to expensive) for an ample brunch with a splendid view of the Chattahoochee River from the big windows of the indoor dining rooms or from the patio. Try to get an outside table where you'll be serenaded by the rushing river, bird songs, and rustling leaves. An architectural masterpiece frequented by the Range Rover crowd, the restaurant features eclectic American cuisine. The brunch menu ranges from pastries to banana waffles to eggs Benedict to grilled fish.

FOR MORE ROMANCE

We go back to the Fourth of July Celebration at Chastain Park year after year and never get tired of it. After all, the performance is different every year, but if you've been there, done that, and want to add more spice to your life by experiencing something different, you can watch the fireworks display synchronized to recorded music bursting over Lenox Square—the largest fireworks display in the Southeast—or see the laser show accompanied by fireworks that concludes the four-day Salute to America celebration at **Georgia's Stone Mountain Park** (770–498–5600).

ITINERARY 5
Three days and two nights

SKULL-DUGGERY

ATLANTA'S HALLOWEEN HAUNTS

*H*alloween just naturally provides a ready-made excuse to throw yourselves into each other's arms. A healthy scare is a surefire way to get lovers to cling to each other. As Halloween becomes more and more an adult holiday, Atlanta consistently meets the challenge for more ghoulish grown-up activities with a diverse selection of spine-tingling events. Expect far more than the amateur haunted house—the city stages a variety of professional spooktaculars. So whether you're searching for treats or tricks, you'll have a shrieking good time here. Of course, the most hair-raising adventures transpire in the dead of night, but we've scared up some related daytime festivities for you as well, and we've selected some equally macabre eateries and nightlife. Fair warning: This adventure is not for the faint of heart.

Practical Notes: This spine-tingling outing isn't restricted to Halloween weekend but generally can be braved any weekend in October. We've listed general periods when the ghostly activities occur but recommend that you call ahead for exact dates to avoid disappointment. Pack something warm for outdoor adventures. If you plan to dress up in costume, bring your own or reserve them ahead of time. (See "Need a Costume.")

DAY ONE: AFTERNOON

Begin your spirited weekend with a stroll through historic **Oakland Cemetery** (248 Oakland Avenue, S.E.; 404–688–2107; free). Because monsters and vampires vaporize in the light of day, this is the least spooky time to visit the cemetery. (Besides that, the gates are locked at night to contain the spirits.) Opened in 1850, but in its heyday at the turn of the century, the cemetery is a treasure trove of excessive Victorian mausoleums and funerary statuary. Oakland is the only graveyard in the country where Confederate and Union soldiers are buried side by side rather than in separate sections. *Gone With the Wind* author Margaret Mitchell, golf great Bobby Jones, and several Georgia governors and Atlanta mayors are buried in these pastoral acres, which offer—to visitors—a splendid vista of the downtown skyline. The visitors center is open Monday through Friday, and you can get a brochure for a self-guided tour of the cemetery or make arrangements for a guided walk.

Romance at a Glance

♥ *Shiver through a Tour of Southern Ghosts.*

♥ *Quake in your boots at Mordred's Haunted Castle.*

♥ *Bite into fright at Agatha's—A Taste of Mystery.*

♥ *Sleep with ghosts at the Village Inn.*

Because it was the only cemetery in Atlanta, virtually everyone who died between 1850 and 1884 when the next cemetery was built is buried here, so it's not surprising that there are some unsavory legends and restless spirits about. Prior to his death, Dr. James Nissen, the first citizen buried at Oakland, was so fearful he might be buried alive that he directed his doctor to sever his jugular vein at the graveside prior to the burial. His wishes were carried out, but Dr. Nissen may not be resting in peace. One of the oldest mausoleums at Oakland, that of the Waid Hill family, contains two tormented spirits condemned to spend the rest of eternity walled up together. So fractious was their living relationship that R. P. Hill shot his brother O. C., but then in remorse he committed suicide. The Union soldiers

Other Ghostly Manifestations

♥ Rally of the Dead: *Visitors to the Civil War section of Oakland Cemetery sometimes report hearing a roll call of otherwordly voices accompanied by the rat-a-tat-tat of phantom drums.*

♥ Phantoms of the Fox: *Legend says that the restless spirit of a former mistress who once occupied a private suite on the seventh floor of the exotic movie palace takes over the elevator and forces it to stop on the seventh floor no matter what button you push. Staff of the Fox also report hearing mysterious creaks and groans, murmurs, cries, sighs, whispers, and footsteps backstage and in the Egyptian Ballroom.*

♥ The Woman in Silver: *On Halloween night, if you come across a distraught young woman in fancy dress at Stewart and Dill Avenues and offer her a ride home, you may be in for a shock. Numerous good Samaritans report that when they reach her address, she has vanished from the car. It turns out she died in a car accident in 1927.*

♥ Henry's Haunt: *Henry Heinz was murdered in his mansion at 1610 Ponce de Leon in 1943. Subsequent occupants reported hearing gunshots and footsteps, but there have been no further manifestations since the house was painted pink.*

♥ Margaret Mitchell: *When Mitchell lay dying in the hospital, a newspaper photographer took a picture of the nurse standing guard outside her room. When the negatives were developed, a shadowy image appeared behind the nurse. Was it Mitchell herself or a guardian angel? Mitchell is also reported to wander the rooms of the Lemuel Grant mansion, which she owned.*

buried at Oakland surely aren't too happy about their final resting place. The full-size statue of Jasper Newton Smith atop his mausoleum may give you an uncomfortable turn as he watches your every move. The statue of the mythological Niobe weeping for her slain children will break your heart as will the empty cribs and cherubs mourning lost children.

DAY ONE: EVENING

Dinner

From Oakland Cemetery drive to the nearby funky **Little Five Points** neighborhood—an area where New Age stores, tattoo and body piercing parlors, unusual shops, cafes, and alternative entertainment abound. Although the tattooed and pierced leather-and-studs folks wandering around the area, hanging out on street corners, or entertaining for tips appear to be in Halloween costume, they really dress this way all the time. Poke through the eccentric shops especially the **Junkman's Daughter** (446 Moreland Avenue, 404–577–3188), which has a little bit of everything. Perhaps you can pick up something there to wear for these Halloween activities. (To learn more about Little Five Points, see "Tie-dyed Twosome, or Bring on the Noise, Bring on the Funk.")

We have a fright-filled evening planned for you, so start it out with a hearty meal while you're still in Little Five Points. You'll be walking along Moreland Avenue, minding your own business, joking with each other, and peering curiously into store windows, when suddenly you'll be brought up short by the horrifying visage of a gigantic one-and-a-half-story leering skull with bulging mad eyes. When you've caught your breath and your heart has risen from the vicinity of the floor, step through the gaping mouth into the **Vortex Bar and Grill** (438 Moreland Avenue N.E.; 404–688–1828; inexpensive). The casual interior is dominated by a skeleton wearing a jaunty hat sitting merrily astride a motorcycle. As you can tell, this fun place doesn't take anything but the food and service seriously. You can order breakfast all day, as well as appetizers, burgers, pub-style sandwiches, soups, salads, specials, and desserts. While you're waiting for your order, amuse each other by reading aloud the back of the menu, which is full of such sage admonitions as, "Everything you need to know is printed somewhere on this menu. *Please read it!* If you ask us stupid questions we will be forced to mock you mercilessly." You'll be rolling on the floor by the time you finish the fifteen items, such as the Idiot Policy or the Tip or Die philosophy.

After fortifying yourselves and building up your courage, head to the village of Stone Mountain. If you're brave enough to sleep with ghosts, check into your lodgings, the **Village Inn Bed and Breakfast** (992 Ridge Avenue, 770–469–3459; $85 to $150). Built in 1850 as a hotel, the structure was commandeered as a hospital during the Civil War. Of simple clapboard construction, the inn features heart-pine walls and floors. Guest rooms, which exude Southern charm, are decorated and furnished with period antiques and feature queen-size beds, ceiling fans, gas-log fireplaces, and private baths with whirlpool tubs. Several rooms open onto verandas. At least one ghost—and possibly two (they are thought to be a former owner and a Civil War soldier)—inhabit the house, but do no harm.

When pitch darkness reigns, head for **Georgia's Stone Mountain Park** (U.S. 78; 770–498–5702; $6 per car to enter park, $6 per person for tour) for one of Atlanta's top storytelling events. Nightly from the middle of October through Halloween, ART Station, a contemporary arts center, offers a scary **Tour of Southern Ghosts.** Eerie candlelight tours of the park's plantation grounds and buildings are combined with chilling Southern ghost stories related by costumed storytellers, portraying different eighteenth- and nineteenth-century characters. Stick closely to your guide as he or she leads you by lantern light from one storyteller to another. Otherwise you might get lost in the inky gloom and be snatched up by a malevolent spirit—never to be seen again. Hair-raising stories are related in dimly candlelit rooms or outside in the shadows where wind and rustling leaves combine to help set your nerves on edge. Don't let go of your loved one's hand—this is no place to get separated.

In just one spirited evening, we shivered through the tortured tales of Uncle Monday, the Werechicken, the boisterous ghosts in Savannah's Bonaventure Cemetery, the Confederate Ghost Rider, the macabre Moonlight Sonata, and Sugar Man, who left bloodstains and scraps of fabric below the park's stone carving. It's guaranteed that the hairs will stand up on the back of your neck as you tremble while listening to these stories. Of course, these lurid tales must appeal to varied audiences, including children, so they aren't too grisly. Some hair-raising yarns, in fact, are even quite amusing. Although only six tales are related each night, there are more than six stories. Storytellers rotate over several evenings, so if you're brave enough you and your sweetie could go more than once. Ghostly tours begin at 7:00 P.M. with additional tours leaving every ten minutes. The box office opens at 6:45 P.M., but lines may form much earlier, so we recommend that you purchase your tickets by mail before you get to Atlanta. Contact the ART Station in Stone Mountain Village (5384 Manor Drive; 770–469–1105). Your blood-curdling tour ends with a visit to the old schoolhouse where you can shake off the terrors and purchase delicious hot cider, Halloween decorations, and gift items, including a large selection of ghost-story books.

In addition to the frightful spirits you'll hear about during the Tour of Southern Ghosts, the plantation at Stone Mountain Park has three permanent resident ghosts: Agnes Dickey, the former owner of the antebellum main house; a little blond girl who died in the Thornton House; and a caretaker who committed suicide in the carriage house. Learn more about their manifestations during the regular daily tours of the plantation. (For more about the resort, see "Rock Solid Love Affair.")

With your nerves thoroughly raw now, return to your B&B and hope its resident ghosts let you sleep.

DAY TWO: MORNING

Breakfast

Assuming that the spirits haven't been abroad throughout the night, awaken refreshed, then enjoy a bountiful breakfast in the formal dining room.

⌒⌒⌒

Yesterday you ventured into the horrors of a nineteenth-century cemetery and plantation. Today, travel even farther back in time to the Middle Ages—an era particularly noted for its bloodthirstiness and extreme forms of torture—by transporting yourselves to the

Georgia Renaissance Festival (exit 12 of I–85, Fairburn; 770–964–8575; $12.95, with discount tickets available at Publix). You'll have a frightfully good time by making your anxious way locked hand-in-hand through the eleven fright-filled rooms of Mordred's Haunted Castle where darkness and terrifying special effects reign.

DAY TWO: AFTERNOON

Lunch

Once out of the plagued castle, life takes on a less petrifying aspect. In case racing pulses and rushes of adrenaline induced ravenous appetites, an inexpensive lunch at the festival will return your bodies to a normal state. An event in itself, lunch choices range from huge turkey drumsticks to Shepherd's Pie to Steak on a Stake to Dragon Bits. Desserts and other treats range from apple dumplings a la mode to gigantic pickles to funnel cakes. A tea room offers a more refined atmosphere.

⟞⟐⟜

Spend the remainder of a rollicking day exploring the medieval village of Nottingham, where costumed characters include not only King Henry VIII, one of his queens (they change from year to year just as they did in real life), chivalrous knights, and tender ladies in waiting, but also nefarious characters, such as the wicked sheriff of Nottingham; a black-hooded, axe-carrying executioner; a repulsive rat catcher; hags; crones; and other sinister characters. This is a perfect place to express your fantasies by dressing up—no matter how outlandish your attire, you'll fit right in with the regulars.

Continuous daily shows on ten stages include storytellers, jugglers, jousting knights, and magicians, to name just a few. More than one hundred costumed crafters offer their hand-created wares—mostly themed to the Middle Ages—from quaint medieval-style stalls. With all the jewelry, leather, clothing, costumes, swords, wind chimes, calligraphy, instruments, and much

more, you'll surely find one or more mementos to take home to remind you of this getaway. The festival takes place weekends only in October and usually the first weekend in November.

Return to the present on your way back to your Halloween hideaway to see if the resident spirits are still benevolent and to change for dinner (nice casual attire or a costume appropriate to the show in which you'll participate).

DAY TWO: EVENING

Dinner

If you still haven't been scared enough yet, attend a dinner and Halloween-themed, audience-participation mystery show at **Agatha's—a Taste of Mystery** (693 Peachtree Street, N.E.; 404–875–1610; $47.50). Find out in advance what time period the mystery is set in and dress in costume if you like. This past year's Halloween offering was *A Deadly Day in the Neighborhood*. You get the picture—the mysteries are heavy on satire. A core of three or four professional actors move the show along between courses, and audience members assume small roles to play if they're game enough. Be sure that one of the professional cast will die early on, and that anyone could be the murderer. It might even be you. Do you have nerves of steel to help you through the murder, the investigation, and the final solution? As long as your honey is there to hold your hand, you'll be brave.

After the show, return to your lovenest where you and your paramour can celebrate the success of your superb investigatory powers by continuing to play dress up in a more private setting.

DAY THREE: MORNING

Breakfast

Sleep late and linger over your sumptuous breakfast while you chat with your hosts and other guests. After breakfast, it's time to pack and return to the "real" world.

FOR MORE ROMANCE

Here are some other Ectoplasmic Extras:

Fright Fest at Six Flags (Six Flags Parkway off I–20 West; 770–271–9897): Dr. Fright and Arania the Black Widow Bride host one of Atlanta's biggest Halloween parties. Festivities include live shows, creepy streetwalkers, a zombie jamboree, and Dr. Fright's Frightorium haunted house. This spookfest occurs the last three weekends in October and the first weekend in November.

The Haunted Islands at Lake Lanier Islands (6950 Holiday Road, Lake Lanier; 770–932–7200): Events include the terrifying Hotel Scream, Hobgoblin Hayrides, and Scareview Fair, which features monster makeovers at Madame Maggot's, creepy crafts for sale at the Monster Maul, and wild rides. The Haunted Islands runs weekends from early to mid-October, then nightly through Halloween.

ITINERARY 6
Three days and two nights

YULE TIME WITH Y'ALL
ATLANTA CHRISTMAS

$\mathcal{C}$an anything surpass the level of excitement and anticipation you felt as a child in the delicious days leading up to Christmas? Recreate that exhilaration and expectation with an enchanted Christmas getaway for two. Although Christmas in the South seldom includes a dusting of sparkling new snow, the season brims with magic and merriment that can add a jingle to your relationship. Southerners, in fact, go overboard with decorations and activities to make up for the lack of snow and nippy weather. Festivities, from historic home tours to Christmas lights extravaganzas, begin around Thanksgiving weekend and continue through New Year's Day—although home tours are concentrated early in December. Opulent trimmings; colorful light displays; strains of carols; enticing aromas of freshly cut pine, just-out-of-the-oven cookies, and spicy cider; as well as other seasonal ingredients are guaranteed to make the season bright, raise your spirits, and put you in a Christmas mood. Whether you're looking for the perfect gifts for each other or for other family members and friends, you'll find upscale shopping at the major malls and fascinating little boutiques scattered throughout the city. Numerous cultural events make for busy evenings, and restaurants go all out to provide holiday fare. (Because we're thinking of a romantic weekend getaway, we've described only a few of the many, many Christmas events available—you could spend at least a week going from one to another.)

Practical Notes: Make your hotel reservations early and get your tickets as far ahead as possible—lots of folks from all over the region come to the Capital of the New South in December for the best in Christmas shopping, fine dining, and seasonal cultural events. We've provided general time frames in which events occur, but call ahead to verify exact dates to avoid disappointment. Although it's rarely ever uncomfortably cold in Atlanta, you'll be participating in several outdoor activities, so come prepared—layers are best. For a complete list of Christmas festivities, contact the Atlanta Metro Travel Association at the Atlanta Convention and Visitors Bureau (233 Peachtree Street, N.E.; 404–521–6600) for a brochure.

Romance at a Glance

♥ *Enter a winter wonderland at the Festival of Trees.*

♥ *Join the frivolity at Holiday in the Park.*

♥ *Waltz around the Coke on Ice rink.*

♥ *Indulge in upscale shopping.*

DAY ONE: AFTERNOON

Kick off the Christmas season by arriving in downtown Atlanta in the early afternoon. Register at your holiday hideaway, the luxurious the **Ritz-Carlton Downtown** (181 Peachtree Street, N.E.; 404–659–0400; expensive: rooms start at $139 on weekends; suites at $199). As part of your Christmas present to each other, revel in the holiday spirit in one of the hotel's sinful suites. Not only are Ritz-Carlton's renowned for their flawless facilities and superior dining, but also for their not-to-be-topped personal service. Your concierge will be invaluable in making dining reservations and getting tickets for holiday events.

After checking out your accommodations and unpacking, put on your scarf and mittens and begin your wintery weekend by gliding around the outdoor ice skating rink at **Coke on Ice.** Ice skating outdoors in Atlanta? you ask. Yes, you read it here. Through the wonders of modern technology, the **World of Coca-Cola** (55 Martin Luther King Jr. Drive, S.E.; 404–676–5151),

Rich's Great Tree

Rich's department store began erecting a gigantic downtown Christmas tree for the enjoyment of Atlanta's citizens in 1947. When the downtown store closed, the annual tree ceremony was moved to the plaza at Underground Atlanta in 1990. The traditional Thanksgiving weekend lighting ceremony of the more than seventy-foot-tall evergreen attracts thousands of viewers. Entertainment is provided by local choruses, church choirs, and soloists.

adjacent to Underground Atlanta, hosts an annual outside skating rink open from Thanksgiving through New Year's weekend. Rental skates are available and rink hours are from 10:00 A.M. to 9:00 P.M. daily. Ninety minutes of skating with skate rental costs $3 to $5 ($2 off with a museum ticket). Don't worry if you think you're the world's most inept klutz. Few Southerners have ever ice skated, and most long-time transplants haven't skated for years. Wobbling around and falling down only add to the hilarity. What better excuse to hold hands or put your arms around each other than to steady your honey? After your icy interlude, sip on some hot chocolate or steaming coffee while admiring Rich's great tree—a longtime Atlanta tradition. If you want to go inside to get warm during the Christmas season, World of Coca-Cola museum ($6/$4 for seniors) features a seasonal display of early Sundblom artwork of Santas with Coca-Cola.

DAY ONE: EVENING

Dinner

Go back to the hotel for a nice warm shower, then wrap up in the lush bathrobes provided by the hotel while you get ready for dinner—you'll want to dress up. Because you're staying at the best, why not have dinner at the best? **The Restaurant** at the Ritz-Carlton Downtown

(181 Peachtree Street, N.W.; 404–659–0400; expensive) is one of only a few restaurants in the state to earn prestigious four-star, five-diamond awards. Exquisite international cuisine guarantees an out-of-this-world dining experience amid luxurious surroundings. Unusual menu items include such specialties as squab, sea bream, and prawn tartar, but always ask about the chef's special, which is sure to be out of this world.

Zip back up to the room and change to comfortable shoes, maybe even warmer clothes, and continue your festive evening by strolling over to **Centennial Olympic Park** at International Boulevard and Techwood Drive, a legacy of the 1996 Summer Olympic Games. Festooned for the holiday season, **Holiday in the Park** is a festival of lights, street vendors, "snow" men, and interactive activities. Join in the holiday mirth by watching children of all ages zooming down a giant sleigh slide or try it yourself.

Wend your way back to the hotel where you can celebrate the season with hot-spiced wine or a hot-buttered rum toddy before drifting off to bed. Share your fervor for the season and each other; then fall into blissful dreams of sugar plums dancing in your heads.

DAY TWO: MORNING

Indulge in a light breakfast or dig into a full meal at the buffet in the **Cafe** at the hotel. In addition to pastries and fruit, you can choose Belgian waffles, omelettes, or eggs Benedict.

One of Atlanta's premier holiday extravaganzas is the Egleston Children's Hospital **Festival of Trees** (404–325–NOEL; admission $8/$5 for seniors), generally held the second week in December, with proceeds going to the hospital. A tradition for more than twenty years, the glittering gala is the largest of its kind in North America. Held at the Georgia World Congress Center adjacent to Centennial Olympic Park, the exhibition features three hundred lavishly adorned trees and wreaths, elegantly decorated room vignettes, and imaginative holiday stockings—all created by the region's best designers and artists, clubs, and school children, and all vying for coveted prizes.

Light Up Your Life

Numerous Christmas lighting extravaganzas make the season bright at night. Here are a few:

♥ *Stone Mountain Park (U.S. 78; 770–498–5702) features a Christmas illumination of the park. The Holiday Celebration at the park features twinkling giant greeting card displays, larger-than-life Christmas toys, and Snowflake Lane, as well as yuletide laser light shows, sing-along train rides to the North Pole past the Twelve Days of Christmas track-side lighting display, horse-drawn carriage rides, Jingle Bell Bonfire with hot cocoa and marshmallows, and visits with Santa. (Friday through Sunday Thanksgiving through mid December, then nightly through December 31.)*

♥ *Life University of Chiropractic (1269 Barclay Circle, Marietta, 770–426–2875; free) presents a display featuring two million lights on a 2.7-mile drive around the campus. Among the scenes are a 150-foot-long, nineteenth-century historic village; a 200-foot-long Nativity scene; 150-foot-long Santa's Flight School; a 65-foot Santa and sleigh; a 60-foot Christmas tree; and seven animated Christmas displays. (Thanksgiving through January 1.)*

♥ *Chateau Elan welcomes the season with Lighting Up the Chateau (100 Tour de France, Braselton; 770–932–0900, ext. 6301), when more than 30,000 lights illuminate the sixteenth-century-style chateau. On select weekends there are hot air balloon glows, tethered balloon rides, helicopter rides, pony rides, music, storytelling, ice-carving demonstrations, Irish dance performances, and hayrides.*

♥ *Lake Lanier Islands Magical Nights of Lights (Holiday Road, Lake Lanier Islands; 770–932–7200), a 6-mile spectacular through the wintery night, is the largest and most elaborate animated light display in the South. Scenes and characters include Teddy Bear Lane, Sailboat Regatta, Nativity, Santa's Workshop, Holiday Village with midway rides, Frosty's Playland, North Pole Express, Santa's Elves at Work, Icicle Bridge, and the Twelve Days of Christmas. After driving through the sparkling winter wonderland, stop by Santa's Workshop, roast some marshmallows, and enjoy seasonal crafts, music, shopping, and foods. (Thanksgiving through New Year's Eve.)*

Hanukkah and Kwanzaa activities abound. Ask your concierge for more details.

Many of Atlanta's private homes are open for tours at Christmas and museum houses are bedecked in their best finery.

♥ *Christmas at Callanwolde (980 Briarcliff Road, N.E.; 404–872–5338), usually held the first two weeks of December, has been a Christmas tradition for more than twenty years. The Gothic–Tudor mansion, which is now a fine arts center, is decorated with lavishly trimmed Christmas trees, floral displays, and glistening lights. In addition, there is constant entertainment, organ music, and refreshments.*

♥ *Bulloch Hall (180 Bulloch Avenue, Roswell; 770–992–1731) was the home of Mittie Bulloch, who married Theodore Roosevelt Sr. in the house on December 22, 1853. They later became the parents of Theodore Roosevelt and grandparents of Eleanor Roosevelt. The house is trimmed by various florists and interior designers as it would have been when Mittie lived there. Teddy bears are often a prominent part of the decorations in homage to the president for whom they were named. Buy gift items, hot drinks, and cookies in a gift shop. Christmas entertainment includes singing groups, and on the weekend closest to December 22, a re-creation of Mittie's wedding.*

♥ *Marietta's Christmas Pilgrimage Tour of Homes, usually held the first weekend in December, permits a glimpse behind closed doors of private historic homes decked out in their Christmas finery. Choose between daylight and candlelight tours of six lovingly restored nineteenth-century homes filled with antique collections, special Christmas charm homes, and six public buildings. Shuttle service is available. Mail-order tickets must be purchased by December 1. Tickets the weekend of the tour are available at the Marietta–Cobb Welcome Center and Visitors Bureau (4 Depot Street; 770–429–1115).*

♥ *Other houses decked out for the season and offering tours include the Governor's Mansion (391 West Paces Ferry Road, N.W.; 404–261–1858), the Swan House at the Atlanta History Center (130 West Paces Ferry Road, N.W., 404–814–4000), and Rhodes Hall (1516 Peachtree Street, 404–885–7800).*

Get fabulous ideas for decking the halls of your own abode for the Christmas season by touring the festival regardless of whether this is your first Christmas with your sweetie or your fiftieth. If this is your first, compare notes on how each of your families traditionally decorate and celebrate. Combine the best of both or start your own joyous traditions.

You can bid on the trimmed trees and wreaths, so you may be lucky enough to acquire one of these gaily ornamented treasures. Imaginatively decorated full-size trees vie with gaily trimmed tabletop trees as well as with sumptuous rooms created by Atlanta's top designers to portray their elegant or whimsical interpretations of the current year's holiday theme. Full-size dioramas depict Christmas traditions in other countries. Many of Atlanta's noted chefs concoct gigantic elaborate gingerbread houses and castles. Almost nonstop entertainment by local and national groups add to the heady holiday spirit. Specialty gift shops afford opportunities to find the perfect gift for each other or for someone else on your list. Last, but not least, selections at the food court may stave off starvation until your next meal.

DAY TWO: AFTERNOON

Lunch

Take Peachtree Street north to the Midtown section around Peachtree and Ponce de Leon. Attached to the Fox Theater is an intimate and sophisticated coffee shop called **Churchill Grounds** (660 Peachtree Street, N.E.; 404–876–3030; moderate). Enjoy a light lunch of sandwiches, salads, or pastas, an espresso or cappuccino, and maybe a dessert if you're feeling naughty.

Go next door to the fabulous **Fox Theater** (660 Peachtree Street, N.E.; 404–249–6400) to attend a matinee performance of **The Nutcracker,** a traditional Christmas favorite. Prices range from $10 to $42. Get there early enough to explore the theater, which is a show in itself. Built in 1929, it is a masterpiece of excess—a Moorish, Egyptian, and Art Deco treasure resembling a fortress courtyard inside. Be sure gape at the sheik's "tent" in the balcony and watch for twinkling stars and the clouds moving across the "sky." In our opinion, the best seats in the house are in the loge or the first dress circle. You can order tickets through the Fox box office or Ticketmaster (404–249–6400).

DAY TWO: EVENING

Dinner

After the performance, treat yourselves to a special dinner at **The Abbey** (163 Ponce de Leon at Piedmont Road; 404–876–8532; expensive). True to its name, The Abbey is located in a Gothic-style church built in 1915. Forty-foot-high vaulted ceilings soar over massive stained glass windows and Gothic furniture. Waiters clad as monks serve you continental/ French cuisine, while a harpist plays softly in the choir loft. The subdued, romantic setting will permit you to share your innermost feelings and dreams with each other. Topping the menu are lobster, a game duo consisting of venison and squab, and duck. The extensive wine list has been voted one of the country's top one hundred by *The Wine Spectator,* while the restaurant itself has been voted one of the top ten restaurants in America by sixty thousand traveling business executives.

Linger over your elegant repast as long as you like, then return to the hotel to create some of your own Christmas memories.

DAY THREE: MORNING

Brunch

For a touch of whimsey have brunch at the **Buckhead Diner** (3073 Piedmont Road at East Paces Ferry Road; 404–262–3336; expensive), a glitzy chrome eatery a la the fifties with an energetic atmosphere where the who's who of Atlanta are often seen supping with sports and entertainment celebrities. It's a great place for people watching, and some mighty fine cars pull up in the crowded parking lot. A modern American restaurant with a creative menu, the Buckhead Diner is also known for its excellent service. Brunch is ordered from the menu, and choices range from Southwestern eggs Benedict to Savannah blue crab to sea bass filet to veal and wild mushroom meatloaf. Buy a baseball cap or T-shirt to take home as a souvenir. Get there early—reservations are not taken.

You've played for two days and reveled in each other. Now it's time for some serious Christmas shopping. Two of the most upscale malls in the Atlanta area are located across the street from each other at Peachtree and Lenox Roads (popularly known as the intersection of Ecstasy and Nirvana), near the Buckhead Diner. Not only do these malls have the most authentic Santas in town and the most opulent Christmas decorations and activities, but they both boast some of the swankiest names in retail, valet parking, concierge service, personal shoppers, food courts, and world-class dining. (Learn much more about the attractions of these malls in the "Adding Sparkle to Your Life" itinerary). If your tastes run more to art and antiques, off-the-beaten-track Bennett Street is crammed with small shops and galleries.

With your spirits soaring from your Christmas trip to Atlanta, with memories made, and perhaps all your gift shopping done, the rest of the holiday season should be a breeze.

FOR MORE ROMANCE

Although Atlanta offers dozens of theatrical performances every single week throughout the year, the Christmas season overflows with traditional works and some new pieces. Among the old standards are a Gospel Christmas with the Atlanta Symphony Orchestra (ASO) at the Woodruff Arts Center, Christmas with Robert Shaw and the ASO and guest choirs, the *Messiah* with the ASO and the Robert Shaw Chorale, *The Nutcracker* at the Fox Theater, *A Christmas Carol* at the Alliance Theater in the Woodruff Arts Center, *The 1940s Radio Hour* at

Theater on the Square in Marietta, and *An Appalachian Christmas Homecoming* performed by the Georgia Ensemble Theater at the Roswell Cultural Arts Center. For laughs, thrills, and chills, try the Christmas-themed mystery-dinner show at Agatha's—A Taste of Mystery. Check with your concierge for dozens of other suggestions.

HEARTS AND ARTS

ITINERARY 7
Two days and one night

A FEAST FOR THE EYE
THE VISUAL ARTS

*P*icture this: a weekend for two dedicated to discovering the overflowing palette of Atlanta's colorful arts community, its art museums, chic galleries, avant-garde exhibitions, and art for public spaces. We'll also introduce you to one of the city's most artistic restaurants, which is located in a historic facility renovated with the artist in mind, a restaurant priced for the starving artist, and an art studio where you can create your own masterpiece. If your love affair, like history's great works of art, has stood the test of time, but your sense of romance has faded like an old master that hasn't been cared for, then this artful weekend getaway may help the two of you bring bright color back to your masterpiece. If your passion hasn't cooled over time, this holiday weekend will surely add fuel to the fire.

Practical Notes: We've planned this weekend for a Saturday and Sunday, when hotel rates are cheaper, but you can enjoy this artsy getaway any two days of the week. If you're seriously considering the acquisition of any sizable artwork, be sure to bring some packing material so that you can get your treasure home safely. The King Plow Arts Center Gallery isn't open to the public when there's a special event going on there, so check ahead with the Bold American Food Company (404–815–1178) to be sure it's going to be open. If it isn't, don't go to the arts center until it's time for dinner. Your hotel is directly across the street from the MARTA Arts Station, which makes access to some areas of the city easy, and you'll be staying within two blocks of the Woodruff Arts Center. Nonetheless, you'll need a car for most of this artsy vacation. As an added bonus, if you can plan your getaway in the fall or spring, strolling through the city during those colorful seasons is like being part of an impressionist painting.

Romance at a Glance

♥ *Indulge your passion for masterpieces at the High Museum of Art.*

♥ *Dine on food as art at The Food Studio.*

♥ *Nibble on starving artist portions at Cafe Tu Tu Tango.*

♥ *Revitalize your romantic energies with the sheer joy depicted at Folk Art Park.*

♥ *Shop for an important piece of art for your own gallery of romance at Nexus Contemporary Art Center.*

♥ *Create your own work of art at Wired & Fired: A Pottery Playhouse.*

DAY ONE: Afternoon

When you arrive in downtown Atlanta, head for your weekend abode, the intimate Spanish-inspired **Granada Suite Hotel** (1302 West Peachtree Street; 404–876–6100; $99–$199). A small work of art in its own right, the hacienda began life in 1922 as an apartment house, but ten years ago it was transformed into a boutique hotel with guest rooms, suites, and penthouse suites. True to the Spanish style of architecture, the hotel wraps around a charming courtyard enhanced with a bubbling fountain. The lobby, which faces the courtyard, is furnished with its own collection of Spanish artwork and opulent Victorian furnishings. Take advantage of the weekend Honeymoon package ($159), which includes champagne, Godiva chocolates, and a bubble bath for the Jacuzzi tub in your suite.

Once you've checked in and gotten settled, you'll be ready to head out to explore some of the city's art galleries. If the

King Plow Arts Center Gallery is open, you won't be returning to the hotel before an early dinner and a play, so you'll want to wear something nice that will make the transition from afternoon to evening. If the gallery is closed, you can come back to the hotel to relax in the Jacuzzi before dinner.

Atlanta boasts dozens of large and small galleries and this afternoon's art-lovers' adventure searches out and explores some of them. The **Art Gallery Association** (770–396–8010), a professional organization of Atlanta's finest galleries—all of which are open to the public free of charge—has prepared a map/brochure to the galleries, which is available through the Atlanta Convention and Visitors Bureau (233 Peachtree Street, N.E., Suite 100; 800–ATLANTA) and many hotel concierges.

Here are some highlights and other places you might want to visit: The twenty-two artists of the **Artists' Atelier of Atlanta** (800 Miami Circle; 404–231–5999) invite you to come and smell the paint at the cooperative's galleries, working studios, and gift shop. Take your time and stroll through the wonderful, eclectic medley of different art forms presented here. Talk to the artists and share their love of shape, color, and technique. Look for a special piece to add to your personal collection as a reminder of your romantic weekend or something to give as a gift to your favorite art lover. Linger as long as you like, but remember you have other galleries to visit elsewhere.

When you can tear yourselves away, it's time for you two to heat up your relationship at your next stop: **Frabel** (695 Antone Street; 404–351–9794; free). At Frabel, the world's largest torch-working glass art studio and gifts gallery, you can watch one-of-a-kind sculptural flame-work glass art masterpieces in the making. Many of Frabel's sensual pieces reside in prestigious museums and are owned by celebrities. Although many sculptures are on display, the pièce de résistance is the replica of Queen Elizabeth's *Palm Tree*.

When you're ready to cool down a little and move on to visit the galleries, studios, and artist press at the **Nexus Contemporary Art Center** (535 Means Street;

404–688–1970; $3). At the highly recognized multidisciplinary arts establishment, the emphasis is on experimental visual and book arts. This is a place to let your imaginations run wild. Today's art is so much more up close and personal than that of the old masters, so indulge yourselves. Located in renovated historic warehouse, Nexus is the anchor of the growing Marietta Street Arts Corridor. Before you enter, however, take time to admire one of the city's public art projects in the Nexus Contemporary Art Center Plaza. Twelve Georgia artists were commissioned to create a variety of designs for forty-two-inch-tall bollards lining the entrance to the arts center. Founded in 1973 by a group of photographers as a place to exhibit their works, Nexus began humbly as a revolution against the status quo in an art world that didn't recognize photography as an art. Always cutting edge and just the place to stimulate your awareness of the many styles of art and beauty, Nexus showed Mapplethorpe before he became a politically incorrect issue and showed the first Kara Walker silhouettes of racial stereotypes. Call for times of scheduled gallery tours.

Your next stop is the **King Plow Arts Center** (887 West Marietta Street, N.W.; 404–885–9933). Housed in an award-winning, artfully restored historic structure, the arts center was once a factory where plows and other agricultural equipment were manufactured. Today the ninety-plus-year-old buildings retain turn-of-the-century artifacts and industrial characteristics, such as arched windows and doorways, twenty-eight-foot ceilings with clerestories, and heart pine and steel columns and trusses. Handmade brick delineates the patio, central courtyard, and commons areas. The multiuse complex, created by the original owner's grandsons, is home to offices, loft apartments, an art gallery, the Actor's Express Theater, and your destination for dinner: The Food Studio. The gallery is free and displays the work of local artists as well as serving as an avant-garde venue for parties and special events. This out-of-the-way location is well worth seeking out for its urban chic.

DAY ONE: Evening

Dinner

Dinner is at **The Food Studio** (887 West Marietta Street, Studio K-102; 404–815–6677; moderate to expensive), one of the linchpins of the King Plow Arts Center. Exterior and interior spaces, furnishings, and food and its presentation are all forms of artistic expression, and rarely are they married so well as here. Dine on the high art of innovative regional American cuisine artistically presented in the eclectic setting of a stunning converted warehouse, winner of the 1997 Urban Design Award. Spacious and raw, the restaurant's look has the Spartan look of an artist's studio merged with a retrofit warehouse. Brick walls, massive exposed wooden beams and machinery gears, bold brushed-steel detailing, dark wood, and a deep blue and burgundy color scheme create a seductive backdrop for your romantic tryst. Flickering light from dozens of candles and oil lamps (and from the fireplace in season) adds to mysterious sexy atmosphere.

The culinary formula used at The Food Studio blends art, culture, fashion, and entertainment to create a fresh culinary montage of American regional tastes, textures, and traditions presented with artistic care. Specialties we recommend include black sesame bread sticks, Navajo fry bread, grilled Alaskan halibut, tequila- and ginger-cured salmon, seared mushroom-encrusted talapia, braised rabbit enchiladas, and apple-stuffed smoked pork loin. Among the seductive desserts are warm berry soup and chocolate truffle cake. Although some diners prefer to watch the show by sitting near the exhibition kitchen, while others join the lively throng at the cosmopolitan wine bar, for the height of romance, ask for a cozy table by the fireplace in the upstairs loft or outside on the intimate patio with its lush landscaping and tinkling fountains. The patio's twinkling fairy lights and the city lights flickering in the background provide a nighttime landscape any painter or photographer would covet. (Reservations are recommended.)

If you two art lovers are also budding culinary artists, Chef Chris Brandt offers monthly interactive cooking lessons, allowing you to work hand in hand with him in his award-winning exhibition kitchen. At the culmination of this hands-on epicurean experience, you're served the meal you just prepared along with appropriate wines.

Nightlife

Having sated your appetite for gastronomic artistry, stroll back to the center of the complex to one of the city's fifty-plus studios for a theatrical performance. Here you can snuggle together while you're transported to the never-never land of a theater at the **Actor's Express** (807 West Marietta Street, 404–607–7469). When the play is over, return to your love nest.

Enjoy a nightcap in the courtyard if the weather is nice. Drink in the beauty of the setting as you share your feelings about the art you've seen today. Finally, return to the privacy of your suite to create your own special form of art.

DAY TWO: MORNING

Breakfast

Enjoy some early morning snuggle time with your sweetheart; there's absolutely no reason to get up early. When hunger finally forces you out of bed, share the continental breakfast included in your weekend package. After all, considering your work-of-art repast last night, a simple breakfast is called for.

※

This morning will be devoted to viewing one of the permanent legacies of the 1996 Centennial Olympic Summer Games. Downtown where Baker Street meets Piedmont, a pair of bridges cross over the I–75/I–85 connector. This intersection is the home of **Folk Art Park,** a permanent outdoor tribute to Southern folk art, which contains designs by some of the South's best outdoor artists. As art lovers, you'll get a real kick out of this outpouring of playful images. Two of Georgia's most creative folk art geniuses are Summerville's Howard Finster and the late Eddie Owens Martin of Buena Vista, the self-styled St. EOM. *Homage to Reverend Howard Finster,* by the artist's grandson, uses found objects and concrete, metal, glass, and marble to create cast materials similar to those found in Finster's Paradise Gardens. The quixotic, brightly painted concrete figures in *Homage to St. EOM's Pasaquan,* replicate the visionary environment in which the late artist lived in south Georgia. Other works include *Quilt Traditions,* a series of quilt pattern motifs by nine quilters cut out in the stainless steel roof of a sunshade structure; the *Sculpture Garden,* which several artists have rendered in a variety of mediums; and *The Gourd Tree,* made of steel and plastic gourds, which houses Brazilian purple martins. On the Courtland Avenue bridge at Ralph McGill Avenue (part of the same intersection), painted steel *Windmills* gyrate cheerfully in the breeze. *Rolling Hills of Georgia* is the work of three artists, which they executed in concrete, glass marbles, and painted steel. Drink in the unadulterated joy and delightful energy these exuberant creations evoke, and let the whimsical art feed the romance in your own souls. Linger awhile. This is a wonderful place to take pictures of each other amidst all this creativity.

DAY TWO: AFTERNOON

Lunch

Because you had a light breakfast, hunger will eventually strike; that means it's time to experience another of Atlanta's clever fusions of art and food. **Cafe Tu Tu Tango** (220 Pharr Road; 404–841–6222), in the heart of Buckhead, is funky, smart, innovative, and dedicated to the proposition that even poor artists should eat well. The multiethnic eatery resembles a

Ten Most Romantic Pieces of Art at the High Museum

Dr. Ned Rifkin, director, and the curators at the High Museum rated these works as the most romantic in the permanent collection:

1. Eternal Spring, *Auguste Rodin*
2. Paris and Oenone, *Pieter Lastman*
3. The Funeral of Atala, *Anne-Louis Girodet de Roucy Trioson*
4. Hang Him, *Nicholas Africano*
5. Hit My Summer, Hard and Fast, *Jim Dine*
6. Red Canna, *Georgia O'Keeffe*
7. Number 73, *Mark Rothko*
8. The Heart Knows No Control, *Hollis Sigler*
9. Life Saver, *Man Ray*
10. Bench House, *Jackie Ferrara*

Spanish artist's studio. On the menu created for starving artists, fifty items are served as appetizer-sized portions meant to be shared, so you can both try a little bit of everything. Specialties include Cajun chicken egg rolls, Oriental steak skewers, Mediterranean spinach dip, and Barcelona stir fry. Save room for the guava cheesecake. Cheerful yellow accents and simple mission-style tables and chairs provide a friendly environment, one where local artists work, display, and sell their works. Outdoor seating is a pleasant alternative on nice days. (Reservations aren't accepted.)

With lunch nicely finished, it's time for Atlanta's main art event. Return south to the **High Museum of Art** (1280 Peachtree Street, N.E.; 404–733–4444; admission $6/$4 for seniors). When the museum's collection was moved into its award-winning, sleekly modern edifice, itself a work of art designed by Richard Meier in 1983, it was extolled by the *New York Times* as "among the best museum structures any city has built in at least a generation," but it took traditional Southerners some time to get used to it. Further lauded by professional groups, it was named by the American Institute of Architects as one of the "ten best works of American architecture of the 1980s." Take a few minutes to walk around the grounds to enjoy the outdoor sculptures.

Inside, the museum's permanent collection of more than ten thousand objects includes a significant collection of American paintings of the nineteenth century and works of major contemporary artists. The American collection also includes paintings, sculpture, and drawings from the West Foundation Collection, which is on extended loan. Critically acclaimed, the Virginia Carroll Crawford Collection of American Decorative Arts documents styles from 1825 through the early twentieth century. The Samuel H. Kress Foundation has added Italian paintings and sculpture from the fourteenth century through the eighteenth century to the museum's collection, allowing you the opportunity to examine the details of various masters' hands. In addition, the museum houses European masters, English ceramics, prints of French and German impressionists, and Sub-Saharan African Art. The long-term "About Masks" exhibition helps visitors of all ages look at art through participatory activities. An array of very special traveling exhibitions have recently included the works of Monet, Matisse, and Picasso, as well as a selection of pieces from the Pierpont Morgan Library. If you need a respite from the intense power of so much art, the High Cafe features an assortment of coffees, bakery items, and sandwiches; the High Museum Gift Shop sells quality jewelry, art, and art-related merchandise. (Free on Thursday from 1:00–5:00 P.M. On fourth Fridays, there's live musical entertainment and a cash bar in the evening.) Located next door in the Atlanta Memorial Arts Center is **Gallery One** where cutting-edge student work from the **Atlanta College of Art** is displayed. Folk art is a growing area of the museum's collection. It and photography are exhibited at the museum's branch facility, the **High Museum of Art Folk Art and Photography Galleries,** located downtown at the Georgia-Pacific Center.

After all the artistic inspiration you've gotten this weekend, it's your turn to eat, drink, and be creative at one of Atlanta's paint-your-own-pottery studios, which sells the joys of participating in the artistic process. In general, they follow the same concept: You select a piece of white, unglazed pottery and let your impish imagination run riot as you create your own memento of this weekend of romance and the arts. Even the artistically challenged klutz can adorn plates, mugs, bowls, candlesticks, platters, pitchers, you name it with colorful glazes. Leave your masterpiece to be kiln fired, and a few days later you can pick up the finished product. Prices for the pottery pieces range from $4 to $50 in addition to the $8 per hour to paint. **Art & Soul: An Arts and Crafts Cafe!** (Brookwood Square Shopping Center, 2140 Peachtree Road; 404–352–1222) offers other crafts, including mosaics, glass painting, beaded jewelry, painting terra cotta pots and birdhouses, making sand castles, and tie-dying fabric. It also serves munchies, cookies, coffee, tea, and sodas. **The Painted Biscuit** (247 Buckhead Avenue; 404–869–0411), which is near Nickiemoto's and Cafe Tu Tu Tango, allows customers to bring in food from those establishments. **Wired and Fired: A Pottery Playhouse** (279-A East Paces Ferry Road; 404–842–1919), also serves lavish desserts, coffee, beer, and wine. The arts and crafts emporium also has menus on hand from nearby restaurants so that customers can bring in food of their choice.

FOR MORE ROMANCE

Like its astounding array of theatrical and musical offerings, Atlanta offers an extraordinary number and variety of arts venues, so if you two art connoisseurs have more time or can plan more than one visit, here are some more suggestions. The **Robert C. Williams American Museum of Papermaking** (Institute of Paper Science and Technology Building, 500 Tenth

Street, N.W.; 404–894–6663) charts the chronological history of papermaking, including the introduction of books and printing. The **Oglethorpe University Museum** (4484 Peachtree Road, N.E.; 404–364–8555) is dedicated to figurative and realist art that is international, spiritual, and/or mystical. The **Michael C. Carlos Museum** (571 Kilgo Circle, on the Emory University campus; 404–727–7522) brims with art from the ancient world. **Callanwalde Fine Arts Center** (980 Briarcliff Road, N.E.; 404–872–5338), a work of art itself, is a fine arts center located in a magnificent Gothic-Tudor mansion built in 1920 by Charles Howard Candler, eldest son of the founder of Coca-Cola. Located on twelve acres of sculptured lawns and formal gardens, the mansion is listed on the National Register of Historic Places. Check local newspapers or ask your concierge for a schedule of exhibitions. Other places to look for art are **City Gallery at Chastain Park**, **Bennett Street** (see "Beverly Hills Southeast"), **Marietta Museum of Art** (see "Love Squared"), **ArtWalk at Lenox Square, Spelman College Museum of Fine Arts, Spruill Gallery and Historic Home, Gwinnett Fine Arts Center,** and the galleries of Roswell: **Heaven Blue Rose, Potters Guild, Artistic Glass, Gallery V Ltd., Anne Jackson Gallery,** and the **Raiford Gallery.** (In addition, check out the "Atlanta's Cultural Heart," "The Magical Emerald City," and "Tie-dyed Twosome, or Bring on the Noise, Bring on the Funk" itineraries to learn about walking tours to view public art.)

ITINERARY 8
Two days and one night

ALL THE WORLD'S A STAGE
ATLANTA'S THEATER SCENE

*D*o the crash and clank of ferocious sword play, beautiful period and contemporary costumes, and the brilliance of the Bard's dialogue set the stage to light the fires of your passion? When the theater lights dim and the velvet curtain rises, do your hearts begin to flutter in unison? Then it's obvious you're smitten by that special kind of magic that only live theater can evoke. This weekend, you will headline your own romantic production of several acts by attending two different performances of Shakespeare's works at different venues, staying in the style of a star at the historic Biltmore Suites, dining at exciting restaurants, and spending the *entre acts* creating your own body of work.

Practical Notes: This holiday for the soul must be scheduled during the summer (mid-June through mid-August) or in October when the Georgia Shakespeare Festival is in residence, and it must be arranged for Saturday–Sunday, so you can see the Sunday matinee. Because the productions are done in repertory, if you can come on Friday for a three-day weekend, you can see a different play at the festival in the same getaway. Although you might think attending Shakespearian plays is a formal affair, you'll only need casual clothes for this dramatic weekend—both theater venues are extremely informal. Also, for those brave enough to take a chance on last-minute plans, you can purchase tickets for a variety of performances around town for half price on the day of the performance at ½ **TIX,** but tickets must be purchased between 10:00 A.M. and 6:00 P.M. for evening events and between 10:00 A.M. and one hour before the performance for matinees. Purchases are cash only, so that means you must make a personal appearance to get them. These half-price tickets are available from **TicketMaster at Blockbuster Music** (2099 Peachtree Road, Buckhead; 404–605–7131). We strongly recommend, however, that you purchase tickets in advance to avoid disappointment.

Romance at a Glance

♥ *Set the stage for romance at the Shakespeare Tavern.*

♥ *Raise the curtain on comedy or tragedy at the Georgia Shakespeare Festival.*

♥ *Take center stage in a penthouse Jacuzzi suite at the Biltmore Suites.*

♥ *Savor an entre-act meal at the Horseradish Grill.*

DAY ONE: AFTERNOON

Take center stage in your own drama at the **Biltmore Suites Hotel** (30 Fifth Street, N.E.; 404–874–0824; $149–$299), a fine old dowager of days gone by. Created as a magnificent set for countless comedies and dramas in 1924, the hotel almost became its own tragedy when plans were made to tear it down. Although 75 percent of it sits empty while being converted for mixed use, one end is an intimate all-suites inn. For this special weekend, splurge and reserve one of the nine rooftop suites ($229–$299): eight are trilevel and one is bilevel. If you don't have that much backing for your production, choose one of the eighteen one-level Jacuzzi suites, which offer wonderful views of downtown ($149–$189). Although a little dated, the suites have a delightful retro Art Deco feel (but are undergoing renovation) and include at least one bedroom with a brass or mahogany bed, a bath, a living/dining area, and a kitchen or kitchenette, allowing you to bring in snacks, drinks, and breakfast fixings. If you arrive early enough, you can rehearse for later activities in your rooftop Jacuzzi before you have to get ready for dinner and a magical night of theater.

DAY ONE: EVENING

Dinner

Eat, drink, and be merry at a play performed in the casual atmosphere and Globe-like ambience of the **Shakespeare Tavern** (499 Peachtree Street, N.E.; 404–874–5299; $16.50 Thursday, Friday, and Sunday; $19.50 Saturday, dinner an extra $10–$15 per person), home of the Atlanta Shakespeare Theater. Designed to resemble a tavern of the Elizabethan period, the pub will be the scene of both your dinner and the play. Before the performances order British-pub menu choices, such as Cornish pasty, Cornish gobble, or the King's Supper, along with soups, sandwiches, desserts, and Irish ales and premium brews. Thus fortified, turn your attention to the stage and the Elizabethan set; the culturally diverse ensemble, wearing hand-crafted Renaissance or Medieval costumes; live acoustic music, and the boisterous action of another of the master's works. (In addition to Shakespearian plays, the tavern also stages original plays, variety shows, and classics by the likes of George Bernard Shaw, Christopher Marlowe, Albert Camus, and Moliere.) (Doors to the tavern open forty-five minutes before the performance.)

Nightlife

After the curtain calls, drop in at **Cafe Intermezzo** (1845 Peachtree Road, N.E.; 404–355–0411) for a nightcap and live entertainment, then return to your penthouse suite and become the only two members of the cast of your own production. After all, part of romance is the art of make believe. The rooftop Jacuzzi with its spectacular views of the downtown skyline is sure to create a scene in which you kindle your ardor for each other.

DAY TWO: MORNING

Brunch

Sleep late, read the morning papers, nibble on something you brought in or run downstairs for coffee and a Danish to tide you over until brunch. Last night's performances should have stimulated your desire for more Shakespeare, but as the morning rolls on satisfy your appetites at the **Horseradish Grill** (4320 Powers Ferry Road; 404–255–7277; expensive), located in a chic Buckhead barn. Named one of the "Top 25 Restaurants in the Country" by *Esquire* and "Top Thirteen Restaurants in the Country" by *Bon Appétite*, the Horseradish Grill is true to its authentic southern cooking traditions, creating simple but cleverly prepared regional dishes and homemade desserts. Order brunch specialties including pecan waffles, omelet of the day, chicken-liver salad, potato hash—from the à la carte menu. French windows look out onto a shady scene: an outdoor stone-floored terrace where you can choose to dine in good weather. (Reservations suggested.)

Alternately, you can take a picnic purchased in the gourmet deli at a grocery store or gourmet takeout place to enjoy at the outdoor tables on the lawn or terrace before the play.

DAY TWO: Afternoon

The castle- and battlement-like structures and fluttering flags of the beautiful campus of Oglethorpe University announce the home of the **Georgia Shakespeare Festival** (4484 Peachtree Road, N.E.; 264–0020; $18–$24). Whether you've brought a picnic or not, come early enough before the production to relax and people watch out on the patio or on the ground surrounding the theater. Part of the festival experience is the raucous preshow on the lawn.

During midsummer and in October, the Bard's historical opuses, comedies, and classics come to life on the stage of the **Conant Performing Arts Center.** For eleven years, plays were enacted in a tent—much to the delight of audiences—but sultry Atlanta summers and some tempestuous storms finally drove the performances inside. In 1997, the intimate 510-seat arts center was built—a worthy stage for any company enacting one of the Bard's works. In keeping with its heritage, the exterior of the center was

created to resemble a cheery, circular, yellow-and-white tent on the outside, and in fact, the side walls can be raised on pleasant evenings to re-create the traditional outdoor ambience, but much to the relief of actors and audience alike, on hot days and nights everyone can enjoy the production in air-conditioned comfort. In addition, the new theater permits improved acoustics and better views of the stage. So successful is the new venue that tickets sales increased by 20 percent the first year. Now a magnificent set for love's labors, the center is a perfect place to share the thespians' art with your own personal producer.

And now for the main event: the play. When the lights dim, take your seats and your sweetie's hand, for a demanding highbrow production that is often brilliant. Powerful, timeless themes and magical theatrical effects combine to create an unforgettable experience for you and your leading man/lady.

As the curtain falls on your weekend of make believe, return home to your own balcony scene.

FOR MORE ROMANCE

If your hearts aren't set on Shakespeare, Atlanta has so much fabulous live theater to offer (fifty theater companies; yes, count them—fifty), you could plan a theater outing any weekend, indeed any day of the week, throughout the year. The Shakespeare Tavern is open year-round, so you can still get a fix of the Bard by combining a performance there with any weekend of other theatrics. If you two are totally enamored with live theater, it's possible to plan a weekend during which you'll immerse yourselves completely in dramatics by seeing a play Friday evening, a matinee and evening performance on Saturday, and a matinee and evening performance on Sunday—for a total of five different theater experiences in five different venues and still not have begun to scratch the surface of the quality and quantity of what Atlanta offers the theater lover. Several nationally and internationally known productions, such as *Driving Miss Daisy,* have debuted in Atlanta before heading for the Great White Way. In addition to world-class theaters like the two stages at the **Alliance Theater** (Robert W. Woodruff Arts Center, 1280 Peachtree Street, N.E.; 404–733–5000), the Southeast's premier professional theater where *Miss Daisy* premiered, you can find quality theater at the **14th Street Playhouse, Actor's Express Theater** at the King Plow Arts Center, **The Theatrical Outfit, barking dog theater, Theater Gael, Jomandi Productions, Jewish Theater of the South,** Decatur's **Neighborhood Playhouse,** Marietta's **Theater in the Square,** Roswell's **Georgia Ensemble Theater,** about twenty-five small and alternative theaters, the **Ferst Theater** at Georgia Tech, and theaters at Georgia State and Emory Universities. Blockbuster Broadway musicals and other major traveling shows are performed frequently at the **Fox Theater** and the **Civic Center.**

ITINERARY 9
Two days and one night

LET YOUR HEARTS SING
ATLANTA'S MUSICAL ARTS

*P*repare to be filled with music as you set out on this weekend ode to joy. Although the strains that suffuse Atlanta's music scene range from the ridiculous to the sublime, on this itinerary we'll focus on the sublime. It's no overstatement to say that Midtown is the center of all that's divine in Atlanta, but on this getaway it will be the melodies and harmonies of Midtown's musical world that fill your days and night.

Practical Notes: When planning your euphonious trip to the land of romance, we strongly suggest that you arrange for tickets to the symphony before you arrive to avoid disappointment. There are other alternatives, however. One of the packages at your hotel includes the services of the concierge to arrange your tickets. Half-price tickets are available the day of performance (see "All the World's a Stage" for details). The hotel is located a block from the MARTA Arts Station, making it very convenient to access other areas of the city by rapid rail. You'll need a car, however, to reach most of the sites on this itinerary.

DAY ONE: Afternoon

The classy, top-of-the-line **Four Seasons Hotel Atlanta** (75 Fourteenth Street; 404–881–9898; $210–$525) is your lyrically civilized haven. Hallmarks of grace and intimacy, all Four Seasons hotels are noted for outstanding personal service, incomparable amenities, elegant rooms and suites, and spectacular restaurants. The Atlanta hostelry is no different. From the moment you step into the grand marble lobby, you'll know that this is the very vision of what a gracious hotel should be. Ask for a guest chamber on one of the top floors, where as rulers of all you survey, you'll be rewarded with fabulous sweeping views of downtown and Midtown.

Romance at a Glance

♥ *Stay at the Four Seasons Hotel Atlanta.*

♥ *Savor a masterful pre-concert dinner at the elegant City Grill.*

♥ *Watch fine stringed instruments being handcrafted at Williams Gengakki Violins.*

♥ *Enjoy a classical or pops performance of the Atlanta Symphony Orchestra.*

♥ *Sample après-concert sweets or aperitifs at the cafes and clubs on Crescent Avenue.*

Everything about the Four Seasons seduces lovers to make it their harmonic headquarters, but further enticements include several special weekend packages. The Artful Weekends package ($125), geared to patrons of the cultural arts, includes the services of the concierge to arrange for the best tickets available to whatever cultural events you desire to attend. You'll also be presented with an "artful amenity." This food item is created around a theme relating to some event going on in town. For example, during the recent High Museum of Art's Picasso exhibition, guests were treated to a white chocolate artist's palette. The Weekend package ($170) includes continental breakfast and parking; the Special Occasion package ($250 in a room, $460 in a suite) includes sparkling wine, strawberries on arrival, a Southern breakfast, and valet parking.

Check in, get in tune with your weekend habitat, then get ready for some exploring. Whether you're a musician or not, you might be intrigued by watching violins, violas, and cellos being crafted by hand by the artisans at **Williams Gengakki Violins** (2774 Hardman Court; 404–233–2811). In addition to the intense three-week construction project required to create each fine instrument, the two violin makers and a bow maker repair stringed instruments. How did a fine violin-making concern come to be located in Buckhead? While American Reginald Williams was living in Tokyo and teaching English, he started a violin business. When he returned to this country with his Japanese wife, Gengakki, they picked a city that had a large market for fine instruments. With a clientele of serious students, professionals, and collectors, Williams Gengakki sells instruments ranging in price from $350 for a child's starter violin to hundreds of thousands of dollars for a fine instrument. Williams also acquires antique instruments, such as a Stradivarius, for professionals and collectors.

Return to the hotel in time for an interlude of afternoon tea or champagne in the stunning lounge or a drink in the cozy bar. Let your rhythms slow to a romantic waltz as the two of you tune up for a symphonic evening.

DAY ONE: EVENING

Dinner

Make this a very dressy night out. The prelude begins with an elegant, exquisite dinner at the **City Grill** (50 Hurt Plaza at Edgewood Avenue; 404–524–2489; expensive; reservations are strongly suggested), a swanky, sophisticated restaurant where style, decor, and service blend like a resounding chord to give dining a sense of occasion. Use the restaurant's valet parking. The opulent restaurant is located in an old bank in the historic Hurt Building—one of the most architecturally beautiful buildings in downtown Atlanta. Enter the glass-enclosed atrium, then take the graceful marble curving staircase to the main dining room. This

Books Set in Atlanta

Music may be a symphony for the ears and the heart, but literature is a tone poem for the mind and soul. Here are several works of fiction with Atlanta as a backdrop as well as some memoirs about growing up in Atlanta.

Be Sweet: A Conditional Love Story, *Ray Blount Jr.*

Down on Ponce, *Fred Willard*

Driving Miss Daisy, *Alfred Uhry*

Gone With the Wind, *Margaret Mitchell*

Palindrome, *Stuart Woods*

Peachtree Road, *Anne Rivers Siddons*

Peachtree Street, U.S.A., *Celestine Sibley*

Prince of Tides, *Pat Conroy*

The Roswell Women, *Frances Patton Statham*

Where Peachtree Meets Sweet Auburn, *Gary M. Pomerantz*

Every Crooked Nanny, *and other mysteries by Kathy Hogan Trocheck*

gorgeous room, romantically dim in flickering candlelight, is enhanced by towering ceilings, columns, ornate plasterwork, marble, crystal chandeliers, plush fabrics, and subdued colors—yet, like a Beethoven symphony, it stills manages to be romantically restrained. Salute your darling by toasting each other with a glass of champagne, then peruse the menu. If you can resist holding hands across the table, you're not in tune with the romance of the moment.

The food of love, this imaginative, lyrically conceived and executed updated regional cuisine features a symphony of flavors. Great finesse goes into the little touches of the impeccable white-glove service—the most formal in town. Begin your medley of taste sensations with an appetizer, such as southern fried quail with cream gravy and raspberry black pepper biscuits, then move on to yellow corn and sweet potato soup, and finally to the magnificent entrees featuring quail, seafood, duck, beef, and pork. Just be careful not to eat or drink too much—you don't want to doze off during the concert. Save dessert until after the symphony.

Nightlife

With this fantastic gastronomic prelude under your belts, it's time to move on to the evening's featured performance. Retrace your route, return your car to the hotel (you won't need it anymore this evening), and walk to the Woodruff Arts Center for a stellar performance of the critically acclaimed **Atlanta Symphony Orchestra** (ASO) at Symphony Hall (1293 Peachtree Street, N.E.; 404–733–5000; $19–$48) in all its glory. Glorious harmonies reverberate through the hall during the Master Season, which features popular masterworks, from classic concertos to epic symphonies. These classical masterpieces are offered Thursday through Saturday nights. If you'd like something a little lighter, some weekends are set aside for a pops series, accompanied by coffee and pastries after the Saturday morning performance or by champagne after the Friday and Saturday night performances. Whichever you choose, a night at the symphony is a surefire way to add a special glow to your evening.

Once the crescendos have been reached and the maestro and musicians have taken their final bows, it's time for a passionate discussion of merits of the performance and some lively cafe life. Prolong the evening's delights by working your way down Crescent Avenue's "Restaurant Row" one block east of your hotel for dessert or a nightcap. When the weather is ideal, any of these small gems can be enjoyed al fresco because they all have intimate patios or decks. A drink at **South City Kitchen** (1144 Crescent Avenue, 404–873–7358), located in an updated house, is the ultimate urban escape. Try any one of fifty-four martinis at the **Martini Club** (1140 Crescent Avenue; 404–873–0795). Located in a 1920s home, the club's interior is a striking thirties/forties Art Deco decor. Intimate plush seating near fireplaces, live jazz, and an extensive selection of premium cigars, make this a great place to debate the fine points of the performance. The interior of **Metropoli, A Village Cafe** (1136 Crescent Avenue; 404–873–6307) resembles a street or piazza in a small Italian village. Doors leading to the spacious patio, one of the most attractive and inviting in town, resemble entrances to different shops, such as a bakery or cheese shop. **Vickery's Crescent Avenue Bar and Grill** (1106 Crescent Avenue; 404–881–1106), a neighborhood tradition for the past twelve years, has just enlarged the restaurant, but still retains its flavor as an intimate neighborhood hangout. Rounding out this ensemble of night spots, **Front Page News** (1104 Crescent Avenue; 404–897–3500), the Sunday newspaper of the restaurant world, serves newsworthy food day and night—as well as microbrews and martinis by the huge fireplace or out on the breezy patio.

As your evening of music and romance nears the end of its score, return to the hotel to celebrate your melodious day together by composing some music of your own.

DAY TWO: MORNING

Breakfast

After such a mellifluous night of fine food, memorable music, and high living, there's absolutely no reason to bound out of bed early. Start your day out on the right note by relaxing in your romantic hideaway and sharing the harmony of your spectacular night out. When hunger pangs finally drive you out, slip into some casual togs and walk the block and a half to Peachtree Street to the **Corner Bakery** (Colony Square at Fourteenth and Peachtree Streets; 404–817–7111; inexpensive) for fresh, hearth-baked breads, including flavored breads and baguettes, muffins, strudels, Danishes, and other light breakfast items.

❧

After satisfying the inner you, a magical way for the indulgent to wrap up a visit is by luxuriating in the hotel's state-of-the-art health and fitness spa. The marbled neoclassic facility, one of the prettiest we've seen, is the perfect place for you to do a mild body tune up or simply indulge in some playful high jinks in the pool.

FOR MORE ROMANCE

This itinerary doesn't begin to do justice to the city's extensive and varied musical possibilities. The **Atlanta Opera Company** (1800 Peachtree Street, N.W., Suite 620; 404–355–3311; $16–$115) presents two operas in the spring/early summer season and two in the autumn at the extravagant Fox Theater. Fresh and original musical programming that ranges from classic silent films to modern dance to jazz to blues is presented at the **Rialto Center for the Performing Arts** at Georgia State University (University Plaza; 404–651–4727), a restored movie theater downtown. Any extra nights added to your getaway can be spent at highbrow performances at **Spivey Hall** or **Emory University;** lighthearted musicals at the **Savoyards Musical Theater Company,** awesome pops with the ASO and international artists, coupled with cool breezes and a candlelight gourmet picnic at **Chastain Park** (see "Adding Sparkle to Your Life"); or popular rock concerts at **Lakewood Amphitheater.** During the summer, the ASO also presents several free concerts in parks around the city. If you can expand your musical weekend to include a Friday or a Monday, trace the life and works of Georgia native songwriter Johnny Mercer by seeing the "I Remember You" exhibition at the **Johnny Mercer Museum** (Pullen Library, Georgia State University, 100 Decatur Street, S.E.; 404–651–2477; free). Among the memorabilia are manuscripts, correspondence, photographs, a telegram from Cole Porter, the Academy Award for "Moon River," and the Grammy for "Days of Wine and Roses" (for more about Midtown cultural life see "Atlanta's Cultural Heart," "All the World's a Stage," and "A Feast for the Eye."

ALL AROUND THE TOWN

ITINERARY 10
Three days and two nights

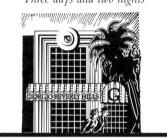

BEVERLY HILLS SOUTHEAST
BUCKHEAD

*U*pscale Buckhead, Atlanta's answer to Beverly Hills, is *the* place where the city's well-heeled movers and shakers of any age—but particularly the young upwardly mobile—live or flock to for outstanding dining, entertainment, shopping, or simply to see and be seen. Among its hedonistic pleasures, Buckhead features the city's highest concentration of fabulous restaurants and trendy nightspots, two tony shopping malls, hundreds of chic boutiques and antiques shops, a wide array of art galleries, and several day spas, in addition to fashionable hotels and ritzy residential enclaves as pricey as the Hollywood Hills (the Governor's Mansion is here as is Elton John's opulent condo). It's no surprise that dozens of foreign countries have chosen Buckhead as the site of their consulates as well. The swanky neighborhood has come a long way, since its humble beginnings as a simple crossroad that got its name from an early tavern that used a mounted buck's head as its symbol. When Atlantans want a fast and fashionable evening or a weekend getaway, Buckhead is usually their preference. This fantasy weekend for high-style pairs is all about pleasure—finding it, sharing it, giving it—and there's no better place for that sensual agenda than Buckhead. This stimulating holiday is strictly fun and games, and you can style yourselves after Oscar-winning Hollywood stars or other celebrities. Whether you and your heartthrob are seventeen or seventy, you'll find style and verve in Buckhead. Because the lively area really sparkles at night, we've highlighted spirited nightlife. Days are lightly scheduled to allow you to conserve energy for the evening and to permit you to sleep in after a late night of partying.

Practical Notes: Buckhead, almost a city within the city of Atlanta, covers twenty-eight square miles and has a population of more than sixty thousand. The area stretches south from the Atlanta/Sandy Springs border to approximately Peachtree Creek and is bounded on the east by the city limits/DeKalb County line and on the west by the city limits/Cobb County line. Therefore, although there are some activities where you can walk from one place to another, for the most part you'll need a set of wheels—whether they're your own or those of a limo, taxi, or a MARTA train or bus. Traffic in busy Buckhead is heavy at all times of day and evening, but it is particularly frustrating during the morning, midday, and evening rush hours, so it's best to avoid driving then. In general, there's plenty of free parking at shopping outlets and restaurants, although some parking decks charge a fee. At the nightspots, however, parking can be very difficult, so many have valet parking. We recommend that you stay at the fabulous **Ritz-Carlton Buckhead** (synonymous with luxury) from which you can walk to shopping malls and to some restaurants and nightspots. You can also avail yourselves of the hotel limo service within a prescribed area or you could call a taxi. The Lenox and Buckhead MARTA rapid rail stations—both of which are within walking distance of the hotel—offer easy access to other areas of the city.

Romance at a Glance

♥ *Shop at antiques and design shops on Miami Circle.*

♥ *Peruse art galleries on Bennett Street.*

♥ *Feast on gastronomic delights at Hedgerose.*

♥ *Party until the wee hours at nightspots like the Cotton Club.*

♥ *Spoil yourselves with a half-day's pampering at Spa Sydell.*

DAY ONE: AFTERNOON

Lunch

Don't even think about your waistline during this weekend fantasy. Diet before you come or after you go home so you can enjoy yourselves without guilt. It's almost impossible to choose only a few eateries from among Buckhead's two hundred trendy dining establishments, but begin your weekend of pleasure seeking by treating yourselves to the soul of Italy in the heart of Buckhead. **Amerigo** (2964 Peachtree Road, N.W.; 404–237–2964; moderate), a casual Italian bistro with American flair, serves a large selection of wood-fired pizzas, pastas, and risotto, as well as beef, chicken, veal, and fish entrees. Its location in a round, windows-encircled building and the availability of patio seating allow you to watch the hustle and bustle of Buckhead from almost any table, while you relax and savor your meal and the glitter of each other's company.

Finish your dessert and coffee, then drive north on Peachtree Street (Atlanta's Rodeo Drive) to your love nest for the weekend—the legendary **Ritz-Carlton Buckhead** (3434 Peachtree Road, N.E.; 404–237–2700; expensive). After being greeted like a celebrity by the nattily uniformed doorman, turn your car over to valet parking and your luggage to the bell captain and prepare for unsurpassed luxury and service. The hotel is a winner of the coveted Mobil five-star and AAA five-diamond awards. It is consistently named one of the ten best in the world by surveys such as those conducted by Zagat and Conde Nast and is always chosen as Atlanta's best hotel. Built and furnished to approximate a very exclusive private club or residence (that is, if your residence is Versailles-like), the hotel is embellished with Italian marble, antique Persian carpets, authentic antiques, and superb, museum-quality eighteenth- and nineteenth-century European and American art.

Surrender to the splendor. If you and your sweetheart really want to pamper yourselves as the rich and famous do, splurge on a room on the Club Level ($255). After all, when you're madly in love, money is no object. In addition to enhanced room amenities, lucky guests on this floor have access to a sumptuous private lounge where five magnificent complimentary food services are provided each day: an opulent continental breakfast, midday snack, afternoon tea, cocktails and hors d'oeuvres, and evening cordials and chocolates. In fact, if you stay on the Club Level, you could truly lose yourselves in each other and never go out at all, but there are so many fabulous restaurants nearby, including the ones in the hotel, that we suggest you restrain yourselves. Just nibble very lightly on the goodies in the lounge and save yourselves for the restaurants.

If it's too early to get into your little slice of heaven, or after you've gotten settled, use the hotel as a headquarters from which to walk to a shopper's paradise—either upscale **Lenox Square,** the largest mall in the Southeast, or the ultraposh **Phipps Plaza.** Rodeo Drive has nothing on these swanky shopping districts. It doesn't matter which fashionable mall you go to first, a shuttle service will whisk you to the other. Between them, the malls house 350 upscale shops; you can find everything from something as mundane as a paper clip to a magnificent Tiffany diamond for your paramour. If your budget doesn't stretch quite that much, shop for sexy lingerie, fresh flowers, chocolates, candles, and other sensual accoutrements to add zest to your getaway—or simply window shop. (For more detailed information about the two malls, see the "Adding Sparkle to Your Life" itinerary.)

If you and your honey are into sharing that fitness thing, after shopping or instead of it, work off your luncheon calories at the hotel's swim and fitness center, which features an indoor heated lap pool, whirlpool, sauna, steam room, and weight machines. You can't even use the fact that you forgot to bring appropriate attire as an excuse for not taking advantage of these perks, the hotel can provide fitness clothes and disposable swimsuits for celebrities like you. Afterward, snuggle up with a glass of wine in plush terry cloth robes.

If you haven't opted for the Club Level, appease an empty stomach or a sugar low at the hotel's comfortably sophisticated traditional **Afternoon Tea** ($16), which is served in the elegant Lobby Lounge. In cool weather, cozy up to the inviting fire in the nineteenth-century marble fireplace and listen to classical music played on the Steinway grand while enjoying a selection of imported teas, accompanied by scones, tea sandwiches, miniature pastries, and tea breads.

DAY ONE: EVENING

Dinner

Late dining is a European tradition, but after the amount of food you've consumed today, you'll probably want to follow that custom. You won't even have to leave your pleasure palace to dine like royalty at Atlanta's finest restaurant. Silk-upholstered seating, grand pieces of art, soft lighting, fresh flowers, and classical music entice lovers into **The Dining Room,** (expensive), the city's only Mobil five-star, AAA five-diamond restaurant.

For many years internationally renowned chef Guenter Seeger guided The Dining Room to its present epicurean prominence, so it was with great care that the company searched for a replacement when Seeger struck off on his own. French-born chef Joel Antunes brings an impressive resumé to the Ritz-Carlton Buckhead. Not only has he worked in some of the foremost restaurants in the world, but he was named one of the top five chefs in the United Kingdom. He blends his French training with subtle Thai influences learned during a stint in Bangkok to create his flavor-intensive "progressive French-Mediterranean with Thai influences" cuisine. Although the menu changes frequently, gastronomic delights might include duck filet in Thai sauce; lobster with Thai spices, bok choy, carrots, and coconut tuile; or more traditional seafood, pigeon, lamb, veal, or venison dishes. Desserts are visually and gastronomically elegant. A three-course dinner without wine or drinks runs about $65. The six-course tasting menu is $75 without wine, $112 with. Of course, in this rarefied atmosphere, coats and ties are required for gentlemen, and although business attire is appropriate for ladies, many opt for an elegant cocktail dress or evening pants outfit. If you have any special proposals or gifts (such as diamond earrings or cufflinks) for your darling, the sense of ceremony and hushed Old World grace make The Dining Room *the* place to make that ultraromantic gesture.

Nightlife

Round out your sybaritic evening by floating across the dance floor in each other's arms until the wee hours to the strains of the hotel's live orchestra.

DAY TWO: MORNING

Breakfast

After a *tres romantique* evening of dinner and dancing, it goes without saying that you'll want to sleep in. If you're staying on the Club Level, whomever wakes first can surprise the other by slipping down to the lounge to bring back hot coffee or tea and a little something to nibble on while you enjoy newspapers or each other in bed. If you're not staying on the Club Level, call room service or enjoy a light breakfast in **The Cafe** or **Expresso's**—a gourmet delicatessen.

∾

Once fortified, perhaps one of your goals for this weekend getaway is to search out that perfect piece of furniture, antique or new; a stunning accent piece; or an important work of art for your sophisticated love nest back home. Whatever your decorating style, you'll think you've died and gone to heaven when you see the quantity and quality of choices in Buckhead. One place to begin is the **Buckhead Design Center** (2133 Piedmont Road, N.E.; 404–876–2543), which features 140 businesses. Other decorator districts include the **Miami Circle Market Center** (2658 Piedmont Road, N.E.; 404–261–3224), where there are 65 businesses; the **Peachtree Decorative Arts Center** (2300 Peachtree Road; 404–352–2577), with 25 businesses; and **Bennett Street** (2110 Peachtree Road; 404–352–5511), with 150 businesses.

Obviously, with almost 400 businesses for you marathon shoppers to peruse, you could spend both entire days of your getaway and hardly scratch the surface. You'll just have to come back again—and again.

DAY TWO: AFTERNOON

Lunch

Serious shopping can take a lot out of you, so if hunger pangs are gnawing again, swim over to **Fishbone & the Piranha Bar** (1874 Peachtree Road; 404–367–4772; moderate), a moderately priced seafood restaurant sure to reel you in with its fun, casual atmosphere. Just to get you in the mood for one of the ten daily fresh catches, the restaurant features a just-for-looking, three-thousand-gallon aquarium where schools of sea life patrol the waters. Get hooked on Fishbone by trying lobster fritters with chili lime sauce, spicy conch chowder, Thai mussel hot pot with red curry, broiled American cold-water lobster tails, or ten-vegetable salad with Peekey Toe crab. Entrees can be served grilled over a live oak fire, steamed, or teppan steel grilled. Accompaniments include shrimp fried rice, tangy slaw, jalapeño cheddar muffins, and crispy garlic baguettes. Dessert specialties include mile-high baked Alaska, Key lime pie, and passion fruit pie. At the Piranha Bar, a spirited watering hole next to the restaurant, a collection of more than one hundred Caribbean rums provide the kick in Mojitas, Rum-tinis, Rum-ritas, Pain Killers, and T-Punch, or you can choose from thirty-five wines by the glass or handcrafted beers. Cool breezes and people watching reward those who dine on the screened porch or open deck. (Open daily 11:00 A.M.–11:00 P.M. Reservations are not accepted.) Complimentary valet parking is offered for cars, jet skis, and fishing boats.

With all the overindulgences you've permitted yourselves so far, and keeping in mind that there's a very energetic evening in store for you tonight, a healthy, but relaxing, afternoon is called for. Have your concierge make appointments for both of you at **Spa Sydell** (3060 Peachtree Road, N.W.; 404–237–2505). Here you can turn your bodies over to a masseuse or beauty technician. Rest while you're being pampered to conserve your energy for an evening of gaiety and pleasure. Not only do treatments make you glow, you'll feel as if you've had a week's vacation. A half day at the spa is $120, as is the His and Hers Body Massage, but single treatments start at $50.

DAY TWO: EVENING

Dinner

You should be feeling lazily content by now. Flaunting the healthy radiance of your recently revitalized skin, get the evening off to a relaxed, elegant start by feasting on an exquisite gourmet meal in a highly ornamented, refined Parisian-like salon at **Hedgerose** (490 East Paces Ferry Road; 404–233–7673; expensive), named for the profuse hedge roses that grow around this 1930s cottage. Savor the flawless Continental/American cuisine, offering choices such as foie gras, potato roll of scallops, roasted truffled chicken, or filet of John Dory, but you need to know upfront to save some room for the dessert specialty, so order accordingly. It wasn't a simple moment of whimsy that made the owners of Hedgerose headline their dessert menu with a sinful chocolate concoction called a Faberge egg. Before the turn of the century, the jewelry artist Faberge created elaborate decorative eggs encrusted with jewels for the czars of Russia. Most of these opulent toys opened to reveal another jeweled surprise inside. The partners of Hedgerose describe the restaurant as "a little jewel box . . . like a Fabergé egg" so it made perfect sense to name the dessert after the whimsical plaything. Indeed, you'll be guaranteed several little surprises at the posh restaurant, but we won't spoil the fun by telling you what they all are. Ask for a table by the fireplace or in a secluded corner where you can shut out the rest of the world to concentrate on each other. (Reservations are strongly recommended.)

Don't get too laid back, though, because now it's time to switch gears. Whether you like hip-hop, rap, rock and roll, jazz, blues, comedy, or some other form of entertainment, Buckhead has something just perfect for you. Half the fun, however, is bar hopping. Buckhead's nightlife is so varied and the nightspots so numerous in such a compact area (Buckhead Village—six blocks on either side of Peachtree at Paces Ferry) that most revelers don't simply go to one place and stay for an entire evening. They spend some time and have a drink at one, then drift to another and another. In fact, from late evening until the wee hours of the morning, so many couples are out on the streets that the entire area almost becomes a pedestrian mall or floating party. (Just remember though, this isn't New Orleans and "go cups" or open alcohol containers are illegal.) Because our space is limited, we'll only list a few clubs that might strike your fancy, or you could simply join a crowd and let it take you where it may.

Remedies (293 Pharr Road; 404–846–0822) has had lines down the block since it opened because it offers something for everyone: two outdoor patios with live acoustic and jazz, cigar and martini lounge, techno/top 40 dance room, sports/games room, and five bars. It is open until 2:00 or 4:00 A.M. depending on the night. A perennial favorite, the **Cotton Club** (1021 Peachtree Street N.E.; 404–874–1993) features up-and-coming alternative and local bands. (For information about other popular clubs and comedy spots, ask your concierge which clubs are currently in vogue.) Wind down the evening on a quiet note by stopping for drinks and/or a dessert fondue while you listen to live jazz at **Dante's Down the Hatch** (3380 Peachtree Road; 404–266–1600), a perennial favorite. The intriguing interior creates the illusion of your being on an eighteenth-century sailing ship surrounded by alligator-infested waters. Dim lighting and live music are conducive to lovers' soft conversations, gazing into each others eyes, and holding hands. Be decadent and feed each other hand-dipped, chocolate-covered strawberries while you sip champagne. You'll be guaranteed to have pleasant dreams. (Reservations are strongly suggested. Live music begins at 5:00 P.M., and there's a small cover charge for sitting onboard the ship.)

DAY THREE: MORNING

Breakfast

If you choose to eat out this morning rather than at the hotel, continue your fine dining experience with "Atlanta's best breads and pastries" (as named by *Atlanta Magazine*) at the **Buckhead Bread Company and Corner Cafe** (3070 Piedmont Road; 404–240–1978; inexpensive to moderate) where you can feast on adventurous morning meals, including award-winning pastries, homemade granola, grits, and fried prosciutto chips accompanied by gourmet coffees.

⌒⊙⌒

Before you leave town, indulge your fantasies by taking the time for a leisurely driving tour around Buckhead's upscale neighborhoods (the traffic on Sunday mornings is light). Your concierge can give you some tips about where to go. Known as Atlanta's silk stocking district, the area boasts fine old mansions on large, heavily wooded and impeccably landscaped estates. The superb architecture of these castlelike villas spans many styles, and the amount of property on which they sit make this real estate the most sought after (and most expensive) in Atlanta. Have fun picking the ones you'd like to buy and spend your future in together when you win the lottery. (After all, the average price is more than $500,000 and many sales easily top $1 million.)

FOR MORE ROMANCE

Check ahead or with your concierge as soon as you arrive to see if a show or concert is playing at the fine old restored **Roxy Theater** (3100 Roswell Road; 404–233–1062), a small, intimate venue where you can sit close to the action. During the summer, the most popular evening activity is an outdoor concert with the Atlanta Symphony Orchestra and a guest artist at the **Chastain Park Amphitheater** (4469 Stella Drive, N.W.; 404–872–1115 or 404–733–5000). (For a complete description of the Chastain experience, see "Adding Sparkle to Your Life." See this itinerary for information about other popular music spots also.)

ITINERARY 11
Two days and one night

TIE-DYED TWOSOME, OR BRING ON THE NOISE, BRING ON THE FUNK

LITTLE FIVE POINTS

*H*ave you two love children ever wished you could go back to the wild-and-wonderful, anything-goes sixties? In that case, this fun-loving weekend offers you a chance to fulfill that wish. Nestled incongruously between Atlanta's magnificent, stately turn-of-the-century residential Inman Park and Candler Park neighborhoods is a flamboyant and slightly seedy realm from another dimension—an exuberant, zesty, superenergized, counterculture domain with an eclectic and fascinating street life of the conventional and unconventional (dominantly unconventional): hippie holdovers in psychedelic tie-dye, street musicians, punk rockers, Boomers, Gen Xers, burly bikers and traditional bankers, liberals and conservatives, straights and gays. A genuine melting pot, funky Little Five Points (known as L5P) is acknowledged as the most unusual commercial district in Atlanta. Truly a Bohemian "Village," hip L5P is an ongoing bazaar of the bizarre—a place where free expression is encouraged and trends are set. This outlandish district's easygoing camaraderie, wealth of local color, and tolerance and acceptance of "anything goes" provide a singular identity that gives the area its high energy. A buzz of creative excitement makes Little Five Points one of the most exuberant shopping, entertainment, and people-watching spots in Atlanta. In addition to the retro bell-bottoms and miniskirts, the well-worn grunge-look baggies and combat boots, you've probably never seen so much studs-and-leather or so many tattoos, body piercings, and spiky multicolored hairdos. As a counterpoint to the offbeat, this weekend excursion offers you ready-to-

Romance at a Glance

♥ *Linger in your Royal Suite at Sugar Magnolia Bed and Breakfast.*

♥ *Immerse yourselves in turn-of-the-century grandeur in Inman Park.*

♥ *Discover funky art during a walking tour of L5P public art.*

♥ *Create your own look at the Junkman's Daughter.*

♥ *Commune with "The King" at his shrine in the Grace Vault at the Star Community Bar.*

take-a-chance lovers a perfect opportunity to explore lovely Victorian-era Inman Park, a vibrant residential neighborhood undergoing an exciting renaissance. Begun in the 1890s, Inman Park was Atlanta's first planned community and one of the nation's first garden suburbs. (Since the early 1900s, L5P has been the commercial district for the Inman Park and Candler Park neighborhoods.) In addition to exploring both the residential and commercial districts, you'll stay in royal splendor at a superb bed-and-breakfast, dine at some local offbeat hangouts, experience some alternative nightlife, and shop for an exotic remembrance of your wild-and-wacky weekend.

Practical Notes: Parking is a serious problem in Little Five Points, so leave your car at the B&B and walk. It's not far, and your reward will be seeing the handsome stately homes along the way. Only casual clothes are needed for this laid-back weekend, the more unconventional the better if you don't want to stand out like a sore thumb. This is a perfect opportunity to wear some far-out things you might never want your nearest and dearest friends and neighbors to see.

DAY ONE: AFTERNOON

Check into your weekend hideaway, the gorgeous **Sugar Magnolia Bed and Breakfast** (804 Edgewood Avenue, N.E.; 404–222–0226; $75–$120), located in Inman Park. The B&B occupies one of the best-preserved and most magnificent Queen Anne Victorian mansions in this large turn-of-the-century district of majestic homes, built by the city's most affluent and influential citizens of the period. This particular gem will charm you lovebirds with its many gables, ornate chimneys, and whimsical turrets. Built in 1892, the mansion is embellished with a wraparound porch, twelve-foot ceilings, grand staircase, six fireplaces, oval beveled windows, hand-painted plasterwork, and the front hall's magnificent crystal chandelier. Today's owners have added modern baths—some with Jacuzzis—as well as ceiling fans, artwork, and antique furnishings.

For your lovers' getaway, we recommend that you splurge on the Royal Suite, a favorite of honeymooners and other romantics, with its sitting area, brass bed in a draped alcove, sunken Jacuzzi tub, and rooftop deck, garden, and waterfall.

Whichever love nest you choose, once you've gotten settled, you could spend the entire weekend strolling hand in hand through Inman Park's tree-lined streets and admiring the varied Victorian architectural treasures, ranging from small bungalows to grand mansions. Inman Park was developed in 1889 and connected to downtown by the city's first electric streetcar line. To create a country setting, developer Joel Hurt built houses on large lots along curving streets and surrounded them with parks. Unfortunately, in later years, as cars made it possible for Atlantans to flee to suburbs farther from the city center, Inman Park and Little Five Points deteriorated drastically; by the 1970s, they were slums. Much of the neighborhood was scheduled to be demolished for a highway, but residents mobilized to prevent this tragedy, new folks moved in and began to rehabilitate the homes, and today the entire neighborhood is listed on the National Register of Historic Places. It's only natural then that the butterfly, which symbolizes metamorphosis, was chosen as the neighborhood's logo. If your relationship has experienced any hard times, buy a butterfly flag to remind you both of your personal growth and this weekend of renewal.

Now characterized as "SmallTown DownTown," more than three hundred of the neighborhood's splendid homes have been restored and are lived in by Boomers or operated as B&Bs. A few as-yet unrestored, down-at-the-mouth Charles Adamesque mansions behind unkempt hedges or creaking iron gates look as if they could still have a few skeletons in their closets. Speaking of ghosts, you'd never guess when wandering by tranquil Springvale Park (intersection of Waverly Way and Edgewood Avenue), that it was the site of one of the bloodiest battles in the Atlanta Campaign on July 22, 1864—one in which staggering losses numbered seven thousand Confederate troops and two thousand Union troops. Do any of their restless spirits wander the park?

❧❦❧

Too much fun awaits in adjacent Little Five Points, though, to spend time exploring Inman Park now, so limit your wanderings to allow yourselves plenty of time in L5P. In fact, on Sundays at 2:00 P.M. from March through November, the **Atlanta Preservation Center** (tour hotline: 404–876–2040) offers walking tours of the Inman Park neighborhood, which highlights such elegant homes as those built by Coca-Cola magnates Asa Candler and Ernest Woodruff and the **King-Keith House** (889 Edgewood Avenue), one of the most photographed houses in Atlanta, so save a more in-depth tour of the residential area for tomorrow.

After making your way through such a staid-and-proper neighborhood as Inman Park, L5P will bring you up short in delightful surprise. A thriving cultural, entertainment, professional, and commercial district, L5P boasts trendy, eccentric galleries; theaters; concert halls; recording studios; restaurants; nightspots; and shops.

Take a firm hold of your sweetie's hand and join in the lively street life, window shop— look for everything from the essential to one-of-kind, retro, or hard-to-find item in the trendy shops—or, if you dare, get some body adornment at **Tornado Tattoo** or **Sacred Hearts**

Tattoo, tattoo and body piercing parlors. If people are staring at you, it's probably because your clothes are just so conservative, so stop in at **Stefan's Vintage Clothing** for the '50s/'60s retro look or at the **Junkman's Daughter,** which must be seen to be believed, for a look you can put together on the spot to remedy the situation. Although the clothing may look like Halloween costumes, it's really everyday wear for the super hip—lots of black, capes, and studs and leather are only a few of the choices. In addition, there's a naughty adults-only room and a cigar room. Climb up to the loft shoe department by mounting stairs concealed in a huge red high-heeled shoe. Once you get there, the shoe department's chairs resemble high heels as well, but the shoes for sale are biker boots and grunge accessories or Frederick's of Hollywood-style slut shoes with stilettos so high you can't imagine anyone could stand up in them. Maybe that's the point—the wearer will spend most of his/her time on his/her back.

Lunch

As you return from the Junkman's Daughter, sidestepping heavily tattooed-and-pierced citizens with startling white skin and black or purple hair, you'll suddenly be confronted with the wonderous image of a monstrous glowering skull with deranged eyes—after all, this is L5P and this is one of its best restaurants. Pop in through the yawning mouth to the **Vortex Bar and Grill** (438 Moreland Avenue N.E.; 404–688–1828; inexpensive) to be confronted with yet another specter: a full-size, motorcycle-riding skeleton. Take a breather from your shopping and order a drink and a snack and then amuse yourselves by taking your food and libations to the upper deck—a great people-watching spot. Read aloud to each other from the back of the menu, which is full of such whimsical advice as their Idiot Policy and their Tip or Die philosophy.

❧

In your wanderings through L5P, you'll want to stop in at some of these other shops and businesses on your romantic roadmap. Now open thirty-four years, **Charis Books,** an alternative bookstore, was the first business to breathe new life into L5P; **Sevananda Natural Foods Co-op,** a health-food cooperative grocery, has been here almost as long. **Little Five Points Station** is a treasure trove of antiques, classic collectibles, and *objets d'art*. Drop in at **Pink Flamingos** for clothing, cards, gifts, and fun (alien garden gnomes, bath fizzies, chamomile satin eye-rest pillows, 1920s style hand-beaded necklaces, huge collection of salt and pepper shakers); **Civilization** for vintage and new furniture, home accessories, aromatherapy candles, and more; **The Home Store** for futons, table lamps, accent lanterns, and paper lamps; **A Cappella Books** for new, rare, and out-of-print books; **Criminal Records** for alternative music, literature, and comics; **Coyote Trading Company** for Native American and Southwestern arts and crafts, including sterling silver jewelry, drums, flutes, bead and bone work, sand paintings, kachinas, and fetishes; and **Soul Kiss** for exotic adornments from around the world, jewelry, masks, statues, incense, and oils. Everything you can imagine, and plenty of things you can't, await visitors to L5P. Watch how many things you buy though—especially if they're heavy; you'll have to lug the bags back to Sugar Magnolia.

At the end of a hectic day of sightseeing, shopping, and people watching in L5P, return to the B&B where, in good weather, you'll want to relax with complimentary tea and snacks on the front veranda or on the Royal Suite's private porch. If the weather is less than ideal, take your tea into the comfy living room or to the cozy second-floor sitting room. Unwind in your sunken Jacuzzi tub before you get ready for dinner.

DAY ONE: EVENING

Dinner

Stroll back to L5P. A must-see, the **Euclid Avenue Yacht Club** (1136 Euclid Avenue, N.E.; 404–688–2582; inexpensive) can be smoky, loud, obnoxious, and filled with bikers at night, but at mealtimes, it's just as popular with locals of all ages who like it for the quality food, the variety of inexpensive beers, and the convenient location near the Variety Playhouse. Nautically themed, the restaurant is known for its quarter-pound Long Island hot dogs, six-ounce patty burgers, quesadillas, chicken salad, Philly cheese steaks, and weekly Blue Plate specials, such as country-fried steak or stuffed cabbage.

Nightlife

Little Five Points is a mecca for small theater companies and music venues, so you should have no trouble finding some stimulating entertainment for the evening. Ask your hosts or check local newspapers for performances at the **Horizon Theater, Seven Stages Theater, Variety Playhouse,** or the **Dancer's Collective.** Named "Best Venue" by both the *Atlanta Journal* and *Creative Loafing* and "Best Sound in Town" by *Atlanta Magazine*, the **Variety Playhouse** (1099 Euclid Avenue; 404–524–7354) books eclectic groups with ticket prices ranging from $15–$25. After the show, visit some of L5P famous hangouts. A funky little honky tonk "where things go twang in the night," the **Star Community Bar** (437 Moreland Avenue; 404–681–9018), located in a bank building, offers live roots music—including rockabilly, country, bluegrass, garage, blues, and swing Wednesday through Saturday nights. Tuesday is disco night.

The first thing you must do, though, is take your honey to the **Grace Vault.** What's that, you ask? An old bank vault that has been transformed into the Grace Vault, a shrine to Elvis is your answer. Inside the vault, which is lit by candles, is Elvis memorabilia and a jukebox that plays "The King's" famous tunes free. After paying your respects to Elvis, check out the **Little Vinyl Lounge** downstairs—a subterranean martini bar with red-and-black vinyl booths. Closed Sunday, the bar is open the rest of the week from 3:00 P.M. until 3:00–4:00 A.M. Billing itself as Atlanta's only rock 'n' roll bar, **9 Lives Saloon** (1174 Euclid Avenue; 404–659–7656) is dedicated to presenting the heavy metal crunch of the Ozzy Osborne,

KISS, and Motley Crue era. **The Point** (420 Moreland Avenue; 404–659–3522), Atlanta's most intimate concert venue and neighborhood bar, offers nightly live progressive and rock 'n' roll entertainment as well as bar grub.

A time will come when you're finally ready to wander back to your B&B, where you can play in the Jacuzzi or try on and model for your paramour any of today's particularly risque purchases from the Junkman's Daughter.

DAY TWO: Morning

After such a late night, sleep in or spend some time cuddling when you awaken. Once you're ready to face the day, breakfast on freshly baked muffins, fruit, and cereal, accompanied by juice and hot beverages. Don't rush off yet; take a last relaxing soak in the Jacuzzi, get dressed in your new L5P duds, then say goodbye to your hosts.

In Little Five Points, it isn't only the people and the merchandise purveyed in the shops that are cutting edge. It should come as no surprise that the art here is avant-garde as well. This morning take a walking tour of the area's public art. Start at the corner of Austin and Euclid at the **Little Five Points Community Center/Horizon Theater** (1083 Austin Avenue). At the front entrance is *Temple of Luv: Shrine to Past Loves,* a garden shrine combining clay and metal elements with organic plant matter. Head east on Euclid to the **Seven Stages Theater** (1105 Euclid Avenue) to see *Crickets,* an assemblage of mixed media on the exterior wall. Continue east to **Sevanada** (1111 Euclid Avenue) to take a gander at *Livin' & Jammin',* three mixed-media pictures depicting African-American music, family traditions, and clothing styles of the forties and fifties created from fabric, fun foam, wallpaper, plastic, human hair, and beads. Turn south on Moreland to the lot between **The Academy** (368 Moreland Avenue) and **Colonial Bakery** (350 Moreland Avenue)—passersby are invited to ring the *Bell Tower,* a set of metal wind chimes, hanging from a steel mast mounted to stone. Also in the lot, a public

Homemade ice cream: *dick and harry's (1570 Holcomb Bridge Road, Roswell; 770–641–8757; $6)*

Creme brûlée: *La Strada (2930 Johnson Ferry Road, Marietta; 770–640–7008; $4)*

Carrot cake: *The Flying Biscuit Cafe (1655 McLendon Avenue; 404–687–8888; $4.25)*

Banana cream pie: *Buckhead Diner (3073 Piedmont Road; 404–262–3336; $5.25)*

Key lime pie: *Indigo Coastal Grill 1397 North Highland Avenue; 404–876–0676; $4.50)*

Chocolate cake: *Bacchanalia (3125 Piedmont Road; 404–365–0410; $6.50)*

Brownies: *The Beehive (1090 Alpharetta Street, Roswell; 770–594–8765; $4)*

Chocolate mousse: *Georgia Grille (2290 Peachtree Road; 404–352–3517; $4.50)*

Bread pudding: *SoHo (4200 Paces Ferry Road, Vinings; 770–801–0069; $5.50)*

All–American pies: *Greenwood's (1087 Green Street; Roswell; 770–992–5383; varies)*

altar called *Native Alteration* provides a stage for periodic performances of choreographed and improvisational works. Turn back north on Moreland to **Aurora Coffee** (468 Moreland Avenue) to study *September Memories,* created from mail, E-mail, and computer-generated art. Stop and have some coffee and a snack while you're here. Continue on Moreland to Freedom Parkway, a major intersection, where there are four pieces of public art. *Fracturing the Facade* is an interactive site projectassembled from glass, wood, newspaper clippings, fabric, plastic, and rope, which humorously depicts some of the glitches that occurred during preparations for the 1996 Centennial Olympic Summer Games. *Towards Milleniallam II: "the wire tornado"* is created from telephone poles, street lamps, circuit breaker boxes, glass, and electric cable. Buzzing noises emanate from a central city-like structure. *Allegro(w)* is a kinetic steel abstract spider sculpture that stands 15 feet high and spans 24 feet. If you don't like spiders, this is your worst nightmare. *Finnibar, 1994,* a kinetic cantilever of steel and stone, captures the poised energy and power of a tethered bull. Go south on Moreland to the **Mean Bean Restaurant** (463 Moreland Avenue). In the window is *Made with a Gift of Simplicity*, which uses created and found objects to explore a theme of misogyny. Turn west on Euclid and return to your starting point at the Little Five Points Community Center.

DAY TWO: AFTERNOON

Lunch

After all this walking, it's time to try some pita on the sunny outdoor deck at **Marco Polo's** (1105 Euclid Avenue; 404–588–0777; inexpensive), which has the best falafel in the city. In addition to club, Italian, Greek, seafood, tuna, and grilled chicken pitas, you can create your own with a choice of any three meats, cheese, a variety of toppings and dressings. In addition to veggie burgers and salads, Marco's offers a wide variety of vegetables.

Do a little more shopping or hang around the little triangular park at the corner of Euclid and Moreland for more out-of-sight people watching. From March through November, return to Inman Park in time to be on hand in front of the **King-Keith House** (889 Edgewood Avenue) at 2:00 P.M. to join in the Atlanta Preservation Center's walking tour (admission $5/$4 for seniors). Once you've picked up your car, drive south on Moreland to visit **The Wrecking Bar** (292 Moreland Avenue; 404–525–0468), a fascinating antiques emporium located in the magnificent 1900 Victor H. Kriegshaber House, one of the finest examples of a great Victorian house left in the city. Specializing in architectural masterpieces, the shop is full of European columns, porch posts, gates, and the like. The friendly staff says the most romantic piece they ever had was a statue of Romeo and Juliet, which was bought by an elderly couple for their garden. Proves that love has no age limits, doesn't it? They tell us that another popular item with couples is pub tables—just the right size for two. Also drop in at the nearby **Christine Sibley's Urban Nirvana** (15 Waddell Street; 404–688–3329) for the enchanting garden ornaments, from plant markers to birdbaths, that Christine and other local artists create.

All good things must come to an end, and so it is with your escape from everyday reality in Little Five Points. Pack up your new funky clothes, your combat boots, your leather and chains, and return home with your romance just a little energized and stronger as a result of your visit to an alternative world.

FOR MORE ROMANCE

If you have any spare time, the inn is located near the Jimmy Carter Presidential Library and Museum (see "Phoenix Rising") and isn't far from the Virginia-Highland neighborhood (see "Cross Streets for Fun"), Decatur (see "175 Years Young and Counting"), downtown (see "The Magical Emerald City"), and several sports venues. Perhaps you can time your visit to coincide with the **Inman Park Spring Festival and Tour of Homes,** held a weekend in late April, which celebrates the spirit that saved the historic neighborhood. Highlights of the festival include a wacky parade, a tour of homes not available to see any other time of year, a juried arts and crafts show, live entertainment, and a street market. Among the parade participants are the beauty queen—Miss Inman Park Butterfly—Seed & Feed Marching Abominables, floats, and local politicians. Miss Inman Park Trash Heap brings up the rear riding on a street sweeper. Paintings, sculpture, glass, ceramics, toys, whimsical nostalgia, food, and drink vie for your attention at the street market. Home tours begin at noon each day. For tickets and information, call 770–242–4895. For even more about Inman Park, see "Skull Duggery.") Little Five Points is also the scene of many local festivals, artists markets, and celebrations, so perhaps you can make your getaway plans to coincide with one of them.

ITINERARY 12
Two days and one night

CROSS STREETS FOR FUN
VIRGINIA–HIGHLAND

*T*his weekend is about having fun and the joy of restoring lost beauty. If you and your heartthrob are into the art of restoration (either architectural or romantic) or simply want to enjoy a carefree getaway, read on. The trendy old Virginia-Highland neighborhood, on the eastern periphery of Midtown, is one of the top three "in" places to go in Atlanta—especially for Boomers and Gen Xers. The other two are Buckhead and Little Five Points. Virginia-Highland has no tourist attractions—this is a place to go to see and be seen at fabulous, informal, moderately priced restaurants and tony nightspots or to shop for unique clothing, accessories, decorative arts, and mementos from a wide range of boutiques and for collectible art at upscale galleries. It's astounding that so small an area (centering on the intersection of Virginia Avenue and North Highland Avenue, which is how it got its name, and including Amsterdam Avenue, Lanier Boulevard, Barnett Street, St. Charles Place, and sections of Ponce de Leon Avenue) can support so many thriving businesses. If the two of you have been bitten by the restoration bug and are working on a project or simply want to find something special for your place back home, check the Virginia-Highland shops for ideas, tools, and accent pieces. If your romantic relationship is getting a little ragged around the edges, this weekend should help to restore its excitement as well.

Practical Notes: Virginia-Highland is a small area, so park your car at the bed-and-breakfast and walk just about everywhere. Not only is walking the best way to see the neighborhood, but it makes it much easier for you to step into a funky shop on a whim.

Romance at a Glance

♥ *Heat up your relationship at the Gaslight Inn.*

♥ *Join in a Virginia-Highland tradition—brunch at Murphy's.*

♥ *Pig out on the wondrous concoctions at The Dessert Place.*

♥ *Linger over a romantic French provincial repast at Babette's Cafe.*

♥ *Revel in the beauty and camaraderie in this reborn neighborhood.*

DAY ONE: MORNING

Time your arrival so you have time to check into your bed-and-breakfast, leave your car, walk down the street, and then chow down on the ample brunch at **Murphy's** (997 Virginia Avenue; 404–872–0904; moderate). Brunch ends at 3:00 P.M., so plan accordingly.

Your weekend love nest, the **Gaslight Inn** (1001 St. Charles Avenue, N.E.; 404–875–1001; $85–$195) is on the left midway down the block. Parking for check-in is on the street. The original granite carriage step at curbside is the first clue that this is a unique and historic inn. A flickering genuine gas lantern draws you up the steps to the inviting front porch of the unassuming 1913 Craftsman-style bungalow. Step inside to the elegance and sophistication of the public rooms and guest accommodations, where the dining room chandelier and wall sconces are still gas operated, and where five working fireplaces throughout the house add to the cozy ambience. Be forewarned, however, except for a quick look at your room when you drop off your luggage, don't spend any time looking around the extraordinary B&B, or you'll never leave. Much more about the inn later. The friendly staff will show you where to tuck your car. Then walk the short distance to the center of the action.

Brunch

Right now your destination is the wildly popular, casual Murphy's restaurant, which has a large, loyal, local following. You'll need the full bellies you'll get here to keep going all weekend. Located in a former wicker furniture store, the simple diner/lunchroom combines classical American/Continental cuisine with Asian and Southwestern influences. Brunch (about $20/$30 with wine) is ordered from the menu and includes Canadian bacon and eggs, eggs Sante Fe, and eggs Murphy (similar to eggs Benedict). Enhance the romance by asking for a table near the French cafe doors that open to a view of river birches and the artsy boutiques of the neighborhood or on the patio itself in good weather. Just in case you don't get enough to eat (simply impossible), a variety of gourmet salads and freshly made breads and pastries are available for takeout.

After brunch get ready for the fun of exploring Virginia-Highland. In case you're not familiar with its history, this cozy neighborhood was the first of the in-town areas to be restored. As such, it has served as a model for the rest of the city. In the late sixties and early seventies, most of the downtown neighborhoods had been abandoned by their original owners and were slums or about to be. About the same time, the city's large population of gays was looking for a place they could live in peace. They bought and restored many fine old buildings, which attracted new residents and created a need for stores and other businesses. The ultimate result is a delightful, quiet area, with its marvelous concentration of superb places to shop, eat, and be entertained.

DAY ONE: AFTERNOON

You'll want to spend the entire afternoon discovering the many boutiques and galleries in the neighborhood. Some stores you'll probably want to browse through include **Atlanta Book Exchange** for used, out of print, and remaindered books; **Bill Hallman Boutique,** an innovative racy boutique carrying men's and women's clothes; and **Chef!** for groovy kitchen stuff, jammin' java, and smokin' stogies. If you're looking for a hard-to-find tool or part, you can probably find it at **Highland Hardware,** which carries the South's largest selection of fine woodworking tools, or at **Intown Hardware,** which features old-fashioned general hardware, gardening tools, and gifts. Go to **Metropolitan Deluxe** for luxurious bedding, linens, bath supplies, candles, wall sconces, and offbeat gift items; **Mooncake** for whimsical clothing and jewelry; **Nature's Art** for jewelry, minerals, fossils, and gemstones; **Readers' Loft** for New Age books, gifts, and psychic readings; **Synergy,** a psychic center and gift gallery; **20th Century Antiques** for fabulous Art Deco, fifties, and other retro-styled decorative accessories and home furnishings; and **Veronica's Attic** for gifts, jewelry, and clothing. **Jules Jewels** is an eclectic gallery/store featuring sterling silver jewelry hand crafted in Mexico, as well as patterned furniture and accessories and fun, colorful paintings. You might find yourselves returning home with a treasure more tangible than vibrant memories.

All this shopping is bound to be exhausting for the two of you, so stop at midafternoon for a pick-me-up. **Arden's Gardens** (1117 Euclid Avenue; 404–827–0424) purveys all kinds of natural drinks, herbs, and vitamins, which should be just the prescription for revving you up for the rest of the afternoon. For a more decadent treat, the **San Francisco Coffee Roasting Co.** (1192 North Highland Avenue; 404–876–8816) serves all kinds of bagels, croissants, pastries, and the popular Yohay cookie scones.

৵৽৹৵

Continue your investigations by poking through galleries such as **Crystal Dolphin** for metaphysical art and gifts; **Eclectic Electric** for functional and fantastic light as art, neon; **Form and Function** for contemporary furniture and functional art; **Gems of Africa** for original artwork, wood and stone sculptures, baskets, and dolls from all over Africa; **Marcia Wood** for contemporary paintings, drawings, sculpture, and prints; **Modern Primitive Gallery** for self-taught, outsider, and folk art; and **Oglewanagi** for authentic American Indian arts and crafts.

For some hands-on fun, create your own work of art to take home as a memento of your romantic weekend from **Wired and Fired: A Pottery Playhouse** (994 Virginia Avenue,

Atlanta Magazine's Sweetest Dessert   Masterpieces in Town

1. *Cactus Pear Soup with Goat Yogurt Sorbet,* Guenter Seeger, **Seeger's,** *Buckhead*

2. *Iberra Chocolate Pudding on Cinnamon Fried Tortillas,* Kirk Parks, **NAVA,** *Buckhead*

3. *Mont Blanc,* Emory Sims, **Brasserie Le Coze,** *Buckhead*

4. *Chocolate Caramel Turtle Torte,* Joan Trotochaud, **Prime,** *Buckhead*

5. *Turtle Ice Cream Pie,* Glenn Powell, **Agnes & Muriel's,** *Midtown*

6. *White Chocolate Raspberry Cheesecake with Almond Crust,* Sarah Koob, **Van Gogh's,** *Roswell*

7. *Lavender Honey Crème Brûlée with Riesling Poached Pear and Chinese Almond Cookies,* Michael O'Connor, **Canoe,** *Vinings*

8. *Mixed Berry Shortcake,* Julie Anne Sullivan, **Horseradish Grill,** *Buckhead*

9. *Pierce Neige,* Joel Atunes, **The Dining Room at the Ritz-Carlton,** *Buckhead*

10. *Star Canyon Apple Spice Cake,* Alena M. Pyles, **SoHo,** *Vinings*

11. *Fabergé Egg,* Kathryn King, **Hedgerose,** *Buckhead*

N.E.; 404–885–1024). Choose unfinished pottery pieces and decorate them using your wildest imagination.

By now you should be all shopped out, so return to your bed-and-breakfast. One of the most outstanding in Atlanta, the Gaslight Inn has been profiled in regional and national magazines and has been featured several times on travel segments aired by CNN. In addition to all its charms, the inn is within easy walking distance of thirty-five fine restaurants and a wide variety of shops, theaters, and art galleries.

Coolly elegant twin parlors make a pleasant, though formal, gathering place for guests. These parlors flow into the formal dining room, where breakfast is served by glimmering gaslight, and continue into the marvelous, less formal sunroom addition, which contains a grand piano, comfortable overstuffed seating, and a generous supply of books and magazines. This lovely room opens into a walled garden—a quiet oasis of abundant flowers, a lush grass carpet, and a tinkling fountain—which has been showcased on several garden tours. Both public rooms and guest rooms are furnished with antiques and reproductions and embellished with sumptuous fabrics and dramatic window treatments.

A variety of lavish accommodations in the main house and the converted carriage house are offered in exquisite rooms and luxurious suites, all of which feature private baths and TV. Each room displays its own personality and features some special attribute, such as original antique light fixtures, a stained glass window, a working fireplace, whirlpool tub, or a private deck. As an added attraction, the Garden Room opens onto a private secret garden. The English Suite features a fireplace, sitting room, a large bathroom with a two-person Jacuzzi, as well as a steam shower, and a private deck overlooking the rear garden. The opulent St. Charles Suite features a private veranda, a living room, a working fireplace, wet bar, and a two-person whirlpool. Ivy Cottage, a suite of rooms in the carriage house, is decorated in light Nantucket style and boasts a bedroom, a living room, and kitchen.

After your long afternoon, jump into the whirlpool tub with your sweetheart and let the pulsating water jets do their own restorative work. With your batteries recharged, slip into something nice, but not dressy, for dinner and entertainment.

DAY ONE: EVENING

Dinner

At night, Virginia-Highland assumes a romantic magic all its own. Of the thirty-five neighborhood restaurants, twenty-eight are clustered around the one intersection of Virginia and Highland, so the only difficulty you should have in choosing eateries this weekend is how to survive without torturing yourselves over the ones you didn't pick. However, as you've already discovered, there is altogether too much to see and do, and too many places to eat to make significant inroads in a single weekend. The only solution is to come back over and over again. We'll take the heat off you this evening, however, by suggesting that you dine at quaint, cozy **Babette's Cafe** (471 North Highland; 404–523–9121; moderate to expensive) for rustic French provincial fare in a charming, intimate, country-French setting reminiscent of the "Left Bank." *Money* magazine calls Babette's "Atlanta's Best-Kept Secret." This is just the place to share a sumptuous meal while staring intently into each other's eyes across a small table. Choose house specialties such as trout with lemon basil sauce or steamed mussels Pabalano. Reservations aren't taken, but you can call an hour in advance and put your name put on the waiting list. (Pass up the mouth-watering desserts because we have a suggestion for later in the evening.)

Nightlife

There's so much more to do before you have dessert and retire for the night. This is the time Atlantans from all over the metro area come out and play in Virginia-Highland. Instead of choosing a nightspot and spending the evening there, bar hop just like the locals do. **Atkins Park** (794 North Highland; 404–876–7249), around since 1983 as a watering hole, helped make Virginia-Highland the happening place it is today. Open from lunch time until about 3:00 A.M., the neighborhood fixture attracts an active happy hour and late-night crowd. **Blind Willie's** (828 North Highland Avenue; 404–873–2583), a nationally renowned, laid-back Southern blues room offers live hot jammin', cool jazz entertainment from local and national acts. There's no better way to describe this great joint than that is a dive, but once you're inside, it's dark and cozy with a party atmosphere. If you aren't too full, try the hot, Cajun-spiced Willie Wings. Come early if you have any hope of getting a seat or be on the sharp lookout for anyone who leaves. A light bar menu is served. **Dark Horse Tavern** (816 North Highland Avenue; 404–873–3607) is a community hangout with live local music in the basement. **Limerick Junction** (822 North Highland Avenue;

404–874–7147) is a true neighborhood favorite with live Irish music nightly. If you want to have a bite to eat, fish and chips, lamb stew, and other Irish staples, along with regular bar grub are served accompanied by Guinness, lagers, and Woodpecker hard cider. The granddaddy of them all, however, is **Manuel's** (602 North Highland; 404–525–3447), Atlanta's most storied tavern. A comfortable old standby for more than forty years, it has always been a local meeting place for journalists and politicos. Jimmy Carter, Bill Clinton, Ted Kennedy, Governor Zell Miller, and dozens of local politicians have sought counsel or plotted strategy at Manuel's. Carter and Walter Mondale celebrated the twentieth anniversary of their inauguration there as well. Authors Pat Conroy and Bill Diehl drop by. Although it probably isn't of immediate interest having just ate, Manuel's is renowned for its great bar food. You'll see anything here from three-piece business suits to shorts. If either of you is a budding journalist or politico, maybe you can start networking. Nearby is the **Red Light Cafe** (553 West Amsterdam; 404–874–7828), a cyber cafe in a SoHo-style loft environment with lots of couches ideal for snuggling while whispering sweet nothings in your honey's ear. While the other customers may be chatting on the PCS, you two can concentrate on a more old-fashioned mode of communication. Simple bar food and drinks range from sandwiches to pasta and desserts, accompanied by beer, wine, coffee, espresso, and cappuccino. Entertainment consists of open mike nights and live entertainment—especially bluegrass, but also acoustic, jazz, and folk music. The Cosmic Sunday Pickin' Hour is a perennial favorite.

Now for why we told you to skip dessert. Before you head back to your B&B, indulge in one of the special confections at **The Dessert Place** (1000 Virginia Avenue; 404–892–8921). They say that chocolate is an aphrodisiac, so be forewarned before you indulge in such as the signature hot fudge cream cheese brownie, Kentucky pie with pecans and bourbon, chocolate cake, and carrot cake. Although you'll be having a blast, don't stay out too late—you want to enjoy each other in the luxury of your suite at the inn.

DAY TWO: MORNING

Breakfast

After your late night, sleep as late as you can. Whoever wakes up first can get coffee or tea for the sleepyhead. Finally, head down to a continental-plus breakfast served in the formal dining room by flickering gaslight. Get the day off to a good start with freshly baked breads, muffins, and pastries, accompanied by fruit, juice, and hot beverages, then return to your room for a final soak in the whirlpool so that you'll be rejuvenated for more shopping and exploring. If this is a Sunday, you needn't be in a hurry because most shops don't open until noon.

～∞～

Stroll back to the business district and continue your explorations. Extend your restorative weekend as long as you possibly can. When you can put the inevitable off no longer, return to the inn, say a fond farewell to your host, and head for home feeling wonderful.

FOR MORE ROMANCE

Dozens of attractions nearby beckon those who have more time to spend: the Jimmy Carter Presidential Library and Museum (see "Phoenix Rising"), Fernbank Natural History Museum and Fernbank Science Center (see "Indulge the Kid in You"), Emory University and Decatur (see "175 Years Young and Counting"), Piedmont Park and Midtown (see "Atlanta's Cultural Heart"), and the Callanwolde Fine Arts Center (see "A Feast for the Eye"). Downtown Atlanta (see "The Magical Emerald City") is only a five-minute drive away.

ITINERARY 13
Two days and one night

175 YEARS YOUNG AND COUNTING
DECATUR

*Y*our romantic destination for the weekend is DeKalb County, Atlanta's next-door neighbor and Georgia's second-largest county. Its seat of government, Decatur, named after naval hero Stephen Decatur, celebrated its 175th birthday in 1998. To the uninitiated, the area may appear to be simply a neighborhood or a suburb of east Atlanta, but it is actually a distinct town, which, in fact, predates Atlanta by thirteen years. (Ironically, if Decatur hadn't turned down a railroad's proposal to build a major station there, Atlanta might never have been born.) Formed at a rise where two Indian trails intersected, Decatur is known for its historic attractions, stately old neighborhoods, plentiful trees, landscaped yards and parks, and international shopping and dining, but it is also the home of the internationally known Centers for Disease Control (CDC), world-renowned Emory University—the Harvard of the South—Agnes Scott College, DeKalb Farmer's Market, Fernbank Museum of Natural History and Fernbank Science Center, Jimmy Carter Presidential Library and Museum, Neighborhood Playhouse, and Atlanta Dream Hostel. DeKalb County is also home to an evolving international village of stores and restaurants springing up to meet the needs of immigrants from many other countries who congregate in ethnic neighborhoods, especially along Buford Highway. Georgia's Stone Mountain Park, the most visited attraction in the state, is nearby. As the two of you explore energetic Decatur, you'll share the irrepressible energy infusing new life into both the town and your relationship. For those who find the Atlanta scene just too much, try this more distilled sibling of the big city. You'll enjoy the many charms of an exceptional bed-and-breakfast, sample innovative meals at some fine restaurants, and engage in some low-key nightlife.

Practical Notes: Because the courthouse welcome center and museum on the square and the Decatur Downtown Development Office, from which you can get a brochure for the walking/driving tour, are open only on weekdays, this getaway has been planned for a Friday/Saturday. If you can't arrange your schedule to include a Friday, you can get copies of the driving tour brochure and cemetery map at the Holiday Inn.

Romance at a Glance

♥ *Lay your head on a soft pillow at the Sycamore House in Old Decatur.*

♥ *Sip exotic teas while you relax amidst the delightfully whimsical folk art at the St. Agnes Tea Garden.*

♥ *Marvel at archaeological wonders of the ancient world at the Michael C. Carlos Museum.*

♥ *Rack up a game of pool at Twain's Billiards and Tap.*

DAY ONE: MORNING

The historic heart and soul of Decatur is its **Old Courthouse on the Square** (101 East Court Square, 404–373–8287; free). As you approach the courthouse from Ponce de Leon Avenue, you'll immediately appreciate the romance of the area when you spy the life-size street sculpture of an elderly couple snuggled up on a park bench, after he's just given her a valentine. This delightful sculpture reminds us all that romance flowers at any age.

Next admire the exterior of the stately Greek Revival-style structure with its ornate temple pediment, sturdy columns, and town clock. Although the courthouse dates from 1898, it is the fifth courthouse on the site—the first was built in 1823. Since the county's official court business moved to another building years ago, this beautifully restored grand edifice now serves as the home of the **DeKalb Historical Society** and as a welcome center. The repository of a fifteen-hundred-volume archives, the courthouse is also the home of a three-room museum about the county and city's history and their roles in the Civil War. Artifacts in the first room allow you to examine the first one hundred years of Decatur's history (1822–1922) and include the first lightbulb and first bathtub in Decatur, as well as other eclectic artifacts and World War I memorabilia. The second room explores Decatur's past from 1923 on. Among the artifacts here are photos from the Crest View Country Club where golf great Bobby Jones played and some of the golf legend's clubs. The third room is devoted entirely to Civil War memorabilia. As you examine these items from different periods of Decatur's past, envision what your life as a couple would have been like during any of these eras. Also don't miss seeing the magnificent courtroom. Outside, monuments, cannons, historic markers, and an old-fashioned bandstand grace the lovely grounds where concerts are held on Saturday evenings during the summer. (The welcome center and museum are only open Monday–Friday 9:00 A.M.–4:00 P.M.)

Downtown Decatur is delightfully walkable. Around the square and on the streets that radiate from it are dozens of quaint restaurants, most of which offer outdoor seating; several nightspots; and a few shops. Don't miss the unique way progressive Decatur has dealt with its MARTA rapid rail station. The line runs right under the plaza and makes convenient access to downtown and other points around the city as simple as pie, while maintaining the historical integrity of the square. Just as with a loving relationship, with a little planning you can have it all.

Take your sweetie by the hand and do a little exploring. Traditionally, the courthouse square served as a community gathering place; in addition to the concerts on the courthouse lawn, it continues to be the site of a Saturday outdoor farmers' market, many festivals, and other special events throughout the year. To find out about these, call the **Events Hotline, 404–371–8262.**

From the square, head for the **Historic House Complex** of the DeKalb Historical Society (716 and 720 West Trinity Place; 404–373–1088; $2.00 donation), another good place to learn about Decatur history. Although it's certainly a walkable distance from the square to the complex, it's just far enough that you might prefer to drive. Four historic structures show how Decatur residents lived in the town's early years. Two log cabins depict the earliest years: the **Biffle Cabin,** which was built by a Revolutionary War veteran, and the **Thomas-Barber Cabin.** The **Swanton House,** a one-story frame cottage that was constructed between 1830 and 1840, is Decatur's oldest house (as opposed to a cabin) and operates as a small museum. Another one-story frame house, the **Mary Gay House,** is named for the author of *Life in Dixie During the War,* which Margaret Mitchell used as a reference for *Gone With the Wind*. Operated by the DeKalb Junior League, the Mary Gay House serves as a special events facility. Although the interiors of these structures are only open to groups by appointment, you can walk around the buildings and peek in the windows. The complex backs onto a small delightful park filled with shade trees. You may want to stroll here or sit on a bench to do some snuggling.

DAY ONE: Afternoon

Lunch

Once you've stepped off busy Ponce de Leon Avenue into the cool recesses of **Cafe Alsace** (121 East Ponce de Leon Avenue; 404–373–5622), just off the square, you can believe you're in a small bistro in the French countryside. Cheerful yellow walls decorated with floral murals create an intimate garden atmosphere. You're sure to want to hold hands with your sweetheart across the small table while you sip glasses of French wine. Serving hearty Alastian regional cuisine, the restaurant features such dishes as quiche Lorraine, a specialty of the Alsace-Lorraine area; spaetzle, a vegetable stew served over Alsatian noodles; and tarte a l'oignon, an Alsatian onion pie, and other French favorites, including crepe du jour, seasoned according to Chef Marceau's mood; boeuf Bourguignon; and French Riviera salad. Or get into a carefree picnic mood by ordering the Tour de France—an assortment of six cheeses served with grapes, walnuts, and a crispy baguette. No matter what dishes you indulge in, leave room to share an espresso, cafe Viennois, or cafe Liegeois accompanied by a sinfully delicious dessert like profiterolles—ice cream–filled puffs topped with hot chocolate sauce, mousse au chocolat, or tarte du jour.

Now satiated and amused, drive to the Emory University campus and drop in at the atrium of the **Robert W. Woodruff Health Sciences Center Administration Building** at **Emory University** (1440 Clifton Road, N.E.; 404–727–5686; free) to see an immense Byzantine-style **mosaic** illustrating the history of medicine. You'll be astonished by the sheer size of it—three stories tall, 68 feet long. Pick up a free brochure that explains what's going on in each of the mosaic's thirty-three numbered panels, each depicting a significant person or event in medical history. Proceeding chronologically, you begin with skull trephining—surgically removing part of the skull—and continue to Frederick Banting and Charles Herbert Best's discovery of insulin in 1922. In between, you'll see Hippocrates, Florence Nightingale, Pasteur, Curie, and a native Georgian, Crawford W. Long, who in 1842 was the first to use ether as an anesthetic. Italian artist Sirio Tunelli created the mosaic using 2.5 million chips of glass in about three thousand colors, shades, and hues. The scenes were pieced together on the floor of his studio and a school gymnasium, then shipped to Atlanta to be mounted on the wall. It can be troublesome to find a place to park on a college campus, but try behind the building.

Next visit the **Michael C. Carlos Museum** (571 South Kilgo Street; 404–727–4282; $3.00 donation), the Southeast's largest archaeological museum also part of Emory University. Located in a stunning building designed by internationally renowned architect Michael Graves, the collections trace nine thousand years of art and art history, including art of the ancient

Mediterranean cultures of Egypt, Greece, Rome, and the Middle East and cultures of the Near East, the Americas, Asia, Africa, and Oceania, through more than 18,000 objects. Among the treasures are an Egyptian mummy, pre-Columbian pottery, and Greek statues. In addition, there are artworks on paper from the Middle Ages through the twentieth century. The museum also hosts special exhibitions from its own holdings and from those of other institutions.

Once you've been properly impressed by these exotic antiquities, it's time to check into your romantic weekend hideaway. Your destination is the **Sycamore House in Old Decatur** (624 Sycamore Street; 404–378–0685; $100), a beautiful and classy bed-and-breakfast, which occupies a magnificent ninety-year-old Prairie-style mansion on a charming tree-lined residential street. Lovingly restored and handsomely furnished, the house contains an eclectic collection of antiques and modern pieces accented by interesting contemporary artwork.

Guests are encouraged to use the formal front parlor, but they are more often drawn to the entertainment-filled great room that is not only an extension of the kitchen, but that seems to flow seamlessly to the outdoors. This room features a fireplace, comfortable seating, a large-screen TV, VCR, CD player, and a surround-sound audio system as well as magazines, newspapers, and books. As appealing as is the interior of the house, the most pleasant surprise is found in the secluded rear garden, which has been transformed into a relaxation paradise. A multilevel deck descends to a patio, a free-form heated pool, a waterfall that cascades over a rocky promontory, and a hot tub—all surrounded by ornamental plants carefully chosen for their color and fragrance.

Accommodations are offered in a suite and a guest room, but for this special weekend, reserve the elegant suite. Located downstairs, the sumptuous pair of rooms includes a bedroom, a private bath, and a comfortable sitting room with a wood-burning fireplace.

Sycamore House is ideally situated within a five-minute walk from either the Avondale Estates or Decatur MARTA rapid rail stations, from which you can catch a train to downtown, many other points of interest, and the airport. The bed-and-breakfast is also a five-minute

♥ *Top of Stone Mountain*

♥ *Summit of Kennesaw Mountain*

♥ *Sun Dial atop Westin Peachtree Plaza, downtown*

♥ *Grand Hyatt, Buckhead*

♥ *Four Seasons, Midtown*

♥ *Rooftop deck of Georgian Terrace, Midtown*

♥ *Rooftop suites at Biltmore Inn, Midtown*

♥ *Top of the Plaza Restaurant atop the First Union Building, Decatur*

♥ *Piedmont Park, Midtown*

♥ *Oakland Cemetery, downtown*

♥ *Japanese Garden at the Jimmy Carter Presidential Library and Museum, downtown*

♥ *Memorial Avenue overpass, downtown*

walk from the restaurants and shops of Decatur and from Agnes Scott College. If you want to explore the neighborhood, you can simply stroll around, but you might want to borrow the bicycles that are available for guest use.

In warm weather, a little time in the pool and hot tub is bound to work the kinks out of tense muscles and relax you to the point of melting into a little puddle.

DAY ONE: EVENING

Dinner

After you've had an ample opportunity to shake off everyday woes, shower and change into casual clothes for dinner at **The Food Business** (115 Sycamore Street; 404–371–9121; moderate) on the square. This funky restaurant is both a destination eatery and a showcase for Decatur. It's hard to know whether to talk about the food or the decor first. Spurred by the increasingly popular fresh-food revolution, the innovative cuisine is described as New American. Among just a few of the recommended dishes are the Maryland crab cakes, roasted beet salad, grilled beefsteak tomato salad, and pork tenderloin. While you're waiting for your meal, devour a variety of four renowned breads that changes often. Order the sampler basket ($3.95), which might include sweet potato biscuits, orange anise bread, ciabatta bread, nut and raisin bread, or whatever strikes the chef's fancy. The awesome knock-your-socks-off desserts are renowned, especially the cookies and cakes, as are the tortes, tarts, and homemade ice cream. Accompany your meal with boutique American wines and locally brewed beers. The portions are so large, you're bound to take some back to the B&B for a late-night snack. As for your surroundings, the three-level contemporary loft is housed in an old storefront building. The bold, original, mod look of the interior is achieved with exposed old brick, stenciled concrete floors, colorful walls, and fanciful art. Frequented by urbane in-towners, inquisitive suburbanites, and alternative couples, the eatery's noise level can get high, so ask for an out-of-the-way table for your private chats. One very nice plus is that the restaurant is entirely nonsmoking. Reservations are not accepted and The Food Business is jammed on weekends, so get there early.

Nightlife

Although you've lingered over dinner, you may still be too keyed up with your weekend freedom to think about turning in yet. In that case, explore some of Decatur's hoppingest nightspots, which are located on the square or nearby. The **Grog Shop** (121 Sycamore Street, 404-687-9353), next door to The Food Business, is a great place to shoot some pool or play darts. **Eddie's Attic** (515-B North McDonough Street; 404–377–4976), around the corner, is the hub of Atlanta's singer-songwriter scene. The metro area's finest acoustic players perform here every night. Relax with a game of pool in the game room or repair to the popular covered deck out back. Just a few blocks away near Agnes Scott College, musicians perform at the **Great Southeastern Freight Room** (301 East Howard Avenue; 404–378–5365) six nights a week. Named for America's most erudite billiards aficionado, **Twain's Billiards and Tap** (211 East Trinity Place; 404–373–0063), which sports twenty pool tables and three dart boards, is a place where you'll want to chalk your cue.

Return to the B&B to take advantage of your suite for whatever your heart's desire dictates. In cool weather, what could be more conducive to love than curling up by your own fireplace?

DAY TWO: MORNING

Breakfast

After a wonderful night's sleep, it will be hard to emerge from the luxury of your suite, but when the tantalizing aromas of a delicious full breakfast start penetrating your domain, you won't be able to resist. Your morning repast can be served in the formal dining room, but when the weather is good, most guests prefer to eat outside in the backyard Eden. In fact, you might be tempted to spend the rest of the day here, swimming, sunning, reading, and enjoying each other's company. That's certainly an oh-so-attractive option.

In case you'd rather do some sightseeing, however, use the brochure of self-guided walking/driving tours of Decatur that you picked up yesterday. This tour guides you past nineteenth-century commercial buildings and residences and to the historic **Decatur Cemetery** (299 Bell Street; free), where you can stroll through the city's past. A woodsy, parklike retreat, on July 22, 1864, the site was the scene of a Confederate victory in a skirmish with Union troops, one of the few Southern victories during the Battle of Atlanta. Today, headstones in the peaceful graveyard progress in style from the crude, moss-covered stones of early pioneers to ornate Victorian monuments, often inscribed with tender sentiments. Continuing the tour, see the 1891 **Decatur Railroad Depot,** which now houses the Great

Southeastern Freight Room Restaurant; the **Oakhurst Neighborhood,** one of the oldest neighborhoods in Decatur; **Historic Sycamore Street,** the location of some of the grandest houses in town; **South Candler Street,** Decatur's first official historic district and home of **Agnes Scott College,** and the unique shops and fine restaurants of **West Ponce Place.**

FOR MORE ROMANCE

If you can stay longer, visit the **DeKalb Farmers' Market** (3000 Ponce de Leon Avenue; 404–377–6400), the largest indoor market of its kind in the world, where you can find a dizzying array of fresh fruits and vegetables and baked goods from more than fifty countries. You'll want to stock up on these exotic goodies to take home with you. Fill additional evenings of your holiday for lovers with performances at the two stages of the **Neighborhood Playhouse and the Discovery Arena** (430 West Trinity Place; 404–373–5311) or productions of the **Beacon Dance Company, Several Dancers Core,** or the **Decatur School of Ballet.** For more about Decatur-area attractions, see the following itineraries: "Indulge the Kid in You," "Phoenix Rising," "Foreign Affairs," and "Rock Solid Love Affairs."

ITINERARY 14
Two days and one night

THE MAGICAL EMERALD CITY

DOWNTOWN ATLANTA

*D*orothy may have followed the yellow brick road to the mystical Emerald City, but all you have to do is follow any street (especially any Peachtree Street), road, or highway to the central point of soaring, gleaming, and architecturally stunning structures, and you'll have located downtown Atlanta. Although destroyed twice by fire, the city has an awe-inspiring tradition of welcoming tough challenges and triumphing through unadulterated enthusiasm. What began as a simple crossroad for two small railroads has evolved into one of the nation's most sparkling and exciting cities. Although it's reported that thirty acres of trees bite the dust every day due to metro Atlanta's zeal for building, when viewed from the air, the city still appears to be a truly emerald city. The modern business and hotel core coexists with an underground area of Atlanta's original streets and railroad yards. Not surprisingly, the most famous of the city's thirty-two Peachtree Streets is the main artery. In downtown Atlanta, you'll find some of the only buildings to survive the Civil War as well as the modern city's most exciting hotels, restaurants, entertainment venues, boutiques, the last remaining downtown department store, the rapid rail and bus hub, and many tourist attractions. It is in the sparkling heart of the city that you'll spend this enchanted getaway.

Just like the Tin Man who was looking for a heart, you'll be looking to find/fill your hearts only to discover that in the end that the magic was really there for the two of you all along.

Practical Notes: This is one of the few weekend getaways in Atlanta that allows you to park at your hotel and then walk to everything. Make use of your concierge and especially the **Atlanta Ambassador Force** (404–215–9600) for directions and suggestions for your meanderings through the city's epicenter. A delightful holdover from the 1996 Centennial Olympic Summer Games, this fifty-plus person squad patrols 120 square blocks of downtown from 7:00 A.M. to 10:30 P.M. Clad in approachable uniforms and pith helmets, the ushers of Atlanta are not police, and they don't carry weapons but do have portable radios. The friendly force keeps an eye out for anyone who looks lost, gives directions, actually escorts visitors to their destinations or their cars, suggests restaurants, relates the history of surrounding buildings, suggests must-see attractions, and tries to deter aggressive panhandlers. Best of all: Their services are free. The north-south and east-west lines of **Metropolitan Atlanta Rapid Transit Authority (MARTA)** intersect at downtown's **Five Points Station.** With 39 miles of track and 1,500 miles of feeder bus routes, MARTA is the least expensive way to get around Atlanta, and it even goes to the airport. Carriage rides may not be available during the hottest days and nights of summer. If you want to include much shopping in your getaway, a Friday/Saturday holiday is preferable to a Saturday/Sunday—although the Underground shops are open Sundays.

DAY ONE: AFTERNOON

Check into your enchanting castle for the weekend, the charming **Suite Hotel at Underground** (54 Upper Alabama Street; 404–223–5555; $135–$210), an intimate boutique lodging that is at the heart of Atlanta near the Underground and the Five Points MARTA station. The hotel is the clever restoration of a historic office building, with the addition of several stories that blend in so well that you'd never know they were added. The magical hostelry, which places emphasis on intimacy and luxury rather than size, has a tradition of fulfilling each guest's heart's desire. With an atmosphere reminiscent of Europe's finest small hotels, the hostelry offers one-bedroom suites graciously furnished with a marble bathroom, honor bar, three telephones, and two color TVS. Five suites even boast Jacuzzis. A full breakfast buffet is served daily in the Dining Room as are cocktails and light dinner fare in the evening. Choose the One Enchanted Evening package, which includes a bottle of chilled champagne and two Suite Hotel logo glasses delivered to your suite on arrival, as well as breakfast delivered to your suite the following morning. The package is $150 per night and can be upgraded to a Jacuzzi suite for an additional $35.

Once you two lovebirds have checked in, gotten settled, and checked out the amenities of your weekend love nest, venture right outside your door to find the city's bewitching **Underground Atlanta** (50 Upper Alabama Street, S.W.; 404–523–2311), a 6-block, three-level, twelve-acre cavernous area of shops, cart vendors, street performers, restaurants, and nightspots. Now in its second reincarnation, Underground is the city's most visited attraction. Is it really underground? Well, not really—just as with all magic, the answer is yes *and* no. The city was originally founded at **Zero Milepost** (you can see it at the 1869 Georgia Freight Depot on the Peachtree Fountains Plaza) and streets radiated from that spot, with businesses growing up along them like kudzu. As a hint of automotive gridlock to come, the trains and horses and buggies caused the first traffic jams. Some enterprising engineer solved the problem by building viaducts over the tracks. Although most citizens cheered the improvement in transportation patterns, the unfortunate adjacent businesses were left with their first floors below the new street level (thus "under ground"). Not to worry. Enterprising merchants simply left the first floor for deliveries and storage and opened new main entrances on the second story. That's why for the last one hundred-plus years, there have been Upper and Lower Alabama and Upper and Lower Pryor Streets. During the sixties, entrepreneurs rescued the long-forgotten underground area and created an exciting warren of restaurants, shops, and entertainment emporiums. Crime—real and perceived—was the death knell for the all except one or two of the enterprises. But a few merchants refused to let the dream die, and with the advent of rapid rail, downtown revital-ization, beefed up security, a much lower incidence of crime (and maybe a few batwings and a little eye of newt), Underground Atlanta took reincarnation in the eighties. Today, Underground Atlanta is filled with more than one hundred specialty shops and streetcar merchants, as well as a food court, several restaurants, and nightspots, all of which keep the place hopping sixteen hours a day. Underground is just the right place to gladden the hearts of soulmates.

Once you've explored the warren of Underground, come back to the light. Across the plaza and in the shadow of the Georgia State Capitol is the **World of Coca-Cola Museum** (5 Martin Luther King Drive; 404–676–5151; admission $6.00/seniors $4.00), which certainly lives up to its international name. Atlanta is the home and world headquar-ters of the almost mythical giant of the soft drink industry, so it was only fitting that a shrine to the magical elixir be in this city. The three-story pavilion, which is the city's most visited indoor attraction, traces the beverage's development from an 1886 Atlanta drugstore drink to its present position as a worldwide phenomenon (an average of seven thousand Coca-Cola beverages are consumed around the globe every second!). Housed in the museum is the world's largest collection of memorabilia from the company's century-old history. You don't even have to peek behind the curtain to find out how it all happens—an unusual kinetic sculpture called the *Bottling Fantasy* gives a fanciful look at the bottling process. A soda jerk in the replica of a 1930s soda fountain shows you how a fountain Coke was prepared and served, while a 1930s jukebox plays rebroadcasts of period radio programs in the background. A ten-minute film takes a sweeping look at Coca-Cola around the globe. The kid in you can't wait to sample soft drinks from around the globe at Club Coca-Cola's high-tech Spectacular Fountain, which wows visitors as it shoots twenty-foot streams of soft drinks into your cups. Neon lights and special sound effects enhance the experience. You can also enjoy twenty-two soft drink brands available only regionally, and twenty-two exotic flavors made around the world but not available in America. Naturally, a wide variety of Coke merchandise is available in the gift shop, Everything Coca-Cola. (Ticket sales end one hour before closing.)

After you've explored these two magical attractions of our Emerald City, return to your hotel to get ready for a mystical evening of food and entertainment.

DAY ONE: EVENING

Dinner

Words can hardly describe **Mumbo Jumbo Bar and Grill** (89 Park Place; 404–523–0330; expensive), but we'll try. Lush, exotic, artful, funky, uptown (but it's really downtown), upscale, ultrahip, eclectic, avant-garde, this classy downtown restaurant is on the leading edge of dining excitement. Interior designer Patty Khrongold says, "I wanted it to be a place that when you walk in, you are slapped in the face with excitement." She has certainly succeeded admirably. Located in a historic building that was once a famous pool hall where the likes of Al Capone chalked up a cue, the site had several other incarnations as restaurants and a nightclub. During these changes, the two-story detached building managed to hang on to its baronial fireplace and an immense old bar, which now share your awe-struck attention with tangerine-colored walls,

Top Places in the Metro Area to People Watch

♥ *Little Five Points—anyone and everyone, pierced and tattooed bodies, skinheads and hippies, street musicians*

♥ *Morningside/Piedmont Park—colorful mix of people, especially on weekends; lots of Frisbee dogs; in-line skaters; alternative lifestyle couples*

♥ *Masquerade nightclub—Heaven, Hell, and Purgatory sections; more women without hair than men; closest thing to New York club scene in Atlanta*

♥ *Virginia-Highland—see-and-be-seen Yuppie/Boomer neighborhood*

♥ *Underground Atlanta/Five Points MARTA Station—evangelists, street vendors, street entertainers*

♥ *Centennial Olympic Park—cross section of Atlanta and the world*

♥ *Woodruff Park—businesspeople, workers, street people, and foreign tourist mix*

♥ *Buckhead Village—Boomers, generation Xers*

♥ *Glover Park, Marietta—good ole boys and girls*

♥ *Zoo Atlanta—compare spectators with animals*

♥ *Chastain Park Amphitheater—especially interesting when spectators dress the part for different forms of music*

♥ *Turner Field—Ted and Jane, Jimmy and Rosalynn, sports and entertainment stars*

white mosaic columns, funky light fixtures, exposed brick, plush suede seats, and interesting art. Packing an unusual level of energy, Mumbo Jumbo takes its food seriously. Contemporary cuisine created by Consulting Chef Guenter Seeger, former chief wizard of foods at the Ritz-

Carlton Buckhead, and laudably executed by Chef Shaun Doty, is a fusion of style, panache, and design. Elegantly prepared and organically grown menu items showcase beef, seafood, venison, chicken, rabbit, quail, and lamb. Among the upscale clientele you'll see are sports and music figures and gallery owners. For the after-dinner crowd, there's a teeming bar scene as well as a DJ and dancing upstairs in the intimate lounge. (Reservations for dinner are recommended.)

Nightlife

Although it's extremely tempting for the two of you to stretch out the evening at Mumbo Jumbo, tear yourselves away and stroll back to Underground Atlanta where you can embark on **Amen Carriage Company's** (290 Martin Luther King Jr. Drive, Unit 7a; 404–653–0202; $25–$30 per person) enrapturing carriage rides through the sparkling fairy lights of downtown and Centennial Olympic Park. Beginning after 6:00 P.M., the twenty- to thirty-minute ride covers most of historical downtown. For $200 an hour you can reserve a carriage to take you anywhere downtown. Top off this enchanted evening by hitting just a couple of Underground's nightspots in **Kenny's Alley. Fat Tuesday** (404–523–7404) is famous for its frozen daiquiri and Margarita bar, festive New Orleans-style decor, and Cajun cuisine. Dance the night away to music selected by the house DJ Monday through Friday nights or the Z103 (radio) DJ on Saturday nights. A live reggae band performs on Sunday nights. If jazz is more your style, you'll feel like a real pirate when you climb down an actual hatch at the original **Dante's Down the Hatch** (Lower Pryor Street; 404–577–1800), a hip underground (literally) restaurant/bar/night club. Inside, you'll be mesmerized with the illusion of an eighteenth-century sailing ship floating on a sea infested by crocodiles. (Yes, the water and the crocs are real.) Lose yourselves in drinks and dessert fondue while listening to live jazz. Open until 12:30 A.M. When your bewitching hour comes, stroll back to your love nest to finish your enchanted evening.

DAY TWO: MORNING

Breakfast

Breakfast in your suite is included in your One Enchanted Evening Package, so take advantage of the luxury of being waited on. After your server leaves, you can even have breakfast in bed.

As we all know, wizardry doesn't adhere to any schedule, so we've planned no specific agenda for today—simply relaxing rambles through downtown at your own pace. First wander over to **Centennial Olympic Park** (285 International Boulevard; 404–222–7275; free), a glorious legacy of the 1996 Centennial Olympic Summer Games and still a work in progress. Once a run-down area of dilapidated buildings, the twenty-one acres are a shining example of urban renewal wizardry. During the games, 2 million people used the park as home base; now you'll find it uncrowded except during special events. What you will see are the people of our enchanted city at play: picnicking, biking, skating, playing in the fountains, or simply people watching. The centerpiece of the park, of course, is the **Fountain of Rings,** designed in the form of the Olympic Rings. In fact, the fountain is the largest depiction of the Olympic logo in the world. Different heights of water jet out of the ground all the time, but hourly there is a dancing waters show set to music. Join all the munchkins as they cool off in Atlanta's own fountain of youth and revive your Olympic spirit by running in and out of the refreshing spray. (Wear something you don't mind getting wet.) Dry off while you stroll through the park; enjoy the five interconnecting quilt-theme plazas and sculptures, which include the *Gateway of Dreams,* featuring Baron Pierre de Coubertin, founder of the modern Olympic movement, stepping up to a Greek gateway topped by the Olympic rings; Billy Payne, the driving force behind Atlanta's participation in the games, standing in the *Quilt of Dreams;* and perpetually racing Greek athletes—contributed by the Greek community in Atlanta—speeding through the *Quilt of Origins.* The *Quilt of Remembrance*, a quiltlike pattern composed of multicolored stone, is positioned over the spot where the still-unsolved bombing took two lives during the games. Among the other attractions of the park is Atlanta's own brick road (although it's red not yellow). Bricks with names and messages from individual contributors around the world helped raise funds for the park. Perhaps you two donated a brick and would like to find it. Just step into the visitors center and use a little computer magic to locate its position, then go back outside to find it. Concerts, festivals, and other special events are often offered free in the park, so check with your concierge. During the summer, enjoy special activities on the first Saturday of the month and "Downtown Wind Down" concerts on Wednesdays.

Just a few blocks away is another downtown oasis. Long before there was Centennial Olympic Park, there was **Woodruff Park,** named for Robert Woodruff, a former president of Coca-Cola, who gave $10 million for the park's creation. Its expanses of green space, lush landscaping, the fabled phoenix statue, and a wall of gushing water have long attracted Atlantans to eat their lunch, read, sun themselves, or people watch here.

This is a perfect opportunity to admire the downtown architecture, which ranges from classic historic buildings, such as the highly decorative, turn-of-the-century **Candler Building;** the **Hurt Building;** and the **Flatiron Building,** to world-renowned Atlanta architect John Portman's contemporary masterpieces, such as the **Westin Peachtree Plaza, Peachtree Center, Hyatt Regency, Marriott Marquis, Marquis Towers, America's Mart, 230 Building,** and **One Peachtree Center.** Also admire the classical **Capitol** and **City Hall,** as well as the snazzy, contemporary **Fulton County Muncipal Center.** Make a game out of searching for examples of public art (some of it classic, some of it abstract, some of it bizarre) that fill the entire downtown area and pop up in some of the most unexpected places.

If you want to take home a souvenir to remind you of your magical weekend in the Emerald City, return to the famous name stores, exclusive boutiques, and galleries of Underground or check out the seventy shops, rich marble walkways, fountains, and quick-bite eateries at the three-story **Mall at Peachtree Center** (Peachtree Street at International

Boulevard; 404–654–1296).The mall's **Touch of Georgia** is the perfect place to find Georgia memorabilia and Georgia products, such as jellies, candies, nuts, and other edibles.

DAY TWO: AFTERNOON

Lunch

Although you're probably not returning to Kansas, before you return to wherever your home may be, you need to get a fix of grandma's (or Auntie Em's) Sunday Southern home cookin' at **Mary Mac's Tea Room** (224 Ponce de Leon Avenue, N.E.; 404–876–1800; inexpensive), an Atlanta tradition since 1945. The restaurant serves heaping portions of fried chicken, chicken and dumplings, meatloaf, fried catfish, turnip and other greens, fried green tomatoes, sweet potato soufflé, and luscious home-baked breads and desserts such as peach cobbler—all with generous helpings of Southern hospitality.

FOR MORE ROMANCE

Capture the magic of folk arts and photography by viewing the changing exhibits at the **High Museum's Folk Art and Photography Galleries** located in the Georgia-Pacific Center (30 John Wesley Dobbs Drive, N.E.; 404–577–6940; free).

Whenever news breaks around the globe, news hounds turn to CNN. See the fast-paced, high-tech, state-of-the art wizardry involved in broadcasting news in the making twenty-four hours a day at the world headquarters of the Turner Broadcasting System at **CNN Center** (One CNN Center at Marietta Street and Techwood Drive; 404–827–2300; admission $7/$5 for seniors). Here, forty-five-minute tours of CNN and *Headline News* are given in fourteen languages. During the tour, you'll have a unique view of news production from specially constructed, glass-enclosed overhead walkways. You'll be invited to reserve a seat in the studio audience for a production of CNN's hot program *TalkBack Live,* where you can voice your opinion to a national TV audience. In addition, you'll see a special exhibit filled with memorabilia from MGM classic movies and popular cartoons from the Cartoon Network. An interactive monitor wall enables guests to simultaneously preview the twelve Turner television networks. The "Milestones" exhibit chronicles momentous moments in the history of Turner Broadcasting. Bring home a piece of your CNN experience, such as a video copy of you reading the news on a CNN news set or a picture of yourself digitally mixed with any one of fifty personalities, including Ted Turner himself, from the Turner Store Tours (open daily 9:00 A.M.–6:00 P.M.). Call for reservations at least one day in advance. Or you could really splurge and for $24.50 take the one and one-half hour VIP Tour and discover all the wizard's secrets. During this small-group tour, you'll actually get to be out on the news floor and explore production areas not normally accessible to the public. Besides eating in the CNN Commissary alongside familiar newscasters, you'll receive a special gift package of CNN-related items to commemorate your visit. Who knows? You might make some news of your own.

ITINERARY 15
Two days and one night

ATLANTA'S CULTURAL HEART
MIDTOWN

If you and your heartthrob love culture, art, and music mixed with some of the city's hottest restaurants, hotels, and nightspots, get to the heart of the matter in Midtown. In the 1890s, a vast amount of land remained undeveloped between the downtown business district and elegant Buckhead. The extension of electric street cars changed all that by opening up new building sites between the two, and the area was christened Midtown. Today tony Midtown, the cultural heart of Atlanta, beats from Ralph McGill Boulevard north to Brookwood AMTRAK station at Deering Road, to Northside Drive on the west, and to Monroe Drive on the east. Midtown pulses with outstanding attractions that draw people from all over the South to the district: the Fox Theater; the Woodruff Arts Center, which houses the Atlanta Symphony Orchestra, Alliance and Studio Theaters, and the High Museum of Art; Rhodes Hall; Margaret Mitchell House; Piedmont Park; Atlanta Botanical Garden; Center for Puppetry Arts; and the William Breman Jewish Heritage Museum. A bustling commercial area, Midtown sheds its business image after dark to become a throbbing nighttime Mecca for theater goers, discriminating diners, and dedicated nightclub hoppers. Your hearts will beat as one when you stay at an exquisite historic bed-and-breakfast, dine on Midtown's "Restaurant Row," and dance the night away at popular nightspots.

Practical Notes: We've planned this getaway for a Friday and Saturday because Rhodes Hall isn't open on weekends, and so you can make a morning visit to the High Museum of Art on Friday. By deleting Rhodes Hall from the itinerary, however, the other attractions would fit nicely into any Saturday and Sunday holiday. The nucleus of Midtown between Ponce de Leon Avenue and Fifteenth Street is walkable; however, to reach some attractions and restaurants in the farther reaches of the district, you will need your car or some other mode of transportation. Midtown is served by four MARTA rapid rail stations: Midtown (at Tenth Street), North Avenue, Civic Center, and Arts Center, which offer quick and easy access to some other attractions within Midtown as well as to downtown, Buckhead, and other areas of the city.

Romance at a Glance

♥ *Celebrate the essence of your romance at the Shellmont Bed and Breakfast.*

♥ *Get right to the heart of Midtown on a walking tour.*

♥ *Nourish your soul and your body at the South City Kitchen.*

♥ *Sip a cool drink on the patio at Einstein's.*

DAY ONE: MORNING

Your first destination: the **Margaret Mitchell House** (990 Peachtree Street; 404–249–7012; admission $6/$5 for seniors), is the former home of one of Atlanta's most illustrious citizens. Along the Peachtree Street corridor from downtown to Buckhead only a few residences remain from the street's heyday when it was one of the most fashionable addresses in Atlanta. Two, now museums, are your goals for this morning. First, see the small apartment in the three-story, turn-of-the-century, Tudor Revival Crescent Apartments where the native Atlanta author wrote *Gone With the Wind*. Imagine how exciting Mitchell's love affair with her husband must have been during that creative time. Among the treasures on display are Mitchell's 1937 Pulitzer Prize and the typewriter she used to transcribe her handwritten manuscript. The adjacent visitors center contains a film, photographs, and displays about the book, the movie, the author's life, and Atlanta during her lifetime. There is also a gift shop where you can purchase a *Gone With the Wind* memento to remind you of your sentimental visit to Midtown.

DAY ONE: AFTERNOON

Lunch

For lunch head for the sophisticated **South City Kitchen** (1144 Crescent Avenue; 404–873–7358; moderate), just the place for two cosmopolitan lovers to lunch. Located in a renovated historic home, the sleek, gutted and opened up, steel-and-glass interior, open kitchen, and long snazzy bar set the stage for a lively atmosphere. Billed as "where the low country meets the high rises," the cheery restaurant showcases eclectic, contemporary, nouvelle Southern cuisine, which marries influences as disparate as Southwestern and Carolina coastal. Lunches are headlined by choices such as Charleston she-crab soup, spinach and watercress salad, and cornmeal-seared trout. Dinner's specialty is skillet-fried crab cakes. Any meal can be accompanied by a selection from the excellent wine list. When the weather's warm and breezy, enjoy a cool drink on the popular patio. The open floor plan does tend to let noises bounce around, so ask for an out-of-the-way table if you want to do anything but stare into each other's eyes.

After feeding the body, it's time to continue the nourishment of your souls. Visit your second house museum, **Rhodes Hall** (1516 Peachtree Street, N.W.; 404–881–9980; $3 unguided, $5 guided). Completed in 1904 by the Rhodes Furniture family, the heavy Romanesque Revival-style home combines the elements of several Rhineland castles Rhodes saw on trips to Europe. The home of the Georgia Trust for Historic Preservation, the mansion's interior is equally lavish in style and embellishment. Try to imagine what turn-of-the-century life would have been like here with your significant other.

The next stop will allow you to get in touch with your roots if you're Jewish or to become better acquainted with that faith if you aren't. The **William B. Breman Jewish Heritage Museum** (1440 Spring Street, N.W.; 404–873–1661; admission $5/$3 for seniors) is the largest museum of its kind in the Southeast. Displays in the museum permit the visitor to explore Atlanta's Jewish heritage from 1845 through the present by examining everyday items such as photographs; newspapers; party souvenirs; signs; architectural fragments, such as stained glass windows; posters; and other memorabilia. Displays interpret Jewish rituals, celebrate prominent Atlanta Jews, and trace the Jewish business presence in the city. Videos explore two tragic episodes in Atlanta's past: the 1913 murder case in which innocent Jewish supervisor Leo Frank was accused of killing thirteen-year-old factory worker Mary Phagan and then was lynched, and the 1958 bombing of The Temple, thought to have been in retaliation for Rabbi Jacob Rothschild's support of integration. No matter what your faith, you'll want to hold tight to your loved one when you encounter displays depicting the heartrending horrors of the Holocaust (Hitler's "final solution") through the story of the Jews in Europe. Although the Holocaust is traced from its historical roots to the Nazi death camps, the exhibit ends on a hopeful note: the creation of Israel and the rebuilding of the lives of the survivors. The museum features a number of exhibits, a hands-on Discovery Center, educational programs, and facilities for genealogical and archival research. Guided and self-guided tours are options.

After experiencing the dedication and resilience of these determined people, it's time for a change of pace by checking into your weekend love nest. At the corner of Sixth and Piedmont is the beautiful **Shellmont Bed and Breakfast** (821 Piedmont Avenue, N.E.; 404–872–9290; $120–$150), an exquisite example of Federalist Greek Revival Victorian architecture, festooned with an Adamesque shell garland and ribbon work and a Tiffany stained glass window. A city of Atlanta landmark building, the Shellmont has won many awards and is listed on the National Register of Historic Places. Inside, twelve-foot ceilings, ornate plasterwork, and corner fireplaces provide a dramatic backdrop for antique furnishings, Oriental rugs, and opulent Victorian wall treatments. Bedrooms have private baths with old-fashioned clawfoot tubs. Extra romantic touches include fresh flowers, a fruit basket, and evening chocolates. If you're all hot and sweaty from a day of heavy sightseeing, take time for a relaxing soak in the clawfoot tub before you get ready for a hearty dinner.

DAY ONE: Evening

Dinner

Now that you're relaxed, prepare for a full and lively evening. For hearty, flavorful, authentic, rustic Italian cuisine in a chic international atmosphere, **Veni Vidi Vici** (41 Fourteenth Street; 404–875–8424) is a delight. (Don't let the fact that this tony restaurant is located on the ground level of a parking deck deter you from dining here. You'd never guess it.) First, if the season is right, sip your favorite drink outside on the patio and steal a kiss or two from your amour while watching casual and serious competitors play on the traditional bocci ball courts. You can eat outdoors if you'd like, or go inside to the large, open dining room for appetizers, including calamari, veal meatballs, and octopus; pastas, wood-burning rotisserie roasted meats, chicken, veal, seafood, soups, salads, sandwiches, and rich desserts.

Nightlife

Culture is what Midtown's all about, so it's only natural to attend a symphony or theatrical performance at one of Midtown's many cultural venues. Both the **Alliance and Studio Theaters** and the **14th Street Playhouse** are located within a couple of blocks of the restaurant. (We've described some of the musical and theatrical offerings in other itineraries, so consult those sections and your B&B hosts for suggestions.)

After the show, upscale Midtown gives trendy Buckhead a run for its money in the nightlife category. Sample one of these happening places or try them all. For slick fifties/sixties cocktail culture swank, stop in at the **Leopard Lounge** (84 Twelfth Street; 404–875–7562) where you can listen to Rat Pack-era Sinatra and Sammy Davis Jr. hits piped in during the week until 2:00 A.M. or a live quartet from 10:00 P.M. until 2:30 A.M. on Friday and Saturday. The **Crescent Room** (1136 Crescent Avenue; 404–875–5252), one of Atlanta's newest in-spots, is a speakeasy with a decor described as industrial flair with heavy opulent undertones, accented by lots of customized art provided by local artists. Of course, what most folks go there for is the live music Thursday through Saturday nights. Go to the **Kaya Club and Bistro** (1068 Peachtree Street; 404–874–4460) for disco on Friday nights or Latin entertainment on Saturday. Dance to the wee hours with your heartthrob; then once you've taken care of your cardiovascular system, return to your hideaway for a little attention to your love life and a peaceful night's sleep.

DAY TWO: MORNING

Breakfast

You'll awaken in the morning to the aromas of coffee or tea left on the second-floor landing. A continental-plus breakfast of cereal, dried and fresh fruit, and an assortment of pastries is served in the formal dining room, with china, crystal, silver, and linens as befits this special weekend.

After a leisurely breakfast, head for the crown jewel of Atlanta's cultural scene, the **Woodruff Arts Center** (1280 Peachtree Street, N.E.; 404–733–4200) where you will spend the morning. Begin at the **High Museum of Art** (404–733–HIGH), the repository of a superb collection of European and American paintings and sculpture, contemporary art, photography, and decorative arts. Located in a stunningly modern facility, the museum often hosts blockbuster traveling shows, such as the magnificent "Five Rings" exhibit during the Olympics, along with exhibits highlighting the works of Monet and Picasso. Take your time and be on the lookout for particularly romantic works that may give you some ideas. If you feel the urge, there are dozens of nooks where the two of you can steal a quick kiss or an embrace. Next door is the **Woodruff Arts Center** is the **Atlanta College of Art Gallery** where innovative student work is shown.

DAY TWO: Afternoon

Lunch

When you feel the need for food, try **Einstein's** (1077 Juniper Street, N.E.; 404–876–7925), a community cafe where intelligent minds and eager mouths make relatively short work of tasty appetizers, pastas, salads, and sandwiches. While you're enjoying your repast, check out the Einstein-like graffiti on the stark white walls. In good weather, dine outside on the tree-shaded patio, consistently voted "Best Outdoor Dining Experience in Atlanta." While lingering over a good meal, share your heart's desires.

જ⊚ે

After lunch, leave your car at the restaurant and walk west one block to Peachtree Street to begin a leisurely **walking tour of Midtown,** which will permit you to admire the varied nineteenth- , early-twentieth-century, and contemporary architecture and the many pieces of public art. Pass the Margaret Mitchell House at Tenth Street. As you continue north on Peachtree, admire the many street sculptures along the way: *Tai Chi,* an abstract bronze, and *Forgotten Alchemy,* a blue-patina bronze square balanced on a sphere, both outside the First Union Plaza building; *Sabine Women,* a geometric steel piece outside Colony Square at Fourteenth Street; and *Trilon,* a three-sided, copper-clad concrete abstract with a pool and fountain at Fifteenth Street. Take a short detour west on Fifteenth and follow the colonnade of the AT&T Promenade building into the courtyard to see *Olympia,* a colorful abstract of painted metal. While you're on this side of the Woodruff Arts Center, view *World Events,* a twenty-five-foot, 4.5-ton youth holding a sphere. On closer examination you see that the entire cast aluminum sculpture is made up of puppetlike human figures welded in a spider web effect. Return to Peachtree and turn north once more to see *Teatro XIX,* an arrangement of bronze architectural elements. On the grounds of the High Museum are *Three Up Two Down,* a colorful stabile; *Red,* a large red rectangular shape of painted stainless steel; a statue of Robert W. Woodruff, a major Atlanta philanthropist; and *L'Ombre,* a bronze casting by Rodin, which was given to the museum by the French government in memory of the 122 Atlanta arts patrons and civic leaders who were killed in a 1962 Paris plane crash.

At this point, most casual visitors will want to skip the upper regions of Midtown and take Fifteenth Street west to West Peachtree and turn south. If you're in really good physical condition, however, and have lots of energy to spare, continue north past Nineteenth Street to the intersection of Peachtree and West Peachtree to see the *World Athletes Monument* commissioned by the Prince Charles and the Princess of Wales Institute of Architecture for the 1996 Centennial Olympic Summer Games. Perched on classical columns, five athletes representing the five Olympic rings support a globe illuminated by an eternal flame. After Princess Diana's death, the sculpture became a mourning place, and the tiny triangular parked was named Princess Diana Memorial Plaza. Take a minute to pay your respects and be thankful for your loved one before continuing the tour. Pass Rhodes Hall. A block north you'll find the imposing **Peachtree First Christian Church** (1580 Peachtree Street) and **The Temple** (1589 Peachtree Street). The 1925 church is modeled after Melrose Abbey, a sixteenth-century cathedral in Great Britain. Its sanctuary contains the largest collection of handmade English stained glass outside of Great Britain. The Temple is the synagogue of the Hebrew Benevolent Congregation, Atlanta's oldest Jewish congregation. Built in 1931, the exterior is classically Southern (Greek Revival), while the interior follows the plan of Solomon's temple in Jerusalem. After your visit, turn south and return

to the *World Athletes Monument* where you will pick up West Peachtree Street. Pass the William B. Breman Jewish Heritage Museum, the **Center for Puppetry Arts,** and continue to Fifteenth Street, where the route joins the shorter tour.

Another detour for the hardy is to turn east at Fourteenth Street or Tenth Street and walk the three long blocks to **Piedmont Park.** Once the site of the 1895 Cotton States Exposition and the driving ground and race track of the Gentleman's Driving Club (horses, that is, not cars), it is now the city's most popular park. Pieces of public art in the park include *Free Nelson Mandela,* made of a granite boulder, barbed wire, and steel pipe; *Playscapes,* a sheet metal and steel pipe playground; and *Peace Monument,* a bronze angel standing over a fallen soldier.

If you skipped the park detour, continue south on West Peachtree and admire the 1941 neo-classical revival **Academy of Medicine** (875 West Peachtree Street). Between Sixth and Fifth Street, you'll see the historic **Biltmore Hotel and Tower,** which was the largest hotel in Atlanta when it opened in 1924. Today 75 percent of it sits empty, awaiting a renaissance as a mixed-use complex, but this end still operates as an intimate inn as recommended in "All the World's a Stage."

Continue south to Ponce de Leon Avenue, and then go one long block east to Peachtree. On the corner are the **Georgian Terrace Hotel** and the **Fox Theater.** The elegant hotel, called a cross between Southern and Parisian architecture, was built in 1911 and is the only hotel in Atlanta listed on the National Register of Historic Places. The Moorish, Art Deco, Egyptian theater was originally (1929) a Shriner's hall and movie theater. Today it hosts traveling Broadway shows. Also admire the Mediterranean architecture of the old **Ponce de Leon Apartments** (75 Ponce de Leon) on the corner.

Continue north to **St. Mark's United Methodist Church** (781 Peachtree). Built in 1902 and 1903, the modified Gothic church features a triple-arched entrance and stained glass and opalescent glass windows. Having now completed a moderate or major circuit of Midtown, return to Einstein's to pick up your car.

We hope Atlanta's display of public art and historic buildings and its rich diversity of musical and theatrical offerings gladdens your hearts and renews your love for each other.

FOR MORE ROMANCE

Choose from among any of the attractions mentioned in the introduction: for example, Piedmont Park and the Atlanta Botanical Garden (see "Full Bloom of Love") or the Center for Puppetry Arts ("Indulge the Kid in You"). For a curator's list of romantic artworks, see "A Feast for the Eye." Take one of the **Atlanta Preservation Center**'s (404–876–2040) guided walking tours of the interior of the Fox Theater, the Ansley Park residential neighborhood, and/or Piedmont Park. If you can make this escape during the week, you can get right to the heart of the local news business by touring the radio and TV operations, including the news rooms and studios of **WSB** (1610 West Peachtree Street; 404–897–7369, free) or the facilities of **WXIA** (1611 West Peachtree Street; 404-892-1611, free).

ITINERARY 16
Three days and two nights

LOVE SQUARED
MARIETTA SQUARE

*S*pend an enchanted weekend together discovering the delicious attractions around what we consider to be the handsomest town square in Georgia (outside Savannah). Glover Park is the centerpiece of the lovely antebellum town of Marietta, and the area around the park will be the nucleus of your visit, but the town also boasts five historic sites, five National Register of Historic Places neighborhoods with 150 antebellum and Victorian homes, and two state parks and historic sites nearby that you'll want to see as well. If you and your loved one fancy digging into Civil War history, poking through out-of-the-way antiques shops, frequenting cultural events, and dining at casual and fine restaurants, all the while staying at one of Georgia's newest luxury resort hotels, you'll treasure this romantic sojourn.

Practical Notes: Parking is limited around the square, so you may have to find a place for your car a block or two away, but strolling back to the square while peeking into intriguing store windows may alert you to interesting shops that you'll want to come back and browse through.

DAY ONE: AFTERNOON

Marietta began as a railroad town before the Civil War and also developed as a summer resort. Prosperous citizens of that era built grand homes, many of which survive. Marietta's golden age ended drastically in 1864 when Union troops battled their way south toward Atlanta, occupying the town, and destroying many buildings.

Today, modern Marietta blends the romance of nineteenth-century history with the conveniences and attractions of the late twentieth century to establish and maintain its own distinct personality—and this in the face of being swallowed up by the gargantuan and rapacious sprawl of metropolitan Atlanta.

The Marietta square is located 2–3 miles west of the Big Chicken (more about it later). If possible, park at or near the square; then prepare to step back in time with your sweetheart by visiting the **Marietta Welcome Center and Visitors Bureau** located just off the square in the quaint 1898 Western and Atlantic passenger depot (Four Depot Street; 770–429–1115 or 800–835–0445). Watch a video about the town's history and pick up information including brochures for self-guided walking and driving tours. Morning and afternoon guided walking tours are also available by reservation only.

Romance at a Glance

♥ *Luxuriate at the Marietta Resort and Conference Center.*

♥ *Clip-clop around the square in a carriage.*

♥ *Feast at local restaurants.*

♥ *Time travel through history.*

♥ *Browse in antiques shops filled with treasures.*

To learn about one of the most infamous episodes in Marietta's past, go next door to the second floor of the Kennesaw House to visit the **Marietta Museum of History** (One Depot Street: 770–528–0431 or 770–528–0430; admission $2). The venerable structure, built in 1850 as a warehouse, was converted to a hotel in 1855. It was during an overnight stay in 1862 that Union spy James Andrews and some Union soldiers disguised as civilians plotted to hijack a train and flee north to

Chattanooga, burning bridges and tearing up track behind them in order to disrupt the South's war effort. The successful hijacking of the locomotive, the *General*, and its subsequent recapture by the Confederacy created one of the most exciting and enduring tales of the Civil War—memorialized in two movies. Later in the war, the hotel served as a hospital first for the Confederacy and then for the Union. Sherman commandeered it as his headquarters. It was here that he devised the downfall of Atlanta. Steal a lingering kiss in the elevator as it creeps to the second floor.

Display space in the museum is devoted to memorabilia about Marietta and Cobb County from the Creek/Cherokee Indian period to the present. An entire room is devoted to the story of "those people" (the Yankees) who hatched their nefarious plot there. Special exhibits change periodically, and the gift shop contains helpful books about the area's history.

After your museum visit, return to the square and wander through **Glover Park.** The romantic, Victorian setting is guaranteed to make you want to hold hands or share a kiss. Land for the park was donated in 1852 by Marietta's first mayor, John H. Glover, who shrewdly stipulated that if the land were ever used for any other purpose, it would revert to the family, thus ensuring its continued existence as a park. Lush landscaping encloses a turn-of-the-century-style gazebo and bandstand as well as a fountain, statues and historic plaques, benches, and a children's playground with a replica of the famous locomotive, the *General*. Numerous special activities and concerts draw visitors to the park—particularly on weekends—so if your timing is good, your visit may coincide with an art show, festival, or performance. It's no surprise that the square is also the scene of many picturesque weddings.

If shopping turns you and your paramour on, spend the remainder of the afternoon drifting through the shops and boutiques located in the historic buildings surrounding the square and the streets that radiate from it. Perhaps you and that special someone collect antiques. In that case, you'll think you've died and gone to heaven to find so many antiques shops (twenty-one) within such a small area. Whether your interest is in furniture or collectibles, museum-quality pieces or country crafts, you'll discover myriad treasures. Remember your romantic getaway with a meaningful piece to add to your collection. Pick up the brochure *Antique Shops of Marietta, Georgia* from the welcome center or from the shops themselves. Don't miss **DuPre's Antique Market** (17 Whitlock Avenue; 770–428–2667), a ninety-dealer antiques mall. DuPre's, built around 1880, was originally a general store and Marietta's first unofficial post office, a place where friends could leave messages or packages for each other. You're sure to find something there that you'll both treasure.

Other shops around the square carry a variety of wares: dolls, costumes and magic tricks, trendy clothing, vintage clothing, jewelry, and more. One shop you mustn't miss is the **Brumby Chair Company** (37 West Park Square; 770–425–1875) where the famous rocking chairs are finished and sold. The family business began in 1875, creating sturdy, generous-sized rockers of oak and cane for southern verandas. When Jimmy Carter was president, he introduced the by-then-renowned rockers to the White House. In addition to the jumbo rocker, the company also creates a smaller size adult rocker, baby rocker, footstool, and for lovers of any age, the double-courting rocker. That's the one you'll surely want for future cuddling. The double rockers are $639 stained or $679 painted. No matter which size rocker you buy, it is destined to become a family heirloom. At the back of the store, watch craftspeople hand assemble and cane the acclaimed chairs. Throughout the store, examine antique rockers and the photo collection of noted Georgians in their Brumby rockers.

DAY ONE: EVENING

Register at your weekend love nest, the magnificent new **Marietta Resort and Conference Center** (500 Powder Springs Street; 770–427–2500). Designed to resemble grand resorts, such as West Virginia's Greenbrier, the sweeping Greek Revival structure sits regally on the site of the former Georgia Military Institute and is backed by the championship city golf course. Amidst shiny marble and burnished paneling, large oil paintings, murals, and a life-size diorama depict the period of the property's former life as a military school. You have 200 potential love nests, among the elegantly furnished guest rooms, parlor suites, and the deluxe two-bedroom Presidential Suite, from which to choose. Prices range from $99 to $350, but this is a lover's holiday, so splurge with a suite. Each chamber offers a stunning view of the Atlanta skyline or the golf course and Kennesaw Mountain. Among the facilities at this Eden are the gracious **Hamilton's** restaurant, which serves three meals a day; the clubby **Pub** bar, where you can get light fare and enjoy the billiards, darts, and large-screen TV; lighted tennis courts; a health club with the latest in aerobic and weight equipment; and an outdoor swimming pool with spa and sundeck. In spite of all these amenities, we find the extensive grounds (which are perfect for quiet walks and romantic interludes) most beguiling.

For this evening's activities, nice casual attire is appropriate, but you might want to dress up a bit. Assuming your trip falls on a weekend, return to the square as it begins to get dark and take a carriage ride as the lights begin to flicker on in Glover Park and the surrounding businesses. What a perfect opportunity to nuzzle—especially if there's a nip in the air. A carriage ride will give you lovebirds a head start on an ultraromantic evening.

Dinner

Pamper yourselves with a nice dinner at **Shillings on the Square** (19 North Park Square; 770–428–9520; moderate to expensive). Located in a former hardware store, Shillings is a cozy, intimate place for a dinner for two. In the dimly lighted dining rooms, you can hold hands across the table and gaze into each others eyes, oblivious to those around you. The restaurant offers two dining options. The **Streetside Grill** on the main floor, which serves chicken, steak, and seafood, is more casual and more economical. Upstairs overlooking Glover Park, the more formal **Top of the Square** serves elegant candlelight dinners. Once a month, this restaurant features a four-course prix fixe dinner whose every course is accompanied by an appropriate wine. Call ahead to see if one of these dinners coincides with your visit. Although there are mouth-watering sweets on the menus of both eateries, save dessert for later.

Now that you've fed your bodies, it's time to feed your lust for culture. Cross the square and go halfway down Whitlock Avenue to the **Theater on the Square** (11 Whitlock Avenue; 770–442–8369; tickets $20–$25) for a night of award-winning live theater. Regardless of whether the play is light comedy, a musical, thriller, classic, or new work, you're bound to have a stimulating evening. If you and your honey are dying to talk over the play afterward, cross the street to **Java's Blues** (10 Whitlock Avenue; 770–419–0095) for a late-night cup of coffee and

dessert with musical accompaniment or return to the Pub at your hotel. Enjoy a comfortable night's sleep in your love nest—or whatever your fantasies dictate.

DAY TWO: MORNING

Breakfast

This is a holiday, so be decadent and sleep in. Then get the day off to a good start with the generous breakfast buffet at Hamilton's in your hotel. In nice weather, ask for a table for two on the patio; otherwise request a table in the huge bay window overlooking the golf course.

Before you leave the hotel grounds, visit historic **Brumby Hall and Gardens.** When the Georgia Military Institute existed, Colonel Anoldus VanderHorst Brumby served as its first superintendent, and he built a gracious Greek Revival cottage surrounded by formal gardens as his personal residence. During the Civil War, the school was destroyed with the exception of Brumby Hall—some say because Sherman and Brumby were friends at West Point. The house then functioned as a Union hospital for the remainder of the Atlanta campaign. After the war, the house went through several owners, and the gardens waxed and waned. The most recent restoration used the 1925 drawings of Herbert Bond Owens, founder of the University of Georgia School of Landscape Architecture, to reestablish the lavish boxwood, topiary, rose, annual, and perennial gardens, and a knot garden or maze in keeping with the original displays. Furnished with period pieces, Brumby Hall is open for tours on Thursday, but on other days, you can make an appointment through the hotel to see it. The gardens are always accessible and a romantic place for a clandestine assignation.

Using the *Historic Marietta Walking-Driving Tour* brochure, immerse yourselves in Marietta's past. Of the fifty-seven structures described, most are private residences or bed-and-breakfasts and not open to the public except during the Christmas tour of homes. You can visit the **William Root House** (145 Denmead Street at State 120/Marietta Loop and Polk Street; 770–426–4982). Built in the 1840s, the simple plantation-plain-style home is considered to be Marietta's oldest house. Furnishings depict what the life of a middle-class family was like during the 1850s.

Next explore the **Marietta Cobb Museum of Art** (30 Atlanta Street and Anderson Street; 770–528–1444; admission $4). Originally built as a federal post office, the stately Classic Revival building houses nineteenth- and twentieth-century American art.

DAY TWO: AFTERNOON

Lunch

By now, all this immersion in history has probably fueled your hunger, so take a break. Around the square and down little alleys, you'll discover many appealing options for lunch. When the weather is nice, we recommend **Hemingway's** (29 West Park Square;

770–427–5445) because it has outdoor seating at umbrella tables, which provides an excellent vantage point from which to admire Glover Park and people watch. Although the building in which the restaurant is located is historic, the ambience and menu are pure Key West.

Nearby Kennesaw Mountain experienced three weeks of fierce battles in the summer of 1864. Wounded soldiers of both sides were nursed in Marietta, and many died and were buried there in either a **Confederate Cemetery** (Powder Springs Extension at Cemetery Street) or a **National Cemetery** (Washington Avenue at Cole Street) for Union soldiers. In fact, Marietta is one of the few towns that has both Confederate and National Cemeteries. Both these hallowed burial grounds are quiet, poignant places for a reflective visit and private spots to share with your beloved.

Return to hotel to partake of the sports options at your hotel, or perhaps you'd rather curl up with your partner and a good book.

DAY TWO: Evening

Dinner

Try **Jimmy's on the Square** (164 Roswell Street; 770–428–5627; moderate), which has been a local tradition for a quarter century. Jimmy himself retired recently, and Nick Mandravellos bought the popular restaurant. Since Nick assumed ownership, more Greek and Italian dishes have appeared on the menu. Although the selections change seasonally, some items are always available. Among the appetizer favorites are *kalamarakia* (fried squid) and crab-stuffed mushrooms. You can make a meal out of the restaurant's Greek salad or have it as an accompaniment. Leading entrees include steak Oscar, veal Oscar, and lamb tenderloin. Nick swears that the calories have been removed from the cheesecakes and other rich desserts. Ask for a corner table or one toward the back of the restaurant.

Your evening's entertainment depends on the timing of your trip. From April through August, a monthly concert series is performed in Glover Park. Throughout the year the **Cobb Symphony Orchestra** performs at the **Civic Center** (State 120 Loop; 770–528–8450). Alternately, cuddle on a bench in the park. return to the hotel to rock on the rear veranda while you enjoy the night view, or slip off to your room to create your own entertainment.

DAY THREE: MORNING

Brunch

Arise at your leisure, then indulge in the universal fantasy of the Old South: a visit to a real plantation. Feast on a sumptuous brunch at the **1848 House** (780 South Cobb Drive; 770–428–1848; moderate to expensive) The centerpiece of this estate is a fabulous antebellum mansion that sits on thirteen shaded acres of what was once the three-thousand-acre Bushy Park Plantation. The stunning view of the house as seen going up the entrance drive through a long avenue of overhanging trees is worthy of any scene in a movie about the Old South. Inside, ten tastefully furnished dining rooms and a lounge reflect the period of the mansion's heyday. Two rooms upstairs are set aside as museum rooms. If it's chilly, and you have to wait for a table, snuggle up on a sofa by the fireplace in the lounge. Before you are seated, or before you leave, meander through the grounds to see the original detached stone kitchen and the flower and kitchen gardens. The cuisine is Southern with a sophisticated flair.

Many more shops beckon you to explore them, if you can't bear to end your lovers' getaway.

FOR MORE ROMANCE

If you have more time, look for other Marietta attractions in these itineraries: "That Pyromaniac from the North," "In Scarlett's Footsteps," the "Partners in Crime" mystery weekend, and "Indulge the Kid in You."

ITINERARY 17
Three days and two nights

OUR KIND OF TOWN
HISTORIC ROSWELL

*I*f discovering out-of-the-way places with your sweetheart starts your romantic juices flowing, share an enjoyable low-key weekend exploring a former Southern mill town just north of Atlanta and its adjacent natural attractions. We'll reveal some secrets of our hometown. *Gone With The Wind* it ain't, but the grace and gentility of the Old South flourish in Roswell's antebellum districts, and you'll discover three candidates for Tara. Despite the encroachment of sprawling Atlanta, this bygone mill town *cum* bedroom community clings to its own distinct personality. After twenty years, we can verify why Roswell has often been named one of the top places in America to live, but many of its citizens aren't even aware of all its hidden treasures. We'll divulge these little-known gems, only if you promise not to spread the word too far. Free or very inexpensive activities make this stolen weekend especially appealing.

Practical Notes: Traffic congestion and parking are problems in the core historic areas, so be prepared for some walking. Roswell has several historic districts, and although the separate areas can be reached on foot, it's easier to drive between them. Park at the visitors center to tour the Roswell Square and Sloan Street areas and at your bed-and-breakfast to visit the Heart of Roswell. For the best first impression, arrive in Roswell via Georgia SR 400, exiting at Northridge and following the the signs to the visitors center.

DAY ONE: MORNING

Roswell was founded in the 1830s when Roswell King, a merchant from coastal Georgia, transplanted family and friends here to establish a town and a textile mill. The seed they planted took root, and Roswell became a bustling village with several mills. The Civil War interrupted progress as the mills created cloth for Confederate uniforms. Fortunately, Roswell wasn't in the path of Sherman's march to Atlanta, so it was spared except for the mills. After the war, with the mills rebuilt, Roswell became a small, vibrant community until the 1960s and 1970s when its population exploded as scores of Atlantans moved to the suburbs. Vigorous preservation efforts saved the town's past, and Roswell prides itself on its historic buildings, outstanding parks and trails system, and cultural events. Touring Roswell is not only a perfect opportunity for you two to shrug off your hectic everyday life and indulge in some slow-paced, quality time together, but it is also an ideal occasion to pretend you are Scarlett and Rhett or Melanie and Ashley as you investigate romantic historic areas and natural attractions.

Arriving in Roswell via South Atlanta Street brings you right to the quaint town square, which is enveloped by historic homes and buildings. Presiding over the south side of the square is the gorgeous Greek Revival mansion **Barrington Hall,** Roswell's Tara candidate 1. Built in 1842, the mansion is still

Romance at a Glance

♥ *Drift back in history at Bulloch Hall.*

♥ *Trace Roswell's past at the Archibald Smith Plantation.*

♥ *Amble through city and national parks.*

♥ *Enjoy sweet dreams at Ten-Fifty Canton Street B&B.*

♥ *Feed your relationship at local dining favorites.*

the home of a descendant of the town's founders and is open only occasionally for special tours. A picturesque historic private home on the west side of the square is stately **Holly Hill,** a raised Greek Revival cottage on a generous piece of property.

The remaining sides of the square contain quaint shops for you to peruse—some in historic buildings, others in new structures erected to blend in with the old. Shop for antiques, art, and one-of-a-kind gift items in eclectic shops.

Several days a week guided walking tours depart from the **Historic Roswell Convention and Visitors Bureau** (617 Atlanta Street; 770–640–3253 or 800–776–7935), located in the old city hall. If you'd rather be alone together to explore at your own pace, get a walking tour brochure and depart on foot for a self-guided expedition. Get a map of the parks and trails system too—you'll need it tomorrow.

Stroll arm-in-arm down Bulloch Avenue, just off the square, and imagine yourself and your loved one transported back one hundred years or more. You can almost see the ladies in their hoop skirts and the gentlemen with their top hats and walking canes and hear the clip-clop of horses cantering down the street. Along this quiet, tree-lined boulevard several impressive antebellum and Victorian private residences slumber. The original **Phoenix Hall** burned down; this one rose from the ashes. Historical markers in front of these architectural treasures detail their significance.

Handsome **Bulloch Hall** (180 Bulloch Avenue; 770–992–1731; admission $5), Tara candidate 2, graces the end of the block. Set amidst several shaded acres, the white-columned, Greek Revival mansion perches on a knoll at the top of a circular driveway. A house museum, Bulloch Hall, built in 1839, was the girlhood home of Mittie Bulloch, who married Theodore Roosevelt Sr. Their son Theodore Jr. visited Bulloch Hall in 1905, long after his parents' and grandparents' deaths. Sit a spell in rockers on the verandah beneath the soaring columns and envision the wonderful love affair that took place here. Hint: Warm morning light creates the best opportunity for photographing this house.

One of the highlights is Mittie's bedroom—furnished as it might have been when she lived there. Two rooms are devoted to Roswell's Civil War memorabilia. Bulloch Hall sponsors several active guilds and costumed ladies often demonstrate open-hearth cooking, basket weaving, quilting, and other period crafts and skills. If you're lucky, you might get to taste some gingerbread or something equally delicious fresh from the oven.

DAY ONE: AFTERNOON

Lunch

The aromas of anything cooking at Bulloch Hall will whet your appetite, so return to the square for a delicious lunch at the **Public House** (605 South Atlanta Street; 770–992–4646; moderate), a comfortable restaurant where you and your sweetie can linger over an intimate meal in the elegant ambience of this superb pre–Civil War commercial building, with exposed brick walls, dark beams, hardwood floors, vintage oil portraits, white linens, and upholstered chairs. The imaginative menu runs the gamut from salads to chops and changes often. For a light lunch, you can never go wrong with the generous chicken salad served with fresh fruit and sweet bread. Desserts are to die for, so partake of something sweet, such as their famous chocolate chip pecan pie. Best idea for couples concerned with keeping their svelte waistlines: order one serving to share.

After lunch, work off some of those calories by continuing your walking tour. Saunter down Sloan Street, the nucleus of the **Roswell Historic Mill Village District.** This area was a neighborhood of workers homes, many of which survive as private homes or businesses. Known as the Bricks, two sets of row houses built in 1840 housed workers dormitory style. Farther along, larger cottages accommodated supervisory workers. At the end of the street, the small, shaded **Founders Cemetery** contains the oldest graves in Roswell. Do some rubbings of the aged grave markers.

Classic Couples: Mittie Bulloch and Theodore Roosevelt Sr.

When on a trip to the South in 1850, 19-year-old Theodore Roosevelt called at the Bulloch home in Roswell and met 15-year-old Mittie; it may have been love at first sight for him, but it definitely wasn't for her. She did, however, give him a gold thimble to remember her by. Three years later when they met again at Mittie's sister's home in Philadelphia, it was a different story for Mittie. She was impressed by his strong character, self-assurance, and gentle manner. He melted when she called him "Thee," and, after he traveled to Roswell to ask for her hand, they were engaged. The romantic candlelight wedding was held among the Christmas decorations in the dining room of Bulloch Hall on December 23, 1853. Mittie descended the staircase in a shimmering white silk gown and an illusion veil extending the full length of her train. She carried a white prayer book presented to her by the groom. A lavish wedding supper followed, and then Mittie and Theodore led the dancing. Their second child, Theodore Jr., was born in New York on October 27, 1858. After a twenty-five-year marriage, Theodore Sr. died in 1878. Mittie died in 1884. Neither was to know that their son would become the president of the United States, nor that their granddaughter Eleanor would marry her distant cousin Franklin Delano Roosevelt and become First Lady.

As you return to your car, detour off Sloan Street to see some restored buildings of the former Roswell Mill, now used as professional offices, and the partially restored ruin of an additional mill building. Tiptoe through the kudzu to investigate the abandoned structure. A modern deck added to the ruin overlooks scenic Vickery Creek and provides a private place for some smooching. Even few Roswellians are aware of this picturesque and romantic spot.

Tear yourselves away from your secret tryst and retrieve your car. From the west side of the square, turn right onto Mimosa Boulevard and cruise along slowly to admire the imposing mid-nineteenth-century private homes and buildings, such as **Twin Oaks,** an elegant brick mansion that was one of the original residences in Roswell, and the venerable **Roswell Presbyterian Church,** the oldest church in town, which served as a hospital during the Civil War.

At the end of Mimosa Boulevard, turn right onto Magnolia and immediately left onto Canton Street, which places you in the **Heart of Roswell Historic District.** Continue into the second block and look on the left for the fluttering flags identifying the **Ten-Fifty Canton Street Bed and Breakfast** (1050 Canton Street; 770–998–1050), your weekend hideaway. Built in the late 1800s, this small, simple Greek Revival cottage was owned by a mill supervisor. Owners Susie and Andy Kalifeh created an exquisite three-bedroom B&B where each romantic, high-ceilinged guest room is furnished in turn-of-the-century pieces and features a private bath and a decorative fireplace. An added bonus is that this inn is within easy walking distance of the Heart of Roswell. Check in, get to know your hosts, then leave your car while you tour on foot. Rooms range from $89 to $125 per night.

This section of Roswell embraces an attractive triangular park, and the area is enhanced with brick sidewalks, lush landscaping, and period street lights. Housed in historic commercial buildings are art galleries, antiques shops, gift and clothing boutiques, and restaurants. Stretching north up Canton Street and still within easy walking distance are more antebellum and Victorian homes—some of which serve as businesses, shops, galleries, and restaurants.

Cross South Atlanta Street to the **Archibald Smith Plantation Home** (935 Alpharetta Street; 770–641–3978; admission $5), Tara candidate 3. Amazingly, one family occupied this 1845 house until recently when it was willed to the city with all its contents. Reflecting more than a century and a half of accumulated history, the house features fourteen thousand catalogued items of furniture and memorabilia. Although the plantation's agricultural lands have long since been swallowed up, the family retained the property immediately surrounding the house and preserved the separate kitchen, barn, corn crib, and other buildings, which are worth your time to explore—or step behind for an impetuous kiss. A heavily wooded oasis, the grounds make it hard to remember you're in a busy metropolis.

Some Smith family property was deeded to the city and is occupied by an impressive city hall, the library, and the Roswell Cultural Arts Center—with its small museum and performance hall. Be sure to visit the grounds behind City Hall to see the extremely moving Vietnam Memorial created by two local residents.

If your energy is flagging, enjoy a pick-me-up with afternoon tea at **Mittie's Tea Room** (952 Canton Street; 770–594–8822), then return to your hideaway for some spicy alone time, a nap, or to freshen up for a casual dinner.

DAY ONE: EVENING

Dinner

It's time to let your hair down to explore a more recent past. The funky **Beehive Restaurant** (1090 Alpharetta Highway; 770–594–8765; moderate), named after the bouffant sixties hairdo, takes you back to that era. Located in a lovely Victorian cottage, the staid exterior belies the eclectic, wacky decor inside. Flamboyant painted designs splash across doors, moldings, and light fixtures. Large, gaudy paintings cry out for your attention. Beaded curtains, strings of colored lights, chrome soda fountain stools, Mardi Gras beads, and revolving lamps transport you to the hippie/Motown era. Although the restaurant is crowded and lively, romantics can find a secluded table in a corner of the glass-enclosed front porch or in the tiny nook behind the double-sided fireplace to light their own fires. The diverse menu, which boasts Southwestern and Cajun influences, ranges from sandwiches and salads to appetizers, such as spinach and artichoke queso, to pastas to blue plate specials. Warning: Servings are gargantuan and you must save some room for the banana cream pie.

If after dinner, your lust for discovery isn't sated, find out what cultural events are going on. Orchestra Atlanta performs at the **Roswell Cultural Arts Center** (950 Forrest Street; 770–594–6232), as does the Georgia Ensemble Theater, visiting theater, puppetry, and dance troupes. Two theaters at **Village Playhouses** (617 Holcomb Bridge Road; 770–998–3526) offer comedies, musicals, and dramas. During the summer, concerts are frequently performed on the square.

At the end of a stimulating evening, return to your B&B for more personal exploration in the privacy of your room.

DAY TWO: MORNING

Breakfast

After a good night's sleep, rise and shine. Today you'll switch gears completely to explore Roswell's wonderful abundance of natural attractions. Dress in comfortable outdoor gear for several easy hikes. Although your B&B provides a delicious continental breakfast, you're going to spend a vigorous day outdoors, so stoke up on energy with a hearty Southern breakfast at the **Southern Skillet** (1037 Alpharetta Street; 770–993–7700; inexpensive), a simple down-home eatery. Menu items include biscuits and gravy, eggs, bacon, sausage, grits, and pancakes.

Stop by **Harry's Farmers Market** (1180 Upper Hembree Road; 770–664–6300), an entertainment in itself, to pick up the fixings for a gourmet picnic lunch à deux. You'll find everything from a huge variety of crusty, freshly baked breads, cheeses, fresh fruits and vegetables, and wine to exotic prepared dishes and outlandish desserts. Exercise your imaginations to create your own perfect picnic.

Now it's time to hit the trail. Numerous walking paths wind through the **Roswell Area Park** (10495 Woodstock Road; 770–641–3760) and seven other town parks. The ambitious Roswell Trails System allows you to combine a variety of natural trails, river walks, and historic district strolls that teach about the area's history and flora and fauna. Several city trails link with the more challenging trails of the Vickery Creek Unit of the **Chattahoochee River National Recreation Area** (770–399–8070), one of the best-kept secrets in Atlanta.

DAY TWO: AFTERNOON

Some access points for the national recreation area are hard to find, so use the main entrance and parking lot at the Chattahoochee River (Roswell Road and Riverside Drive). Escape the modern world and hike with your loved one along a dozen secluded trails, which provide moderately demanding hiking through heavily wooded, hilly terrain crisscrossed by gurgling streams. It's hard to believe this wilderness area exists within the city limits. Follow one of two trails leading to the man-made waterfall that powered the mills in the city's textile heyday. Sitting on a stream bank or large overhanging rock while communing with nature just naturally leads to laying your head on a soft shoulder or reveling in a lingering kiss. This might be the perfect opportunity to dig into your picnic lunch. There's nothing saying you have to remain on the marked trails, so take advantage of isolated spots where you and your sweetheart can delight in a private moment.

DAY TWO: EVENING

Dinner

Return to your B&B for rest or play, change into nice casual wear, then splurge on award-winning bold American cuisine at **Van Gogh's Restaurant and Bar** (70 West Crossville Road, Roswell; 770–993–1156; expensive), located just a short distance away. What began as a neighborhood joint evolved into one of Zagat's Top 40 Atlanta restaurants. In addition to imaginative appetizers and soups and salads, the restaurant's extensive menu features chicken, seafood, lamb, beef, veal, duck, and pork entrees. Linen-covered tables for two, chairs covered with tapestry-like fabric, fresh flowers, candlelight, and superb service add to the elegance and formality. Coat and tie aren't expected, however. Ask for an out-of-the-way table in a private nook perfect for lovers. Linger over a luscious dessert or after-dinner drinks in the convivial bar, avail yourselves of Roswell's cultural activities, or return to your room to create your own theatrics.

DAY THREE: MORNING

Brunch

With all the exercise and fresh air you got yesterday, pamper yourselves by sleeping in. We've planned a special midday brunch, but if you wake up early and hungry, eat a light breakfast at the B&B, then bid farewell to your hosts.

Bring your romantic getaway weekend to a perfect finale with a sumptuous champagne brunch at **Lickskillet Farm Restaurant** (1380 Old Roswell Road; 770–475–6484; moderate). Here among several wooded acres along Foe Killer Creek in a tiny pocket of rural landscape on the outskirts of Roswell, you'll find a pleasant 1846 farmhouse restaurant. The vast brunch buffet groans with salads, breads and muffins, breakfast meats, egg dishes, grits, potatoes, vegetables, and pastas. Pork loin, leg of lamb, and made-to-order omelettes satisfy larger appetites. A generous selection of sinful desserts tempt even the strictest dieter. Live piano entertainment and champagne accompany your delightful meal. Wear something nice, but coat and tie aren't required.

Instead of bringing your special weekend to a close, browse through several antiques shops and art galleries for something special to remind you of your idyllic odyssey.

FOR MORE ROMANCE

Time your visit to Roswell to coincide with special events that occur at Bulloch Hall during the year: a quilt show, art shows, Heritage Days complete with Civil War reenactors, and the much anticipated Christmas at Bulloch Hall: the high point of which is a re-creation of Mittie's wedding—a sure-fire way to spark any romantic's imagination. (See the Christmas itinerary, "Yule Time With Y'all.") Learn about the mystery of the disappearing Roswell women in children (in the mystery itinerary, "Partners in Crime").

OUT OF TOWN

ITINERARY 18
Three days and two nights

JOIE DE VIVRE
CHATEAU ELAN

*O*oh-la-la! What does it matter if you can't jet to Paris—the capital of romance—this year? Don't despair. A decadent tryst at a French chateau and winery awaits hedonistic couples right outside of Atlanta. The crown jewel of a three-thousand-acre estate, the sixteenth-century-style chateau at Chateau Elan only hints at the lavish enchantments sweethearts lose themselves in at this four-star resort, the very essence of the French countryside. A long sensual weekend is perfect for you and your *amour* to experience the delights of the winery, restaurants, spa services, accommodations, sports facilities, and maybe even a special event or two—without having to refinance your house to afford it. We've designed a spa weekend with an abundance of pampering to revitalize your bodies, spirits, love life, and anything else that needs rejuvenating. Who knows where your secret whims may lure you? Although the resort boasts a wide range of spa packages, we propose the Spa Getaway ($1,499 for two), which incorporates special accommodations and two days of meals in addition to myriad spa services.

Practical Notes: Chateau Elan (exit 48 on I–85; 770–932–0900 or 800–233–WINE) comprises more than four hundred rooms in a chateaulike lodge, an intimate spa inn, and golf villas; however, for this seductive weekend for two, select the intimate spa building for your accommodations. With only fourteen whimsically themed guest rooms, reservations as far ahead as possible are a must. Schedule spa services ahead of time as well, and arrange tee times and/or court times as soon as you check in. Morning check-in is usually difficult, but, in the meantime, you can begin your spa services or enjoy the resort's many other amenities. The spa furnishes robes and slippers for its guests; you'll see your fellow visitors in this comfortable attire most of the time—even at breakfast and lunch. However, bring at the very least a warm-up suit, workout clothes, bathing suit, athletic shoes, and something nice for dinner.

Romance at a Glance

♥ *Feast on gourmet meals.*

♥ *Luxuriate in spa services.*

♥ *Revel in a themed playroom.*

♥ *Raise a glass at Paddy's Irish Pub.*

DAY ONE: MORNING

Having been fabulously successful in other entrepreneurial ventures here and in Europe, in 1981, Don and Nancy Panoz got the bright idea of establishing a winery and resort in the rolling hills of northeast Georgia. They were convinced that if sweet muscadine grapes flourished here, others varieties would as well. Needless to say, many of their friends and advisors thought they had lost their minds. This was a colossal gamble in an area not typically regarded as good for wine production. However, the dynamic duo forged ahead and planted the vineyards. In 1985, the first wines were introduced and they've garnered awards ever since—250 medals so far from national and international wine events. More than two-hundred acres are cultivated in *Vitis vinifera* varieties and French-American hybrids.

Resembling a fairy-tale castle, the imposing chateau was created in 1988. Believe us, Georgia had never seen anything like this, and the chateau only suggested marvels to come. The first golf course opened in 1989, as did the world-class golf teaching/practice facility.

Almost every year since has brought the addition of another major facility—the free-standing, full-service European-style health spa and uniquely themed guest rooms; more golf courses for a total of sixty-three holes; the charming French country-style inn and conference center, which is still being enlarged; the tennis complex; and the equestrian center. In addition, the resort offers bike and nature trails, paddle boats, and even a ropes course (if you want to get all tied up with each other), so couples can be as active or inactive as their hearts desire.

Get ready for the magic. Once inside the chateau, you're transported to a turn-of-the-century Paris street scene. Brick pavings, iron fences, and vintage street lights create the illusion of nighttime in the out of doors. Large colorful murals intensify the effect.

Behind this fantasy world is a thoroughly modern wine-making operation. Don't miss the video and tour that chronicle the entire process, including pressing, fermenting, and bottling. Of course, the tour ends with sipping several of Chateau Elan's fine wines. Although the chateau produces some dry wines, the majority are sweet. According to the Nielsen Ratings System, Chateau Elan Summer Wine, which has a light bouquet with a slight hint of peach, is one of the best-selling wines in the Atlanta area. With more than thirty medals, Summer Wine leads all Georgia-produced wines. Purchase a sweet or dry Chateau Elan wine to savor in your room as well as some to take home for special occasions.

In addition to wines and an amazing array of wine-related items, browse through the Wine Market for resort clothing, gourmet foods, wine and cookbooks, and more. Exercise your creativity by designing your own personal label for a case of Chateau Elan to take home. These personalized bottles make wonderful mementos and gifts.

Browse through an art gallery that showcases the work of local and regional artists. Who knows? You might discover the works of an up-and-coming artist to collect. A piece of art would be a perfect permanent keepsake of your blissful holiday.

DAY ONE: AFTERNOON

Lunch

Part of the pseudo-outdoor street scene inside the chateau is Cafe Elan, which offers (indoor) patiolike seating overlooking the marketplace. Pretend you're eating a languorous lunch at a little outdoor bistro somewhere in Paris. For a light lunch, choose from salads, soups, burgers, sandwiches, and a few more substantial entrees—accompanied by crusty French bread and one of the Chateau's vintages. Dally over your meal—the vantage point is great for people watching. After lunch, work off those calories with a stroll through the long rows of grapevines, bike through the resort's nature trails, or begin indulging in the spa services.

Check into your fantasy room and get your weekend fling underway. The spa's unique guest rooms are whimsically decorated with a flair for the differences in personal tastes and moods. Fanciful themes and features enhance your experience and appeal to your imagination. For example, the highlight of the exotic Oriental Room, a Far Eastern paradise, is an oriental-style deep soak tub with Jacuzzi. A framed antique kimono and bonsai trees enhance the Oriental theme. At the other end of the spectrum, the Western Room features a cannonball bed, wooden floors, and burlap curtains. Space-age features define the sophisticated Hi-Tech Room, which boasts black lacquer furniture; chrome, green, and black marble; and a full-body massage recliner. The Birthday Room sports a bright red birthday clawfoot bathtub. Other themes include Vintage, Greek, Gatsby, Georgia, Lodge Loft, Art Deco, Victorian Wicker, Fox Hunt, Bacchus, and Country—each adorned to symbolize its name, several of which boast Jacuzzis. We got a kick out of the sleek Hi-Tech Room, but most folks pronounce the Greek and Gatsby Rooms the most obviously romantic. The farther ahead you make your reservation, the more likely you can choose the room that best matches your individual tastes and dreams.

The spa offers all the latest spa equipment and services. For example, it is one of the only spas in the country that offers the Louison BOBET treatment—a form of thalassotherapy hydrotherapy from France, which involves being wrapped in seaweed to improve hair and complexion, invigorate tired legs, and combat overall lack of energy. Several services are geared specifically to men, so the male half of your partnership doesn't need to feel that he'll be left out, or that he'll feel silly. Be on time for your spa appointments—late arrivals don't get an extension of time.

Seven overnight spa packages of various lengths range from $259 to $3,879 and consist of accommodations, specific spa services, and meals. Health-conscious cuisine is served in the spa's own restaurant, Fleur-de-Lis, but other options in your package allow you to choose from the Versailles Room in the inn or Cafe Elan in the chateau.

If the complete spa package prices are a little steep for your twosome, select services à la carte. The package we suggest includes use of all the facilities, facial, pedicure, Swedish massage, thalassotherapy or aromatherapy, underwater massage, salt glow with Vichy shower, make-up application for women, and scalp treatment for men.

You and your honey will be separated from time to time for spa services, so rendezvous in between will be all the sweeter. Meet at the pool and whirlpool, or have an assignation in one of the lounges or the quiet resting room, which is outfitted with divine wicker lounges topped with fluffy cushions. Dim lights and soft music intensify the restful, loving mood.

DAY ONE: EVENING

Dinner

After an afternoon of relaxation and pampering in the spa, dress up (coat and tie for the gentleman) for gourmet dining at Le Clos in the chateau. Although dinner at this exquisite restaurant isn't included in the spa packages, this weekend is so special, you won't mind splurging for this *prix-fixe* dinner (expensive). Believing in the marriage of food and wine, the elegant restaurant serves a magnificent, seven- or eight-course meal expertly coupled with the Chateau's finest wines. The formal, sumptuous French ambience is created with wall coverings and window hangings, crisp white linens, fine china, and crystal. Toast your love for each other over flowers and candlelight.

You may be so relaxed and/or stuffed after dinner that all you want to do is fall into bed to sleep or express your passions for each other. If, however, you're not ready to turn in just yet, switch countries for awhile and experience a touch of the Old Sod at Chateau Elan's newest addition—Paddy's Irish Pub. To ensure an authentic touch of the Emerald Isle, all the pub's furnishings were commissioned specifically for Chateau Elan and imported directly from Ireland. The friendly interior features a rough-hewn, timbered ceiling, barrel tables, slate floors, and a stacked-stone fireplace that burns cheerily whenever there's a chill in the air. In addition to typical Irish fare, the pub serves several Irish ales including Guinness, Murphy's, and Harp. Hear the lilting sounds of local musicians at Paddy's on Friday and Saturday nights.

DAY TWO: Morning

Breakfast

Enjoy a healthful breakfast in the Fleur-de-Lis restaurant. Depending on the spa services included in your package, your morning may be completely mapped out for you. If it isn't, there are other spa activities in which you can participate: an early fitness walk, various types of aerobics, yoga, or relaxation techniques. These activities are offered daily and are complimentary for spa guests. It's your special weekend—do as much or as little as you like or design your own therapy.

Classic Couples: Don and Nancy Panoz

"When Don Met Nancy" isn't the title of a movie, but rather it's a description of the life and accomplishments of two visionary entrepreneurs. When Nancy Hefner was a school girl in West Virginia, she caught the eye of Donald Panoz, a cadet at the Greenbrier Military Academy, and it wasn't long before they married and began a lifelong adventure. Don served his military obligation in Japan, and Nancy worked as a counterintelligence secretary when the couple had the first of their five children. When they returned to this country, they started their business life, opening two drugstores in Pittsburgh. With restless spirits and a penchant for dreaming big dreams, they quickly moved on to found Mylan Pharmaceuticals, now Mylan Laboratories, then moved to Ireland. Here, Don formed Elan Corporation, a pharmaceutical company specializing in drug delivery systems, such as the nicotine patch, while Nancy formed and operated a line of health and beauty aid stores before returning to the United States to form Chateau Elan and Elan Natural Waters. Their next vision is Diablo Grande, a winery, resort, and residential community near San Francisco. Now sharing residences, including a castle in Ireland, a home in Bermuda, and their abode at Chateau Elan, the Panozes believe that their ultimate reward has been their five children and ten grandchildren. They say if Hollywood ever decided to make a movie about them, they'd call it "Two Parents Who Did Okay."

DAY TWO: AFTERNOON

Lunch

Have lunch at one of the restaurants included in your package. Eating at the quiet, intimate Fleur-de-Lis is easiest because you don't have to change out of your robe and slippers. The meals are so delicious and attractively presented, it's hard to believe they're low calorie and low fat.

Your afternoon will probably be filled with more spa services and/or spa activities. For an extra indulgence (additional expense), revel in a massage for two. What could be more luxurious than the total relaxation of a deep rubdown followed by the chance to snuggle with your loved one? Afterward enjoy afternoon tea as a refresher and pick-me-up. Or opt for some golf or tennis. In addition to the marketplace in the chateau, the resort boasts shops in the spa and at the tennis center, inn, and two of the golf courses, so maybe a little shopping will please you.

DAY TWO: EVENING

Choose from Cafe Elan, the Versailles Room, or the Fleur-de-Lis for your evening meal. Drop into Paddy's again for a nightcap. On weekend Saturdays during the summer, Chateau Elan features musical concerts for your listening and/or dancing pleasure. Dancing cheek to cheek is particularly pleasurable after your cheeks have been smoothed with a facial.

DAY THREE: MORNING

Breakfast

Start your day off with a light breakfast at Fleur-de-Lis. You have many options for morning activities: spa services and/or activities: golf, tennis, hiking, biking, or participating in a special event. Chateau Elan hosts numerous activities throughout the year so you may want to coordinate your visit with one of them. February features the romantic Valentine's Day dinner, May the British Motorcar Day, Memorial Day to Labor Day the Swinging on the Grapevine Summer Music Festival, November through December the lighting of the chateau and Holiday Celebration, and the New Year's Eve Black-Tie Gala. Also check for Meet the Winemaker and cooking demonstration events. In addition, the resort hosts the Sarazan World Open Golf Tournament and the American Horse Show Association hunter, jumper, and dressage shows. Some kind of equestrian event occurs almost every weekend. Each July the resort hosts the Volvo Grand Prix Jumping event.

After an idyllic weekend of being overindulged, you're guaranteed to go home feeling years younger and maybe friskier.

FOR MORE ROMANCE

If you share a passion for golf or tennis, design a sports weekend. There are three public golf courses at the resort and the private Legends course where the Sarazan World Open Golf Tournament is played. Overnight guests at the spa or the inn can play on the Legends course within certain time restrictions. In addition, the resort offers a "Wee Links," three-hole short course that tests your putting, chipping, pitching, and bunker skills. Alternately, choose a do-nothing getaway in one of the golf villas at the sprawling inn. Both elegant and casual dining options are available and a free continental breakfast is included at the inn. In addition, the inn features an outdoor Olympic-size swimming pool, as well as an indoor, heated resistance pool, a whirlpool, and a fully equipped workout room.

ROCK SOLID LOVE AFFAIR
GEORGIA'S STONE MOUNTAIN PARK

If you and your loved one are looking for a rock-solid foundation for your relationship, a romantic weekend at Georgia's Stone Mountain Park is a good start. Stone Mountain is literally that—not just any old hill, but one of the planet's most amazing works of nature: the world's largest exposed granite monolith. This masterpiece of nature has attracted visitors since the dawn of time, and if the monolith could talk, it would have a mountain of historic tales to tell. In the early 1900s, the United Daughters of the Confederacy envisioned it as a Confederate memorial, but it took until 1972 to complete the world's largest bas-relief sculpture—a depiction of the mounted figures of Confederate President Jefferson Davis and Generals Robert E. Lee and Stonewall Jackson. In 1958, the Georgia General Assembly bought the mountain and surrounding land and set aside a state park to be used as a recreation and preservation area. A mammoth block of granite isn't the only thing you two rockhounds will discover this weekend. Today the 3,200-acre park is a wonderland of scenic beauty occupied by lakes, meadows, and woodlands, which provide home to a variety of animals and endangered species. Man has added not only the carving, but numerous outdoor recreational and other activities for lovers whose relationship is solid as a rock to discover. Although the park is only minutes from downtown Atlanta, once you've entered its gates, you're far from the distractions of hurried city life and free to be as playful as you like. During this outing at Georgia's most visited attraction, you'll stay in the lap of luxury at the Evergreen Resort, dine at several of the park's casual and elegant eateries, and participate in as many of the park's activities as you can fit into your schedule and still leave plenty of time for romance.

Romance at a Glance

♥ *Lift your love to new heights aboard the Mountain Skylift to the summit of Stone Mountain.*

♥ *Snuggle up on the lawn to watch the Lasershow light up the mountain.*

♥ *Rock around Stone Mountain aboard the Stone Mountain Scenic Railroad.*

♥ *Rocket down the waterslide at Stone Mountain Lake.*

Practical Notes: Although you will remain within the park for your entire getaway, unless you're in fabulous physical condition, you'll need some form of transportation to get to some areas of the park. You'll have your car, but you can bring or rent bicycles to cover long distances or tote along in-line skates for shorter distances. For day visitors who are not staying at one of the inns or at the campground, park hours are 6:00 A.M. until midnight daily. The attractions themselves are open from 10:00 A.M. until 8:00 P.M. in the summer and until 5:00 P.M. the remainder of the year. Remember that the Lasershow is only performed from spring through fall. To view it in comfort bring a blanket and/or beach chairs and insect repellent—all of which will enhance the experience and protect your bodies for other late night pursuits. It is easy to get around in the park; there are signs everywhere directing you to the attractions. The two most important roads are Robert E. Lee Boulevard around the mountain and Stonewall Jackson Drive around the lake.

DAY ONE: Afternoon

To get to the park take U.S. 78/Stone Mountain Freeway east and follow the signs to **Georgia's Stone Mountain Park** (U.S. 78; 770–498–5600 or 770–879–4971; $6). Follow the signs to your lodging—the **Evergreen Resort and Conference Center** (One Lakeside Drive; 770–469–2250 or 800–722–1000; $149–$325), where the Resort to Romance package is sure to win your heart. It includes one night's accommodations, breakfast, champagne, and a special gift on arrival for $129 in a guest room or $159 in a suite. Maybe for this special occasion, you'd prefer to spend a lot of time in your room. In that case, we'd recommend the luxuries of the Mistletoe Honeymoon Suite ($169): a romantic four-poster bed, a cozy garden tub, a snug sitting area, coffeemaker, and small refrigerator. We'll assume, however, that you want to explore the park and take advantage of its activities. For example, if you and your sweetheart have been bitten by the golf bug in addition to the love bug, the Great Golf Escape package includes a round of golf. No matter what package you pick, you weekend mountaineers will enjoy Evergreen's spacious, beautifully furnished rooms with gorgeous views from the balconies, several restaurants and lounges, a double-sided fireplace in the lobby, indoor and outdoor pools and whirlpools, two lighted tennis courts, jogging trails, and an on-site health club. All in all, this is a perfect spot for a romantic getaway.

Once you've settled in, there are several ways to get an overview of the huge park and its many attractions, and we recommend that you do all of them. Head for **Memorial Hall** so that you can begin your odyssey at the **Discovering Stone Mountain Museum** by learning all about the park's history. Exhibits, hands-on models, and full-scale photo murals in the Viewing Gallery orient you lovebirds to the size and scale of the carving, and a video, *How the Carving Came to Be,* traces the entire history of the carving. The Upstairs Gallery features artifacts from an 1860s farm and the Civil War era; other exhibits highlight the unique wildlife inhabitants and natural attractions of Stone Mountain.

You don't have to be experienced rock climbers to take your love to a new level at the top of the mountain. Simply board one of the eighty-passenger Swiss cable cars on the **Mountain Skylift** ($4), located just left of Memorial Hall, for a spectacular ride to the summit, where you'll be rewarded with a stunning panorama of the park, the metro area, and even the far off

Appalachian Mountains. As an added bonus, during the cable car ride, you'll get an up-close-and-personal view of the carving as you pass it on the way up and down the mountain. For those who've visited the park in the past, you'll appreciate the fact that the facilities on top of the mountain have been downsized, and the mountaintop returned to a more natural environment. Stay at the summit as long as you like, take photographs, sketch or paint the scenery if you've brought your art supplies, or simply sit in companionable silence, contemplating the wonders of the mountain and your love. If you're going to stay long, snacks and cold drinks are available, and there are rest rooms.

Once you've decided to come down out of the clouds, you can return to the base of the mountain either by taking the cable car or hiking the path that leads down the southwestern slope, stopping now and then for a hug and a kiss. If you came back via the cable car, walk over to the Memorial Railroad Depot to board the **Stone Mountain Scenic Railroad** ($4.25) for a completely different view of the mountain. If you hiked back, board the train at the **Whistlestop Depot.** Pulled by the *General II,* a replica of the steam-powered *General*, a famous train in Georgia's Civil War history, the nostalgic train ride chugs 5 miles around the base of the mountain, passing a replica of a pioneer town along the way.

Next retrieve your car and drive down to the river boat landing to board a replica paddle wheeler called *Scarlett O'Hara* ($4.25). Relax by the rails or on the top deck as the riverboat plies the waters of 363-acre **Stone Mountain Lake** and provides views of the natural areas of the park, beach and water park, golf course and clubhouse, campground, and grist mill. You'll also get a spectacular view of your hotel and go by the 732-bell **Carillon,** which was donated to the park after being exhibited at the 1964 World's Fair. Stone Mountain Lake is an excellent place to be to get the full effect of the daily concerts that ring out from the bell tower.

Return to the hotel to enjoy some of its amenities or put your love affair on more solid footing by spending some alone time in your room or on your balcony overlooking the lake. Then prepare for dinner and some spectacular entertainment.

DAY ONE: EVENING

Dinner

We've planned a casual outdoor activity for this evening, so dine casually as well. Head back to Robert E. Lee Boulevard where all the action is. We suggest the Southern fried chicken and all the fixins, such as cole slaw and hot biscuits, served at the **Depot Chicken Restaurant** (inexpensive), located in the authentically designed Memorial Railroad Depot near the place where the nightly entertainment occurs. On the other hand, you might be more tempted by the slow-cooked, hickory-smoked beef, pork, and chicken barbecue or ribs slathered in tasty sauce, or Brunswick stew and corn on the cob at the **Whistlestop BBQ Restaurant** (inexpensive) in the Confederate Hall building. Alternately, get takeout vittles from one of these restaurants and settle down on the great lawn for a picnic that will culminate in the night's sensational entertainment.

Nightlife

Whatever your dinner choice, your ultimate destination for the evening is the huge expanse of velvet green lawn in front of Memorial Hall that faces the carving. The lawn will get very crowded by the time it gets dark, so the sooner you've staked a claim to an area, the better. If you want some privacy, pick a spot off to the side, away from the parking lot. Be sure to bring a blanket to snuggle up on. Beach chairs are very comfortable, too. And now for the mesmerizing entertainment. The mountain's north face creates a natural, 1-million-square-foot screen on which the mountain comes to life nightly during the May through September **Lasershow** (free). Colorful laser beams project gigantic dancing images of dramatic stories, historic tales, comical characters, and graphic images onto the screen—all choreographed to musical accompaniment. From jazz to southern rock, country to gospel, rockabilly to rhythm and blues, each year the Lasershow combines old favorites with exciting new selections to create a show that's sure to please everyone.

Stone Mountain   Fun Facts

- *The mountain stands 825-feet tall.*
- *It covers 583 acres above ground.*
- *The mountain's base below ground underlies half of Georgia and part of North Carolina.*
- *Artifacts indicate that humans have lived around the giant outcropping for five thousand years.*
- *Andrew Jackson bought the mountain in the 1830s for the cost of a shotgun and twenty dollars.*
- *Granite was quarried from the mountain beginning in 1845 and used in such projects as the locks of the Panama Canal, the U.S. Capitol building, and the Imperial Hotel in Tokyo.*
- *It took two designs, three master sculptors, and countless workers to create the carving.*
- *The carving covers three acres.*
- *It is recessed forty-two feet into the mountain.*
- *The deepest point is Lee's elbow, which is twelve feet to the surface.*
- *Workers could stand on a horse's ear or inside its mouth to escape a sudden shower.*
- *In the early fall, rare plants such as the cheery yellow Confederate Daisy grow in the mountain's crevices and in wooded areas of the park.*
- *The first use of the mountain as a tourist attraction was in 1838 when Aaron Cloud built a dance hall and a 165-foot tower on the summit (it later blew over in a storm).*

Whether you're a Billy Yank or Johnny Reb, you'll get a lump in your throat and a tear in your eye during the emotional finale when the three mounted horsemen come alive and gallop off to wage the Civil War, which rages on the mountainside until the country is reunited and the horsemen return to their repose. Following the Lasershow, brilliant fireworks burst into the inky night sky above the mountain.

Once the thunderous applause dies down, it's time for you and your favorite mountaineer to return to the hotel to create your own fireworks.

DAY TWO: MORNING

Breakfast

You're sure to have slept well and awakened refreshed and eager for another day at the park after all the fresh air you got yesterday. If you chose the Resort to Romance package, your romantic weekend includes a room service breakfast or the ample brunch buffet in the elegant **Waterside Restaurant**—one of DeKalb County's only white-linen restaurants—overlooking the lake. It's a hard choice and may depend on what other in-room recreational plans you have in mind.

Now it's time to begin today's explorations in the **War in Georgia Museum** ($4.25), located in **Confederate Hall** at the base of the mountain's walk-up trail, to examine the huge three-dimensional map enhanced by lights and sound effects, depicting Sherman's entire Georgia campaign, including the Battle for Atlanta and the March to the Sea. Other exhibits show Civil War uniforms and artifacts.

Next visit an authentic **Antebellum Plantation** ($4.25), a twenty-building complex of fully restored and appropriately furnished structures from eighteenth- and nineteenth-century Georgia, which was created by moving historic buildings from all over the state to the park. Most of the tour is self-guided, but costumed docents give spirited tours of the main plantation house. Be on your toes, this plantation has three ghosts.

DAY TWO: AFTERNOON

Lunch

Just as you've built a strong relationship on a solid foundation, build your own lunch at the **Gondola Grill** (inexpensive) at the base of the mountain. Begin with a burger or chicken breast, then pile on lettuce, tomatoes, onions, and all other manner of accompaniments and condiments to create a substantial sandwich. Add cheese fries, a salad, and a shake and you've got a mountain of a meal.

For a touch of whimsey, this afternoon visit the **Antique Car and Treasure Museum** ($4.25) on Robert E. Lee Boulevard. This nostalgic exhibit of vehicles and collectibles from around America and the world will fascinate both of you. You'll marvel at the forty cars—some of them one of a kind, such as the Buck Rogers' Rocket Car or the Tucker, which was briefly built in Georgia. Other modes of transportation include sixty vintage bikes and fifteen pedal cars. Musically, the museum contains five band organs, twenty-two player pianos, and thirty jukeboxes. There are also period clothing, carousel animals, and thousands of other twentieth-century artifacts bidding for your attention. If you have any time left, visit the wild native species of Georgia and tame farm animals in a natural setting at the **Wildlife Preserve and Petting Farm** ($4.25). Take advantage of the secluded trails in the preserve to pledge your love for each other.

Bid a fond farewell to the park and on the way home stop in **Stone Mountain Village** where more than seventy shops housed in the quaint nineteenth-century village buildings sell appealing wares of all kinds. Stone Mountain leather handbags are a prize every woman would love to own.

FOR MORE ROMANCE

Throw caution (and your wallet) to the winds and stay another night or two to sample more of Stone Mountain Park's other attractions. Always a recreational haven, more and more facilities inspired by the increased interest in physical fitness have been added over the years. So it was no surprise that the Atlanta Committee for the Olympic Games chose the park for three events in the 1996 Centennial Olympic Summer Games: archery, tennis, and track cycling. Pretend you're an Olympic athlete and put your skills to the test at the **International Tennis Center,** a legacy of games. At this superb facility, fifteen of the sixteen Plexi-Cushion courts are available for public play (the stadium court is reserved for tournament competitions and concerts). Racket rentals are $2, and you can take lessons from the head pro, Jay Torrence, for $40 per hour.

But for those of us who aren't world-class athletes but would still like to get some exercise while enjoying the out-of-doors, nature trails for hikers and nature lovers vary from short strolls on flat ground to the challenging, straight-up trail to the mountain's summit. For serious hikers, there's the 7-mile **Cherokee Trail** around the base of the mountain. If you want to cool off in Stone Mountain Lake, there are a variety of ways to do so. Seasonal water activities include a wide beach leading to gently deepening waters and a water slide ($5). The **Rental Boat Complex** offers rowboats, canoes, hydrobikes, pedalboats, and pontoon boats. For a variety of other sports, the park's **Sports Complex** offers eight more lighted tennis courts, softball and baseball batting cages, bicycle rentals, and an eighteen-hole minigolf course. Golfers can sharpen their skills playing up to thirty-six holes of golf on two courses—the Lakemont and Stonemont links. The Lakemont course has been named one of the top twenty-five public courses in America by *Golf Digest*. Play eighteen holes on weekends for $48; on weekdays play eighteen holes for $40, nine holes for $32, or, after 4:00 P.M., as many holes as you can fit in before dark for $32. The golf complex also includes a driving range, putting green, full-service clubhouse, pro shop, and locker rooms.

With careful advance planning you can time your visit to coincide with one of the park's many special events. Among them are the Stone Mountain Scottish Festival, Tattoo, and Highland Games; the twenty-nine-year-old Yellow Daisy Festival; BBQ Pork Cookoff and Springfest; Chili Cookoff; Taste of the South; outdoor concerts; 5K and 10K runs; a Tour of Southern Ghosts at Halloween (described in "Skull-Duggery"); and a month-long December holiday celebration (see "Yule Time with Y'All"). Call the park for a complete schedule of events.

ITINERARY 20
Four days and three nights

FLOAT YOUR BOAT
LAKE LANIER HOUSEBOAT HOLIDAY

*S*earching for a way to spend some quality time absolutely alone together? Yearning to get away from it all? Not even an anonymous, off-the-beaten-track hotel will do, because there will be too many people around? Camping in the wilds is not your idea of a good time? An intimate houseboat holiday on Lake Lanier with your first mate fills the bill for a completely private getaway for two. Rent a luxurious floating palace and set sail for a very private amorous outing. Relax amidst the unparalleled beauty of the great outdoors, while you enjoy all the comforts of home. Spend time lost in each other's charms. Cruise from sunup to sundown or beach your drifting hotel occasionally on an uninhabited island. Curl up with a good book or soak up some sun in total privacy. Cottage watch, indulge in a little nighttime skinny dipping, or watch the moon rise. Most of all, be wrapped up in each other. Complete rest and relaxation from the rigors of modern life will create memories you'll treasure for years. Those who need a little more to do can go ashore occasionally for meals or activities.

Practical Notes: Make reservations for your sailing villa well in advance—especially in the summer. Contact **Forever Resorts** (800–255–5561), which coordinates houseboat rentals on Lake Lanier. Rentals are for three, four, or seven nights. Here, we describe a romantic three-night getaway, which can begin either Thursday or Friday afternoon. If you're simply interested in being alone together and losing yourselves in the tranquility of nature rather than participating in traditional water sports, the winter months are even more idyllic because there is little traffic on the lake, and the rental price is reduced. These magnificent houseboats feature heat and air conditioning so you can enjoy a cruise in any season.

Romance at a Glance

♥ *Set sail for nowhere.*

♥ *Eat hearty.*

♥ *Espy Elvis.*

♥ *Spend an afternoon ashore at Lake Lanier Islands.*

♥ *Play ball (golf or tennis).*

♥ *Saddle up.*

♥ *Play Robinson Crusoe on uninhabited islands.*

♥ *Fly the Jolly Roger.*

DAY ONE: AFTERNOON

Lake Lanier, affectionately known as "Atlanta's Playground," provides endless recreational opportunities. Located just an hour north of the city and nestled in the foothills of the Blue Ridge Mountains, Lake Lanier is 63 miles long and boasts 540 miles of shoreline. Although well-developed, the lake offers many large expanses of undeveloped tree-lined banks as well as one hundred small, uninhabited islands for lovers to discover. Deep waters provide the best in water recreation. The largemouth bass fishing is so good, Lake Lanier is featured on the Bass Master Tournament circuit. Sunny and warm (sometimes hot) summers and mild springs and falls provide nine months of comfortable nonstop outdoor recreation.

Check in at **Lake Lanier Houseboat Rentals at Holiday Marina** (Dock Z, Holiday Road, Buford). The staff can teach you enough seamanship before you set sail on your own to turn even the most dedicated landlubber into an old salt. Although no special boat license is required to operate the houseboat, fishing does require a license. The knowledgeable staff will clue you in about where the area's attractions, restaurants, and gas stations are located and provide some hot tips about where the fish are biting.

You'll be proud to captain and crew your sleek Forever 10 houseboat, but take it easy until you get your sea legs under you. In the spirit of harmony, you two sailors can switch off who's captain and who's mate.

Each vessel boasts one and one-half baths—one with a shower—and a complete kitchen. In addition to the inside helm, the spacious, attractive living/dining area contains comfortable seating, dinette, stereo cassette player, TV/VCR, and grand panoramic views. The palatial craft is stocked with all the gear you'll need from linens to appliances and cookware and utensils. More pleasurable options await outdoors. Discover the play area on the aft deck, which boasts a swimming platform, the full-length, upper-level sundeck with a captain's flying bridge and water slide. The fore deck features a barbecue grill.

Because your floating Shangri-La contains nearly everything you need for your amorous cruise to nowhere, all you need to bring are rations, liquid libations, sunglasses, deck shoes, a camera and film, beach towels, your swim suits (optional), suntan lotion, good books, CDs and videos, fishing gear, a rubber duckie, and any other adult play toys that will make your long weekend à deux truly memorable. For a more carefree weekend—at an additional fee—you can arrange for the boat to be stocked with groceries, wine, flowers, or anything else that sparks a romantic note. You can also rent one or two tag-a-longs—90-horsepower Polaris personal watercraft—to pull behind your houseboat for use whenever the mood strikes you.

Rates range from $895 to $2,195, depending on the season. A hefty deposit and cancellation penalty make this a vacation option for those who are very sure they're going to make it. We recommend that you purchase travel insurance in case you have to cancel at the last minute because of an emergency.

Classic Couples: Elvis Presley and Patsy Cline

Perhaps the decor at the Red Lantern Inn will tip you off to the evening's entertainment. The restaurant is caught in a perpetual time warp, firmly anchored in the late 1950s or early 1960s, and the show is dedicated to "The King" himself. At 10:00 P.M. the kitchen at the Red Lantern Inn shuts down and your chef reveals his true identity—Elvis is alive and well and can be seen here every weekend. This look-alike does a creditable job gyrating and singing the familiar tunes and actually convinces you that he is the King. He's even performed in Atlanta and Las Vegas. Not to be outshone, "Elvis's" daughter does a realistic impersonation of Patsy Cline, belting out some of her signature tunes. So come prepared for a great evening of food, music, dancing, and one of the best shows around Atlanta.

Use the remainder of the afternoon to check out all the amenities of your pleasure palace and stow your supplies and playthings. In the summer, you'll have several more hours of daylight for water sports or simple relaxation out of doors or below deck.

DAY ONE: EVENING

Dinner

Enjoy a leisurely cocktail, then grill some steaks on board and accompany them with a salad, some nice crusty French or Italian bread, and a good wine. Serve your intimate meal outdoors or indoors by candlelight. Add a sinful dessert and you'll have all the ingredients for a spicy evening. If, however, your notion of a romantic vacation doesn't include a tour of duty in the galley, several good restaurants are within a short sail of the marina. You can dock at some of them or beach your boat on shore at others and walk a short distance to the restaurant.

For example, you can pilot your craft over to Big Creek and beach it while you savor a quiet dinner at **Crocker's Place** (3050 Big Creek Road; 770–932–0201). A great favorite of locals, the casual restaurant is sometimes called the best-kept secret on the lake. Not surprisingly, the menu features many varieties of seafood, but the restaurant is best known for its baby back ribs smothered in a rich barbecue sauce and grilled to perfection. You can order a full or half rack as an appetizer or gorge on the Slap Yo Mama dinner, which includes a vegetable, potato, and salad. In addition to seafood and ribs, other menu choices include numerous cuts of steaks, a variety of chicken dishes, and salad entrees. An average dinner for two including drinks runs about $60.

After a relaxing dinner, cruise back out onto the lake, pick a spot, and drop anchor for the night. Take a nightcap out onto one of the decks and cuddle up for some star gazing. Most of the motorized sounds will have abated for the night, and you can relax to rhythmic sounds of splashing and lapping waves against the hull. If the night is hot, you have the whole lake to cool off in.

DAY TWO: MORNING

Breakfast

For this hedonistic holiday, let yourselves be gently rocked to sleep in each other's arms, then sleep late. Having supplies onboard for a simple breakfast is ideal. You don't even have to get dressed while you enjoy your morning repast, or you may want to live in your swimsuits all day long. Take advantage of the cool of morning by carrying your breakfast to the flying bridge and lingering over it. For a special treat, what could be more sybaritic than accompanying breakfast with mimosas or Bloody Marys with which to toast your love for each other?

Unwind from your hectic everyday life by spending endless hours outdoors together with a good book, a fishing pole, or binoculars. Remain anchored or sail off for a desultory exploration of the lake. Just remember to use plenty of sun screen—a bad sunburn could put a real crimp in an otherwise idyllic amorous weekend. Who knows though, applying sunscreen to each other's hard-to-reach places might lead to full-body massages, and you might never get back outdoors.

DAY TWO: AFTERNOON

Lunch

When your stomachs tell you it's time for some grub, land ho! Pull up on a stretch of mainland wilderness or in a secluded cove of a deserted island for a relaxing picnic lunch, then wander around your private world to catch a glimpse of its feathered or four-legged inhabitants. Many species of migratory birds often touch down on the islands; an isolated expanse may yield sightings of squirrels, rabbits, deer, fowl, turtles, and other fauna.

For the more adventurous or those simply unable to do nothing, this afternoon offers numerous opportunities for swimming, diving, or fishing. There's a huge lake out there just waiting for the two of you. Your activities are limited only by your imaginations. The heat of the day is a perfect time for indoor recreation.

DAY TWO: EVENING

Dinner

Freshen up and cruise to the Brown's Bridge area. Go under the bridge and around the peninsula to dock your boat at the **Red Lantern Inn**'s dock (Brown's Bridge Road; 770–887–3080). If the dock is full, simply beach your boat. Then walk across the street for a fun-filled evening at the restaurant, a thirty-three-year-old Lake Lanier tradition, whose every employee is a family member. On the weekends, the Red Lantern offers an enormous, 32-

foot buffet that groans with catfish, flounder, boiled or fried shrimp, crab, ribs, baked chicken, fried chicken, sliced pork, and more, more, more—plus a salad bar, a selection of vegetables, and the cobbler of the day. Dinner is served from 5:00 to 10:00 P.M. and is all-you-can-eat for a fixed price (the astoundingly low price of $17 per couple at press time; beer is $2.50 per mug). Don't be too late getting there because the live band starts playing at 8:30 P.M., and although the restaurant can seat three hundred people, it can still get crowded. There's a special show ahead at 10:00 P.M.

When the show is over, be careful getting under way in the crowd of other boats. Once you're anchored, tempt fate by putting *Titanic* or *The Poseidon Adventure* on the VCR. The suspense is guaranteed to make you cling to each other.

DAY THREE: MORNING

Breakfast

Savor another restful breakfast on board, either indoors or out, before continuing your exploration of the lake. If you're looking for activities, Lake Lanier Islands is the hub of the lake. **Lake Lanier Islands Beach and Water Park** (770–932–7200) offers a beach, several gargantuan water slides, wave pool, other water activities, paddle boats, sailboats, canoes, ten sensational thrill rides, minigolf, and more. Admission to the park is $18.95 each. In response to the newest fitness craze, the park even features a rock climbing wall. (The park is open daily from Memorial Day to Labor Day and weekends in May and September.) Think how heavenly it would be to watch and listen to summer concerts and fireworks displays from the comfortable privacy of your boat anchored offshore.

Both the **PineIsle Resort** (770–945–8921) and the **Lake Lanier Islands Hilton Resort** (770–945–8787 or 800–768–LAKE) occupy part of Lake Lanier Islands, so you can conveniently enjoy their restaurants and other amenities as well. You can tie up at either of the hotel docks, however, only if you are eating a meal there. To visit the water park or engage in one of the other sports options, you can beach your boat between the two hotels and saunter the short distance to one of the venues.

The **Emerald Pointe Golf Club,** adjacent to the Hilton, features a par-72 championship course. Thirteen of its holes have lake views. For tee times, call 770–945–8789. The **PineIsle Golf Course,** with eight holes on the lake, is noted for its spectacular scenery and challenging holes. For tee times, call 770–945–8921. An eighteen-hole round of golf with carts costs $143, and it's best to have reserved your tee times well in advance. Golf is not your thing? Imagine you and your sweetheart horseback riding over miles of scenic trails along the lakeshore. Horseback riding costs $25 per person. Contact the **Lake Lanier Islands Stables** (770–932–7233). Bikes are available for rent there as well for $10 a day. Golf, tennis, horseback riding, and biking are available year round.

Several festivals and other special events spice up Lake Lanier Islands even more during the year. Perhaps your visit will coincide with one of them: Haunted Islands runs through October; the Magical Nights of Lights Holiday Spectacular—an animated lights extravaganza from Thanksgiving through the New Year.

DAY THREE: Afternoon

Lunch

If you're partaking in some of the activities at Lake Lanier Islands, snack at one of the golf courses, or, if you're beaching it, you can choose **Papa Coots Beachside Cafe, Munchies Beach Cafe,** or the **Island Grill.** For a more formal meal, you can dine at one of the hotels. Otherwise eat on board or find another one of the many secluded islands for a picnic.

Share more activities at Lake Lanier Islands or vegetate on your houseboat recharging your emotional batteries. Let your imaginations and fantasies loose.

DAY THREE: EVENING

Dinner

A captain's tradition on board cruise ships is to have a formal meal, but because you won't have a full crew of kitchen help on board to prepare it for you, for the last evening of your romantic getaway dine at **Breezes** at the PineIsle Resort (770–945–8921). Tie up at PineIsle Resort's dock and let the dock attendant know that you're going to Breezes for dinner. The understated but elegant lounge and dining room overlook sweeping vistas of the lake. Dress is likely to range from very casual to formal depending on what events are scheduled at the hotel that day. We suggest nice casual attire. Ask for a candlelit table for two by the window and let the staff spoil you. Check what the special is that night. Various chefs take turns setting the special, and it is either one of their favorites or a new dish they are experimenting with—either way you can't lose. An average meal with drinks for two runs about $60.

Nightlife

Linger over an after-dinner drink in the lounge and dance to a small live band Tuesday through Saturday evenings from 9:00 P.M. until closing, or return to your private palace, put on your favorite CD, light some candles, and entertain one another.

DAY FOUR: MORNING

One last breakfast aboard and then, sad to say, it's time for you sailors to pack up and return your waterborne hotel to Holiday Marina. If you've stayed out on the lake all three days instead of coming ashore occasionally, remember that when you get back on dry land, you're going to be rubber-kneed for awhile.

ITINERARY 21
Three days and two nights

INDULGE THE KID IN YOU

FUN AT ANY AGE

*D*oes love bring out the kid in you and your favorite playmate? Indulge those inner children this weekend by playing hookey together and reveling in all kinds of frolicsome things, while you recharge your batteries and reclaim your youth. This fun-filled stolen holiday takes you to several of Atlanta's museums for the young at heart, to a world-class zoo, and, if you're traveling from spring through fall, to Atlanta's outstanding amusement and water parks. You'll be staying in a hotel with a fantasy, space-age look and dining on lighthearted meals in comfortable, fun-loving restaurants. Just remember to leave plenty of room in your carefree schedule for spontaneity.

Practical Notes: You won't need any fancy duds for the uninhibited fun of this getaway—it's all, oh so casual. Go early to any of these venues to be as little inconvenienced as possible by traffic, parking, and long lines. Wear comfortable clothes and shoes and bring a camera. Don't forget the sunscreen, a hat, insect repellent, and water for outdoor activities. The zoo is open year-round, but can it be unpleasant when the temperature soars into the nineties. The other three seasons are preferable for visiting the animal kingdom—it's less crowded during those seasons as well. The theme parks are only open spring through fall.

DAY ONE: AFTERNOON

Begin your weekend of animal attraction by taking a walk on the wild side at **Zoo Atlanta** (Grant Park, 800 Cherokee Avenue; 404–624-WILD; admission $9/$6.50 for seniors). Located in a Victorian neighborhood, which unfortunately limits its size, the zoo is one of the ten oldest, continuously operating zoos in the country. The old Atlanta Zoo went from having the shameful distinction of being one of the worst in the country to its highly acclaimed status now as one of the best. More than one thousand exotic beasts roam freely in several simulated environments, such as the Ford African Rain Forest and the Masai Mara African Plains. In the rain forest, you'll see Zoo Atlanta's favorite resident, Willie B., a silverback lowland gorilla, as well as his consorts, children, and playmates. A colony of orangutans and other primates keep visitors entertained with their kidlike activity. Emulate the obvious affection our simian relatives display. Elephants, including the noted artist Scarlett, and giraffes, zebras, rhinos, tigers, lions, and other creatures inhabit the plains.

During your lighthearted wanderings, if you get hot or tired, snuggle on a bench in one of the shady areas or share a cool drink or iced dessert that you can purchase from one of the many vendors. If real hunger strikes, there are two casual sit-down restaurants. Whether your particular passion is birds, reptiles, gentle farm critters, or other fauna, you'll find what you're looking for at Zoo Atlanta. (Admission gates close one hour prior to the closing of the zoo grounds.)

Romance at a Glance

♥ *Test your love on "Batman the Ride" at Six Flags Over Georgia.*

♥ *Stroll like Tarzan and Jane through the African jungles and plains of Zoo Atlanta.*

♥ *Play kid games at SciTrek.*

♥ *Get up close and personal with the dinosaurs at the Fernbank Museum of Natural History.*

Check in at your pied-á-terre, the **Hyatt Regency** (265 Peachtree Street, N.E.; 404–577–1234; $99–$139) and unleash a little animal passion of your own. Regress to your

Classic Atlanta Love Stories: Willie B. and His Harem

Celebrating his fortieth birthday in 1998, Willie B. (named for former Atlanta mayor William Berry Hartsfield) was rescued by Zoo Atlanta at age three from the seedy zoo that had brought him from the wilds of Cameroon. Unfortunately, rescue is a relative term. Willie B. spent the next twenty-seven years alone in a cage with only a TV for company in the old down-at-the-mouth Atlanta Zoo. When the new and vastly improved Zoo Atlanta opened with an African Rain Forest habitat, Willie B. was released into the out of doors and introduced to other gorillas for the first time. With the possible exception of President Clinton's sex life, never has there been such attention to any creature's libido. Billboards even trumpeted the question on everyone's mind: Willie or Won't He? TV cameras recorded the event and champagne corks popped when Willie mated for the first time with Choomba. Their first offspring was a cute female, who was named Kudzoo through a community contest. They've recently had another daughter, Sukari. Willie B. has mated several more times and has fathered a daughter, Olympia, with Mia Moja, and his first son, Kidogo, with Machi. At forty, Willie B. is one of the oldest living western lowland gorillas in captivity and the oldest one still producing offspring. Zoo officials expect Willie B to be around for another ten to fifteen years, capturing the hearts of visitors as well as his mates.

childhood at one of the most imaginatively designed and most readily recognizable structures in Atlanta. The futuristic, blue-domed flying saucer balanced atop a slim pedestal crowning the hotel reminds you for all the world of something from a science fiction movie and is sure to appeal to the kid in you. Actually, it's the Polaris revolving restaurant and bar, which was once the tallest vantage point in Atlanta. This comfortable hotel makes an ideal place for your weekend playground. Spoil yourselves with the Romance package, which includes accommodations in a suite for $150 per night, or upgrade your room for an additional $35 per night to the Regency Club, where you can enjoy the continental breakfast, beverages, light hors d'oeuvres, and the services of a special concierge. In addition to an outdoor swimming pool and a fitness room, the hotel has three restaurants: Kafe Kobenhaven, Avanzane, and Polaris. It also has two lounges for the "lounge lizard" in you: one in the Polaris; the Parasol Bar in the lobby is the other.

DAY ONE: EVENING

Dinner and Nightlife

Just a few doors south on Peachtree Street, the Boomer generation can take a walk down rock 'n' roll memory lane at the **Hard Rock Cafe** (215 Peachtree Street; 404–688–7625; inexpensive to moderate), which offers juicy burgers, fries, soups, salads, and sandwiches and pop/rock decor. Ogle the memorabilia of American icons the likes of Elvis and British stars such as the Beatles and the Rolling Stones, then buy each other something from the ever-popular clothing line, ranging from T-shirts to jackets, a reminder of your free-spirited visit to Atlanta. Stick around for live jazz, blues, or rock on Friday and Saturday nights at 10:00 p.m.

Before returning to the private playground of your guest chamber to indulge in some fun and games, zip up to the revolving Polaris Lounge located in the blue bubble. While you have a nightcap, watch the world revolve below you. Pretend you're E.T. keeping an eye on the natives.

DAY TWO: MORNING

Breakfast

Hop right out of bed and prepare for another action-packed day, but first, breakfast. The child in you is bound to be intrigued by the **Flying Biscuit Cafe** (1655 McLendon Avenue, N.E.; 404–687–8888; inexpensive) in Candler Park. When the owners were thinking about opening a restaurant, their signature recipe was for really good biscuits. Friends kidded that the biscuits were so light, they could fly—and the rest, so they say, is history. Go there for what else?—the biscuits—but if you're really hungry, try the made-to-order omelets, the tasty black bean and cornmeal pancakes, or the oatmeal pancakes with special stuffings and toppings, like tomatilla salsa. Although the restaurant's motto is "no pig, no cow, no human," it isn't totally vegetarian. They do use chicken and fish in some dishes. Although space is limited, the fragrant aromas of homemade goodies make a wait for a seat in the cool-hip-funky spot well worthwhile.

Kids have an insatiable appetite for finding out how things work. Feel childlike again—and satisfy *that* appetite—as you cavort from one of the 150 permanent interactive exhibits to another at **SciTrek, Atlanta's Science and Technology Museum** (395 Piedmont Avenue; 404–522–5500; admission $7.50/$5 for seniors), one of the country's top ten science centers. Rest assured, there are no DO NOT TOUCH signs here—this is science you can handle. And don't worry, you won't be the only adults here unaccompanied by children. You'll see plenty of other kindred spirit couples of all ages. Take a "cyber-safari" in the Information Petting Zoo—fourteen ever-changing, user-friendly exhibit stations stocked with "beasts" that demonstrate applications of the information superhighway, including the newest in multimedia, computer, and Internet technologies. Get a charge out of the Electric-Magnetic Junction where you can close a circuit with your own body. Never been to Paris? Get someone to take a picture of the two of you in front of the Eiffel Tower—only this 40-foot-tall replica is made from 18,762 Erector Set pieces, and is the largest Erector Set model in the world. Freeze an eight-shaded shadow of the two of you hugging or kissing on a glowing phosphorescent wall in the Color Factory. Watch yourselves appear to shrink and grow like Alice in Wonderland as you walk through a distorted room in Perceptions and Illusions. Learn how machines help make work into child's play at Simple Machines. Use whisper dishes to tell your playmate at the other end of the museum how much you love him or her without everyone in the room hearing. Find out what it's really like to drive while impaired by alcohol and/or drugs at "Impact! A Crash Course . . ." in driving straight. Lift a race car engine with one hand; blend your face with that of your beloved, you've always felt as one anyway; see yourselves reflected into infinity like your love affair. Watch or participate in live science shows in the Coca-Coa Science Show Theater. There's so much more to do—the sky's the limit when it comes to what science and technology can do for us. Just remember, you have to share with the little kids.

Think puppets are just for little tykes? Guess again. Couples of any age will be agog at the **Center for Puppetry Arts** (1404 Spring Street at Eighteenth Street; 404–873–3089; admission $7.50/$6.50 for seniors), a museum containing the largest collection of puppets in the country. There's enough magic here anytime to delight you and that special someone. Gape at the two-story-tall puppets seen around the world in the opening ceremonies of the 1996 Centennial Olympic Summer Games in Atlanta. Check out more than 200 puppets from around the world—many of them one of a kind. You'll be amazed at how many different types of puppets there are. Put yourself into the action with interactive displays. Remember Madame and her "escort," Waylon Flowers, that saucy, naughty, octogenarian puppet who often appeared on the *Ed Sullivan Show*? Her R-rated exhibit at the center is strictly for big kids. A variety of puppet shows entertain the young at heart of any age, but some performances are for adults only.

DAY TWO: AFTERNOON

Lunch

Go south on Spring Street to North Avenue where you can relive your youth by experiencing the world's largest drive-in restaurant, **The Varsity** (61 North Avenue at Spring

♥ *Send cupid's arrow (actually a paintball hit) into your loved one at Fitness Games, Paintball Atlanta, or Q-Zar.*

♥ *Experience the Lost City of Atlantis at Virtual Reality of Underground Atlanta.*

♥ *Fly a kite.*

♥ *Take a spin on a bicycle built for two.*

♥ *Lie on your backs and tell each other what you see in the clouds.*

♥ *Settle down on the grass for an evening's free entertainment in one of Atlanta's parks.*

♥ *Skate away any extra carbs you may have ingested this weekend trying in-line skating.*

♥ *Splash fully dressed through the spectacular Rings Fountain at Centennial Olympic Park.*

♥ *Relive drag racing or try Grand Prix, sprint track, or road racing at Malibu SpeedZone.*

♥ *Make an appointment to have artist Chris McGehee draw a joint caricature of your dynamic duo (404–873–DRAW).*

Street; 404–881–1706; inexpensive), a college hangout grown to gigantic proportions. Located near Georgia Tech, The Varsity is probably one of the few drive-ins still in existence. An essential Atlanta experience, the casual eatery has been serving chili dogs, onion rings, and fried pies and other fast foods, such as burgers, barbecue, chicken and ham salad, fries, slaw, and the frosted Varsity Orange drink for seventy years. Can you imagine that The Varsity sells 2 miles of hot dogs, 300 gallons of chili, 2,000 pounds of onions and 5,000 fried pies, or that it feeds 12,000 to 15,000 hungry people every day? Enjoy the curb service in your car or step up to the 150-foot-long stainless steel counter to place your order. To handle the crowds inside and keep things moving steadily, customers are advised to "have their order in mind and their money in hand" when the superfast counter clerk bellows, "What'll ya have?" And pay attention—the clerks have a language all their own. "Walk a dog sideways, bag of rags" is a hot dog to go with onions on the side and chips in Varsity-ese. Eating in your car is a more laid-back and nostalgic experience.

Thus fortified, head for the largest natural sciences museum south of the Smithsonian, **Fernbank Museum of Natural History** (767 Clifton Road; 404–378–0127; admission $9.50/$8.50 for seniors). Begin in the soaring, glassed-in Great Hall, then take "A Walk Through Time in Georgia," beginning at the planet's birth, then moving into the age of the dinosaurs. There are artifacts from the earliest inhabitants of the state to those of the present time from Georgia's seven geographic regions. "First Georgians: Indigenous Societies of Georgia A.D. 900–1540" includes more artifacts of early residents. "The World of Shells" features a one-thousand-gallon living coral reef aquarium. Interactive science and technology exhibits are carefully geared to different age levels, but since you're just kidding around, try all of them. You'll also love the big-screen movies in the IMAX theater ($7 additional).

Next it is time to do some star gazing at nearby **Fernbank Science Center** (156 Heaton Park Drive; 404–378–4311), which has one of the largest planetariums in the country. In addition, the center sports an observatory, woodlands, a greenhouse, nature trails, a rose garden, and an exhibit hall, featuring dinosaurs, native birds, and animals. Admission to planetarium shows is $2; seniors are admitted free. All the other attractions at the center are free. Each attraction is open at different hours, so call to check on the ones you're interested in.

After a day of studying the earthlings' science, it's time to return to your spaceship at the hotel to freshen up for a dinner of earth-spawned food units.

DAY TWO: EVENING

Dinner

Eat and play this evening at **Dave & Buster's** (2215 Dave & Buster's Drive; 770–951–5554). Here you'll enjoy a dinner of casual restaurant/bar food, such as Jack Daniels barbecue ribs or oven-baked ravioli or Parmesan chicken (your main objective here isn't the food). After you've wolfed down your dinner, get involved with the state-of-the-arts interactive games at the huge nightclub and entertainment extravaganza. This is a stay-all-evening destination where big kids love the play-for-fun blackjack casino, karaoke, world-class pocket billiards, the extensive game room called Million Dollar Midway, seven bars, and live entertainment.

Even after all the fun and games at Dave and Buster's, once you return to the hotel, there might be time for private games of your own.

DAY THREE: MORNING

Breakfast

Although energetic children usually bound out of bed at the crack of dawn, rise and shine whenever the time is right for you. When the appetite moves you head for the **Tasty Town Grill** (67 Forsyth Street; 404–522–5865; inexpensive) for waffles, pancakes, and other breakfast treats.

If your peppy playtime getaway is in the spring-through-fall time frame, by all means spend a day at one of Atlanta's two outstanding amusement parks. A ticket to **Six Flags Over Georgia** (7561 Six Flags Drive, off I–20, Austell; 770–948–9290, admission $34/$23 for seniors, $6 parking) is a thrill-seeker's passport to fun. The gargantuan park got even bigger in 1998 with a spiffier new main entrance through the Promenade at Six Flags, the addition of the park's tenth themed section where Old South and New South are reflected in traditional architecture, up-to-date food shops, and a gazebo where you can relive your childhood by getting your picture taken with Looney Tunes characters. Although the park features six thrills-and-chills roller coasters, the Great American Scream Machine, Georgia Cyclone, Viper, Ninja, Mind Bender, and Batman the Ride, it is Batman the Ride that challenges even the most hearty thrill seekers. After leading you would-be riders through Gotham City's dark streets to the Batcave and scaring you silly with costumed villains, the park's first "suspended" roller coaster sits daring riders such as yourselves in ski liftstyle chairs hanging from a track with your legs dangling free. You'll reach a dizzying 105 feet in height and a breakneck speed of 50 miles per hour during the two-minute ride, so hang on for dear life. Those brave enough to try it experience four times the force of gravity and weightlessness as they speed through corkscrews, vertical loops, and a zero-gravity spin. What all this means is that as you careen around the outside of the loops, you feel as if you're surely going to fly off into space. Cool? Awesome? Terrifying? It depends on your frame of reference, but then again, being in love makes you feel as if you can do anything.

Although Batman the Ride is the centerpiece of the Gotham City theme area, there's plenty more for adventurous lovers to do there. Gargoyles and other brooding postindustrial decorations create a murky fantasy world based on the movies. Stick as close to your hero or heroine as you can because in these shadowy streets you'll be confronted by Mr. Freeze, the Joker, the Riddler, and their nefarious underlings. Don't worry, though, Batman and Robin will save the day. Because this is just a lark, volunteer to be among the audience members who participate in the crashes and explosions of the Batman Stunt Spectacular, where Batman battles the Joker to rescue intrepid girl reporter Vicki Vale.

DAY THREE: Afternoon

Lunch

If you crime fighters are still intrigued by the foreboding Gotham City, but hunger pangs are starting to intrude on your fun, the **Gotham City Eatery** is a great choice for a simple inexpensive midday meal. If you're ready to say goodbye to Gotham City, try food outlets in the other themed areas of the park. Barbecue is the specialty at Miner's Cookhouse, and Dee Jay's Diner takes you back to the 1950s. If you're feeling particularly lighthearted, dine with Bugs Bunny at the Carrot Club. Remember, you're being kids today, so forgo sophisticated iced lattes and instead share an ice cream soda or sundae, just as youngsters did in simpler times.

Six Flags also boasts four water rides, ninety other exciting rides, and entertainment on ten stages that lasts until late at night, so have a blast as long as you like. (Open daily from mid-May through the first weekend in September, and weekends from the first weekend in March through mid-May and the first weekend in September through first weekend in November. Discount tickets are available at Publix; watch for other special promotions.)

Alternately—and especially if it's a sizzling summer day, take a plunge at splashtacular **WhiteWater** (250 Cobb Parkway North, Marietta; 770–424–WAVE; $21.99), a water theme park, which has been called the most scenic water park in the country by *USA Today*. Providing all the necessary ingredients to cool you off during hot summer days, the park features more than forty water adventures and is truly a place where you can float your worries away. One of the most popular attractions is the Dive-In Movie, sure to get you reminiscing about dating in your teen years. New in 1998 are Flash Flood Canyon, with the 90-foot Cliffhanger, a body flume, and Run-A-Way River, an enclosed raft ride through a 735-foot tunnel filled with curves and dips guaranteed to make you clutch your sweetheart.

All good things must come to an end, even for you love-struck kids, so pack up your kid stuff and head back to the adult world with your relationship rejuvenated.

ITINERARY 22
Two days and one night

GOTTA DANCE!
ATLANTA DANCE WEEKEND

*W*hen the lights go down, those with the beat in their feet take to dance floors all over Atlanta to boogie to disco, big band, swing, cocktail music, golden oldies, international folk, ballroom, country line, west coast swing, hip-hop, reggae, you name it. This is the weekend for the two of you to let your Fred Astaire and Ginger Rogers alter egos out to play. With a love built on a shared passion for dancing, you'll be swept away by the sexually charged clinches of touch dancing. In addition to spending from early evening to the wee small hours of the morning tripping the light fantastic in some of Atlanta's hottest clubs, you'll dance through the following day in the city's newest hot spot, up-and-coming East Atlanta. To round out this fun-filled weekend, you'll stay at a B&B with a naughty past and dine on cuisines as diverse as French and "twisted" soul food. So dust off your dancing shoes and head for the bright lights and loud music.

Practical Notes: Because most of the dance halls in Atlanta are at their peak on Friday and Saturday nights, we suggest that you plan your dance getaway for either of those nights. More clubs offer dancing on weekend nights, and they stay open later as well. Don't write off midweek, however, if that's more convenient for you. Many dance halls have exciting weeknight programs, often with lessons, and more actually feature live bands during the week than on weekends. If one night of dancing isn't enough for you two "gypsies," stay another night or two.

Romance at a Glance

♥ *Cut a rug at Swingers.*

♥ *Dance 'til dawn at Masquerade.*

♥ *Shag, jitterbug, or twist at Johnny's Hideaway.*

♥ *Dance cheek to cheek at the Ritz-Carlton Buckhead.*

♥ *Experience the marriage of France and Georgia at the Frog and the Peach Bistro.*

♥ *Savor the ecclesiastical drinks at Sacred Grounds Cafe.*

♥ *Stay at Atlanta's Woodruff B&B, a former massage parlor/bordello.*

♥ *Discover Atlanta's newest "in" neighborhood, East Atlanta.*

DAY ONE: Evening

Begin your hoofer's holiday by checking into **Atlanta's Woodruff B&B** (273 Ponce de Leon Avenue; 404–875–9449; $79–$149), a bed-and-breakfast "with a past." The legend is that in the forties and fifties, many of the city's power brokers met for lunch at the old-standby eatery—**Mary Mac's Tearoom.** It's reputed that before returning to the office, some of these officials would slip across the street to Bessie's massage parlor to have their stress relieved. It was widely and openly accepted that Bessie's girls were doing a bit more than giving simple massages, but the city turned a blind eye because so many officials were involved. The elaborate board that showed which ladies were "occupied" remains as a conversation piece.

Well, that was then and this is now, and today Bessie's is occupied by the delightful bed-and-breakfast—perfect for a lover's tryst. Originally built as a multifamily dwelling at the turn of the century, the house has been faithfully restored and updated with the addition of modern amenities. Guest rooms and suites are large and high ceilinged. For this sybaritic weekend, choose one with a Jacuzzi. Arrive at the B&B in time to check in and perhaps unwind in your Jacuzzi before dinner. If you and your paramour have ever fantasized about the world's oldest profession, this is the time and place to let your imaginations have free reign.

Dinner

If you can tear yourselves away from your bordello-like love nest, it's time to visit a winsome little tucked-away restaurant created by a talented gastronomic couple. A French man (the frog) and his Georgia-born wife (the peach) have married their two native cuisines at their upscale restaurant **The Frog and Peach Bistro** (3167 Peachtree Road; 404–261–4466). Share your hosts' love affair with their cuisine by trying something like *Feuillantine de pommes* (thinly sliced apples with smoked salmon tartar drizzled with citronelle sauce), *Tournedos de saumon sauce Canaille* (salmon with Rascal sauce), or *Filet d'agneau en croute* (lamb tenderloin in puff pastry). Linger over dinner in an out-of-the-way corner or on the patio and let the fine food settle; most of the dance halls don't get underway until 9:00 P.M. or later. When the time comes, grab your partner and get ready to boogie.

Nightlife

Those with twinkle toes will find a variety of dance halls that suit their fancy in Atlanta. Your ultimate decision about which clubs to choose will be defined by your age (either your chronological age or your at-heart age) and your taste in music. Just in time for this lovers' holiday, all kinds of touch dancing are back in style. Currently, swing's the thing and not just with the middle aged. Although it's been more than thirty-five years since Duke Ellington uttered, "It don't mean a thing if it ain't got that swing!," the swing craze is, in fact, so popular with younger and younger participants that many couples are dressing the part with retro-style full skirts, two-tone shoes, zoot suits, and super-long watch chains.

Here are just a few suggestions of dance clubs offering a variety of musical styles. Buckhead Village is the center of the action, and you can walk from many clubs to others nearby. Twirl together and apart and back together again to the music of the '70s and '80s, surrounded by '70s nostalgia such as go-go cages, lava lamps, and Twister games at **Bell Bottoms** (225 Pharr Road; 404–816–9669). **SoHo The Nightclub** (3259 Roswell Road; 404–239–0202) is a disco in a former storage facility known as "The Vault." The newest craze in town is **Swingers** (3049 Peachtree Road, N.E.; 404–816–9931), where young people go to "cut a rug" to '20s music that might have been popular with their grandparents or even great-grandparents. If this latest fad doesn't prove that what goes around comes around, we don't know what does. Boogie flirtatiously to the house band at the **Celebrity Rock Cafe** (56 East Andrews Drive; 404–262–7625), which plays hits from the '70s through the '90s.

In the outskirts of Buckhead, **Johnny's Hideaway** (3771 Roswell Road; 404–233–8026), a wildly popular, smoky, hole-in-the-wall in Buckhead, has traditionally played primarily music of the '40s to '60s and attracted a middle-aged crowd to twist, jitterbug, and shag the night away. Recently, however, the old-standby club has begun attracting younger crowds by playing music popular up through the '80s. If you can stay over a Sunday night, a popular new addition is "Baby Boomer Sundays," with a different band playing each Sunday. The **Ritz-Carlton–Buckhead** (3334 Peachtree Road; 404–237–2700) appeals to those of any age looking for superromantic, cheek-to-cheek dancing with their sweetheart in elegant surroundings. During this upscale evening, a quartet plays in the lobby lounge for dancing on Friday and Saturday. Best of all, couples can whisper sweet nothings to each other over a glass of bubbly rather than trying to shout to each other over the din, and they won't expire in the can't-cut-it-with-a-knife clouds of smoke so typical of most nightclubs.

Elsewhere in the city, **Masquerade** (695 North Avenue; 404–577–8178) is a twentysomething hot spot known for rock and alternative music. The bartenders and waitresses with their blue, green, or red hair are almost as much fun as the entertainment. Alternative bands play on Friday nights and techno bands on Saturday night. Swing Sundays transform the club into a forties dance hall, with single-time swing, jitterbug, and fox trot. Lessons are given from 8:30–9:30 P.M. Boogie at the **Blue Moon Supper Club** (Market Place, 1255–1 Johnson Ferry Road; 770–579–3131), an upscale food and dance club, which features dancing to live music midweek and to a DJ on weekends. Country music fans can kick up their heels at **The Buckboard** (2080 Cobb Parkway; 770–955–7340). Depending on your sexual persuasion or sense of adventure, **Fusion** (550-C Amsterdam Avenue; 404–872–6411), the former March, is a gay/straight hip-hop dance club. Just so you'll be prepared for what you'll encounter there, Wednesday has evolved into white straight night, Thursday black straight night, Friday white gay night, and Saturday black gay night.

When your legs finally give out or you've worn out your dancing shoes like the princesses in the fairy tale, return to the B&B to make up some special steps for your own private dance of desire.

DAY TWO: MORNING

Breakfast

You'll surely be so exhausted from last night's exertions that you'll sleep late whether you planned to or not. When your stomachs start dancing with hunger, feast on a full Southern breakfast of eggs, bacon, toast, grits, fresh fruit, and hot beverages to restore your energy. Don't worry about the calories or cholesterol—you danced off more last night than you're going to ingest today. After breakfast, jump in the Jacuzzi to work out any sore muscles from last night's danceathon.

Pack up your dance togs and say goodbye to your hosts, so you can spend the day dancing through **East Atlanta** (Flat Shoals Road at Glenwood Avenue), a once-dead district, now newly energized. A strong community of longtime and new residents is putting their hopes and faith into achieving an economic renewal similar to that attained by the Virginia-Highland and Little Five Points districts. In fact, dancing in the streets could be called a tradition in East Atlanta. It's reported that in the twenties, residents frolicked on the newly paved streets when street lights were installed in the thriving business district.

Unfortunately, like many in-town neighborhoods, the district saw rapid decline in the sixties precipitated by the construction of I–20 and white flight to the suburbs. In the eighties, however, residents began to organize and ask for assistance to rejuvenate the neighborhood. Their initial success generated new interest and attracted new residents. Neighbors pitched in to help each other renovate spaces, revealing their antiquated charm, and even donated furniture and art to help decorate them. Today East Atlanta is growing by leaps and bounds as the rest of Atlanta finally clues in.

Celebrities, artists, Boomers, and street musicians comingle for sidewalk dining, shopping, and night life. Just a few of the trendy shops to visit are **Verdi O,** an upscale furniture store and art gallery, for kitsch and European-influence items; **Resurrection Antiques and Other Worldly Possessions; Creative Accents** for fifties and retro stuff; **Village to Village** for masks and folk art; and **Traders of East Atlanta Village** for furniture, candles, candle holders, paperware, and silver jewelry. Mixed in with these trendy establishments is the storefront **Body of Christ Christian Church,** a mattress wholesaler located in an ornate old theater, hair salons, and the **Hungry Rush-In,** a deli, grocery, wine store.

DAY TWO: AFTERNOON

Lunch

When hunger pangs strike, head for the **Heaping Bowl and Brew** (469 Flat Shoals Avenue; 404–523–8030), the first successful restaurant in the rejuvenated area. Identified by

the colorful childlike paintings on the front windows, the restaurant is a fifties kind of place, with Formica-and-chrome retro furniture, which serves primarily Southern vegetarian cuisine. The signature dish is a bowl of greens and beans, and other healthy offerings include roasted Portobelo ravioli, spicy vegetables, fried green tomatoes, grilled asparagus, and sweet potato french fries. The restaurant serves beer and wine and, during Saturday and Sunday brunch, Bloody Marys with saki and mimosas.

If you don't have to leave for home yet, continue exploring the small shops and galleries of East Atlanta. When you need a pick-me-up, stop in at the **Village Ice Cream Shop** for a root beer float, or better yet, at **Sacred Grounds Cafe** (Flat Shoals and Glenwood Avenue; no phone) for a coffee treat and a sweet. This establishment's lighthearted sense of humor is evident in its coffee concoctions, such as the Snickering Monk, Frozen Envy, Papal Passion, Fuzzy Friar, Frigid Sister, Raspberry Rector, and Holy Cow—desserts in themselves. Hardcore dessert seekers, however, can also choose from an array of goodies including cakes, pies, and cookies. Decorated with couches and chairs to resemble a warm, comfortable living room, the space is also adorned with large pieces of sensual art, sure to give you ideas.

If you can stay through dinnertime, head for one of the smallest restaurants you've ever seen. **Edible Arts** (481-A Flat Shoals Avenue; 404–586–0707), identified by the artist's palette sign and the red with black-and-white polka dots storefront, has a minuscule dining room (decorated with splashy murals) with eight tables, but Atlantans are beating a path to its door for cuisine the owner likes to call twisted soul food—Southern staples prepared with extra flair. For example, try the fried green tomatoes with goat cheese, Twisted Soul Salad with shrimp and corn bread croutons, fried chicken with macaroni and cheese, or the sweet potatoes with apple chutney. Right now, it's BYO beer or wine.

All too soon, it's time to take off your dancing shoes and head for home.

FOR MORE ROMANCE

If you can plan a visit to Atlanta during the week, social dance classes meet every night of the week at low-to-no fee. **English country dances** are held the second Sunday of each month at Messiah Lutheran Church, 465 Clairmont Avenue; 404–351–DANC ($5). **International folk dancing** lessons are given Mondays at the Leafmore Hills Clubhouse, 1372 Altamont Road; 404–351–DANC ($2). **Tango** and **swing** lessons are given on Tuesdays at LoCurto's Ballroom Dance Studio, Toco Hills Shopping Center, 2991-D North Druid Hills Road; 404–636–7433 ($15 couple). **Big band swing** dances are held the last Tuesday of the month in the smoke- and alcohol-free City Lights Dance Club, 5441 Buford Highway, N.E., Suite B; 770–451–5461 ($7). On Saturday nights, there are dance parties with lessons for beginners; each week there is a different dance focus. **Scottish country dances** are held Thursdays at the Leafmore Hills Clubhouse (see international folk dance mentioned earlier, $5). **Contra dancing** (a hybrid of Irish, English, and rural folk dancing) lessons at the

Morningside Baptist Church, 1700 Piedmont Road; 404–351–DANC. And finally, Cajun dance parties are held some Saturdays, featuring live music and Cajun food, at the Knights of Columbus Post 660, 2620 Buford Highway; 404–636–9237 ($10–$12). Call the Dance Hotline (404–351–DANC) for a schedule.

ITINERARY 23
Three days and two nights

PARTNERS IN CRIME
MYSTERY TOWN

challenging mystery provides a double-barreled opportunity for you and your favorite sleuth to explore the hidden aspects of your love. Not only does a good puzzle with a few unexpected surprises get the adrenaline going, but it gives the two of you a chance to combine your investigative talents as you try to sort through the clues and discover "who dun it." Couples who are mystery buffs will find plenty of riddles to keep them entertained in Atlanta. Style yourselves as Nick and Nora Charles, Mr. and Mrs. North, or any of the great male-female detective teams as you try to solve three different mysteries. You'll have plenty of time to ruminate over the evidence as well as to experience first-class ambience that will encourage you to discover more about each other.

Practical Notes: Go to the library and get a copy of Frances Patton Statham's *The Roswell Women* to read before your trip so you'll be familiar with the mystery of their disappearance when you go on this crime-solving weekend.

DAY ONE: EVENING

Begin your inquisitive weekend in Atlanta by arriving in the late afternoon and checking into your base of operations, the regal **King-Keith House Bed & Breakfast** (889 Edgewood Avenue N.E.; 404–688–7330; $75–$175) in the historic Inman Park neighborhood. Atlanta's first planned suburb, the entire area is on the National Register of Historic Places. One of the oldest houses in Inman Park, this opulent Victorian mansion was built in 1890 in the highly articulated and angular Eastlake style. The exterior of the house is ornamented with delicate wooden lacework and is painted a warm peach color accented in several bright hues as was typical at the turn of the century. Inside, the house retains its high ceilings, original hardwood floors, ornate moldings, and massive pocket doors. The Keiths, who are only the fifth owners of the house, have furnished it with a magnificent collection of heavy Victorian pieces and extravagant accents that they've acquired over many years. Particularly notice the old prints, ornate frames, and colorful pieces of majolica. Make your reservation far enough in advance to get the garden cottage with its Jacuzzi and fireplace or the master bedroom in the main house, which features a stained-glass window and a big private bathroom with a clawfoot tub and shower. Either will serve admirably as home to your detective agency.

Romance at a Glance

♥ *Make the King-Keith House your base of operations.*

♥ *Murder is served with dinner at Agatha's—A Taste of Mystery.*

♥ *Sharpen your investigatory skills at Dave and Buster's.*

♥ *Brunch with a ghost at the 1848 House.*

Dinner

Your first crime scene is also your destination for dinner. **Agatha's—A Taste of Mystery** (693 Peachtree Street, N.E.; 404–875–1610; $47.50), named for Agatha Christie, the queen of mystery writers, has been mystifying Atlantans and visitors for ten years. At the interactive dinner theater, murder unfolds every night between five courses. Done with tongue in cheek, mayhem, mirth, and melodrama are presented by a core cast of three or four actors with help from the audience. Practically everyone is given a few lines to say at an appropriate time. All the diners are suspects, but you have your sweetie to give you moral support (unless your loved one is the perpetrator). On the other hand, you might be the murderer yourself. Will your darling stand by you then? The professional and amateur sleuths at Agatha's have never failed to nab the bad guy/girl by the end of the evening.

DAY TWO: MORNING

Breakfast

Coffee appears in the upstairs hall for those who have to have their jolt of caffeine before they can appear in civilized company. Later a full breakfast is served in the formal dining room. This is a perfect opportunity to get to know your hosts and your fellow guests.

After your leisurely breakfast, drive north of Atlanta to Roswell, the scene of your second mystery. The events of this unsolved puzzle took place in and around **Roswell Mill** (85 Mill Street; 770–642–6140) in 1864 and have never been solved to this day. Roswell was a textile mill town, and, during the Civil War, the mills produced cloth for Confederate uniforms. With all the able-bodied men in town off to war, the women and children pitched in and kept the mills going. In 1864, as Sherman's Union troops advanced toward Atlanta, he sent a detachment of troops to Roswell to burn the mills. Not content with simply destroying the buildings and machinery, fearing that somehow these plucky women would find a way to continue making uniform cloth, the troops rounded them up along with their children and marched them to Marietta—a railhead Sherman had already captured. They were put aboard trains as prisoners of war and sent north into Union territory. Although the war was over only nine months later and prisoners were exchanged, the Roswell women were nowhere to be found. None of them ever returned to Roswell nor wrote to their families back home. There is neither a record of a train wreck in which they might have all perished, nor any hint of atrocities in which women and children were killed. Yet it's hard to believe that they could have become so acclimated to the North in such a short time that they stayed there voluntarily and didn't let their families back home know what had become of them. What could have happened? We'll probably never know, although you two could earn fame and fortune by solving the mystery.

Investigate the mill site. Perhaps you will unearth some clues missed by previous sleuths. The mill building you see today replaced the one that burned during the war, and there is a ruin of another mill building close by that you can explore. We hope you've read the fictionalized account in Frances Patton Statham's *The Roswell Women*. Search out the buildings and landmarks around Roswell that still survive: the **Bricks**, the route the prisoners took to Marietta (now State Route 120), **Bulloch Hall, Barrington Hall, Twin Oaks,** the Roswell Presbyterian Church, and other historic buildings near the town square. You can get a brochure for a self-guided walking and driving tour of the city's several historic districts at the **Roswell Convention and Visitors Center** (617 Atlanta Street; 770–640–3253 or 800–776–7935) near the mill. (For more about Roswell, see the "Our Kind of Town" itinerary.)

DAY TWO: AFTERNOON

Lunch

Take time out from your investigations for lunch at **Mittie's Tearoom** (952 Canton Street, Roswell; 770–594–8822; moderate), located in a restored turn-of-the-century commercial building in the Heart of Roswell Historic District. Although the restaurant serves steaks, seafood, pasta, and lighter selections, it has been recognized by *Appetit* and *Knife*

Did He or Didn't He?

In 1913, thirteen-year-old Mary Phagan toiled long hours at the National Pencil Factory downtown. On April 26, Confederate Memorial Day, she came to pick up her wages and was never seen alive again. Her body was found the next day by Newt Lee, the factory's Black night watchman. Lee immediately became a suspect, as did Leo Frank, the Jewish supervisor she went to for her pay. Two notes found on the scene pointed to Lee, but anti-Semitism was so strong that the focus of the investigation settled on Frank. Corroborating evidence seemed to clinch his guilt, although much of it later turned out to be false. Even when Jim Conley, a Black janitor, confessed to writing the notes, and a foreman said he saw Conley washing blood out of his shirt, Frank remained under suspicion. At the trial, Conley testified against Frank and accused him of aberrant sexual practices. The combination of being Jewish and being labeled a sexual deviant convicted Frank. He was sentenced to hang, but because there were so many irregularities in the trial, the governor commuted his sentence to life imprisonment. Two years later a group of vigilantes calling themselves the Knights of Mary Phagan broke into the jail and seized Frank. They took him to an area near Mary's grave and lynched him. In the 1980s, Alonzo Mann, who had been a young employee of Frank, testified that he had seen Conley with Mary before her death, which seemed to exonerate Frank, who was pardoned by the state of Georgia in 1986. The story continues to fascinate generations who weren't even born at the time of the killing, and it has been the subject of several books and movies. Many are still convinced that he did it, although many more believe in his innocence. What do the clues tell you?

& Fork for its superb chicken salad, so at least one of you should try that. Afterward, browse through the nearby boutiques, antiques shops, and art galleries for one-of-a-kind gifts.

Continue to search for clues to the whereabouts of the Roswell women to your hearts' content. When you can unearth no more, return to Atlanta and spend time browsing through the city's specialty bookstores for mysteries by your favorite authors and perhaps some new ones. The natural place to start is at the **Mystery Bookshop** (2000-F Cheshire Bridge Road; 404–634–3226), which stocks twenty thousand titles. Collectors will unearth many hard-to-find titles in the Collectors Corner. Celebrity authors visit three or four times a month for readings and signings. There are also several Barnes & Noble and Borders bookstores around town. Check the newspaper to see if any of your favorite authors are making appearances. If you haven't discovered her mysteries already, try one by Kathy Hogan Trocheck, whose stories are centered in Atlanta. If you have a favorite mystery author whose works are no longer in print, or you're trying to ferret out a signed first edition, visit **C. Dickens** (3393 Peachtree Road, N.E., in Lenox Square; 404–231–3825 or 800–548–0376), the purveyor of rare and collectible volumes. Helpful salespeople can probably track down what you're looking for. A visit to the shop is a visual treat even if you're only browsing. Burnished paneling, brass accents, and Victorian furnishings are surrounded by thousands of rare books.

Return to your B&B to compare notes with your partner and maybe return to last night's personal investigation to reconfirm some of the clues.

DAY TWO: EVENING

Dinner

This weekend's next crime will take place this evening outside Marietta (the town where the Roswell women were last seen) at **Dave & Buster's** (2215 Dave and Buster's Drive, S.E., off I–75; 770–951–5554; admission $38). An adult entertainment emporium, Dave and Buster's offers a little bit of everything for inquisitive guests: music, dancing, video games, and dinner theater. Tonight you and your partner will visit the Mystery Dinner Theater, where another crime will confound you. Naturally you'll solve it. After the show, you two might want to indulge in some of the fun and games and could end up staying here until the wee hours of the morning. We know how you detectives leave no stone unturned.

DAY THREE: MORNING

After a very late night and all the mental and physical exertions of a weekend of crime solving, you'll want to sleep late this morning. After all, you've resolved two out of three of the cases you came here for. Don't feel bad about the third—in 134 years no one else has found out what happened to the Roswell women. Besides that, you've done some sleuthing of a more personal nature and have discovered even more reasons to love each other.

Brunch

As a grand finale to your mystery weekend, indulge yourselves with a long, lingering brunch at the **1848 House** (780 South Cobb Drive; 770–428–1848; moderate). In addition to touring the magnificent house and grounds and feasting on the opulent brunch, you'll find another mystery here—the antebellum mansion has a ghost. Two rooms upstairs, furnished as they would have been during the period when the house was built, serve as museum rooms. Several staff members and some diners claim to have seen the apparition of a woman in a long gown in the red room. Any house that's almost 150 years old is bound to have witnessed some tragedy, and this home did serve as a hospital during the Civil War, nevertheless, no one knows who she is. Those who have seen her, are convinced she isn't malevolent. Perhaps she'll make an appearance for you as well.

ITINERARY 24
Two days and one night

THE FULL BLOOM OF LOVE
GREEN ATLANTA

*A*tlanta may be an ever-burgeoning city, constantly tearing down and building, but the city is still well known for its ample greenery. Despite the seemingly unstoppable inundation of buildings and highways, there are still multitudinous shady glens, flower-packed expanses, and profuse vegetation that have not only been preserved, but perpetuated. We know of no other city where opulent landscaping is such an integral part of the development of most apartment complexes, residential neighborhoods, office campuses, shopping centers, and the like. Atlanta may not have New York's Central Park, but the city boasts Piedmont Park and numerous large and small preserves perfect for strolling or sitting with your sweetie. Blessed with a mild climate, flowers blossom luxuriantly year-round. Spring is a fairy land of budding trees—Bradford pears, dogwood, and azaleas predominate, but there are lush beds of daffodils, tulips, and other early bloomers as well. Summer follows with creamy white magnolias and swarms of bright red impatiens, varicolored canna lilies, and flamboyant annuals. Fall is splashed with the bright hues of chrysanthemums and nature's palette of psychedelic leaves. Winter's chill is perfect for saucy pansies and handsome camellias. You can go back to nature and enjoy the peace and serenity of rustic settings or spend languid times in formal gardens. The city's parks and gardens range from tiny, almost hidden treasures to vast acreages, so you won't have to look very hard to find an oasis where the two of you can amble at a leisurely pace and perhaps steal a kiss now and then. Atlanta is a perfect place to plant the seeds of romance in a new loving relationship or nurture a full-blown love affair.

Practical Notes: Because different plants and flowers bloom at various times, you may want to make some adjustments in this itinerary depending on the season. In the spring, add an extra day just for driving around Atlanta's neighborhoods taking in the explosion of blooms.

Romance at a Glance

♥ *Revel in nature in all its glory at the Atlanta Botanical Garden.*

♥ *Celebrate the flowering of your love at the Carter Center's Japanese Garden.*

♥ *Steal a kiss in any of Atlanta's colorful pocket gardens.*

♥ *Luxuriate in the sights and aromas of Atlanta's best floral displays at the Atlanta Flower Show.*

♥ *Cultivate your relationship in the gardens of the Atlanta History Center.*

DAY ONE: AFTERNOON

Check into your secret garden, the **Ansley Inn** (253 Fifteenth Street; 404–872–9000; $99–$119 garden rooms, $129–$159 main house), with your favorite horticulturist. A boutique lodging, the small hostelry is often called the Ritz-Carlton of Atlanta inns. Located in the tony Ansley Park area of Midtown, the inn occupies an elegant and beautifully restored English Tudor mansion filled with museum-quality paintings, crystal chandeliers, Oriental carpets, and quality antiques. Each exquisite guest chamber boasts a Jacuzzi in addition to a private bath. Each has a gas-log fireplace as well. Bed chambers in the main house are furnished with antiques and four-poster beds. The Romance package includes champagne, a gift basket, and fresh flowers for $195 per night. The Ansley Inn is a perfect place for the blossoming or reblossoming of your love affair.

By staying at the Ansley Inn, you're within walking distance of two of Atlanta's most popular attractions. The **Atlanta Botanical Gardens and Fuqua Conservatory** (Piedmont Avenue at the Prado north of Fourteenth Street; 404–876–5859; admission $6/$5 for seniors) is a tranquil haven bordering Piedmont Park. Surrounded by urban Midtown, the garden's thirty acres bloom year-round with rose, fragrance, herb, spring and summer bulb, ornamental grass, dwarf conifer, and vegetable gardens, as well as a diminutive, but picture-perfect Japanese garden, just right for the two of you to commune with nature and each other. Fountains and sculptures scattered throughout the various gardens add to the charm without competing with the colors, textures, and aromas of the flowers and plants. Examining a botanical garden is not the same as ambling through a public park; you need to literally stop and smell the roses.

Variety is the spice of romance, so make a detour from the formal gardens to the fifteen-acre urban forest with a nature trail through woods, a wildflower trail, and a wooded overlook.

If your tastes run to exotics or if it's chilly outside, a visit to the $35-million Dorothy Chapman Fuqua Conservatory will whet your appetite for more. The immense glass conservatory overflows with more than seven thousand exotic tropical plants, such as palms, cycads, ferns, orchids, and air plants; its Desert House showcases exotic and endangered succulents such as *lithops* (living stones) and *welwitschia,* a bizarre plant with no living relatives. Another big hit is the terrarium filled with poison dart frogs from Central and South America.

You could spend as little as an hour or as much as a day in the gardens, and each season brings new colors, fragrances, and sounds guaranteed to stir your imaginations and inspire concepts for your own gardens.

In addition to its everyday attractions, the garden offers classes, social events, plant sales, festivals, demonstrations, and plant and flower shows throughout the year. Check with the garden or your innkeeper for a schedule. The research library and a gift shop abounds with unique items with a botanical flair. Between April and October lunch is served on the Lanier Terrace overlooking the rose garden.

Backing on to the botanical garden is **Piedmont Park** (Piedmont Road at Fourteenth Street; 404–876–2040; free). Almost every Atlanta couple can report at least one romantic memory that has its roots in this wonderful park. The city's answer to Central Park, the preserve, with 180 acres, is the largest in Atlanta as well as one of the oldest. The grounds were the site of the 1895 Cotton States Exposition (for which John Philip Sousa wrote the *King Cotton March*), and the grounds were laid out by Frederick Law Olmsted, who designed Central Park in New York and the magnificent formal and informal park lands surrounding the Biltmore estate in Asheville, North Carolina. Olmsted, whose philosophies were avant-garde in the time of Victorian excess, believed that the best way to manage a landscape (public or private) when there were limited funds to do so, was to leave it alone. For designed spaces, he indulged his penchant for curving vistas on gentle slopes and far–near, vanishing-point perspectives. You can admire examples of Olmsted's forward-thinking ideas at Piedmont Park.

The preserve formally became a city park in 1904. Not simply a place to admire the landscaping, the popular sanctuary is the scene of many of the city's major cultural festivals throughout the year. In addition, on a daily basis, fitness buffs—walkers, runners, joggers, in-line skaters, and cyclists—make good use of the paved paths throughout the park, while those whose purposes are more sedentary make ample use of the vast expanses of lawns for picnics and people watching. Stroll around cheery little Lake Clara Meer, relax under the ancient trees, or rent bikes, in-line skates, or roller skates at Skate Escape. The only drawback to visiting the park is parking of which there is very little, but you don't need to worry about it since you are parked at your inn.

Return to the inn for afternoon hors d'oeuvres and then get ready for dinner.

Say It with Roses

If your sweetie brings you roses, this is what he or she is saying:

- ♥ *Red roses are for love and respect.*
- ♥ *Tea roses mean "I'll always remember."*
- ♥ *White roses represent innocence and purity.*
- ♥ *Yellow roses signify joy and gladness.*
- ♥ *Thornless roses mean love at first sight.*
- ♥ *Single roses say "I love you."*
- ♥ *A bouquet of roses indicates gratitude.*
- ♥ *A mixture of red and white roses indicates unity or an engagement.*

DAY ONE: EVENING

Dinner

Because this weekend is about plants, it's only natural that you eat at the **Kudzu Cafe** (3215 Peachtree Road; 404–262–0661; inexpensive to moderate). For any readers who aren't familiar with kudzu, it's that seemingly innocuous leafy green ground cover that was imported from Asia to control erosion, but it ended up eating the entire South instead. Away from the city, you'll see it rapaciously enveloping trees, telephone poles, and even whole buildings. Don't worry though, the kudzu in the restaurant is strictly under control. The chic eatery's casual yet sophisticated style is reflected in the large central bar, open kitchen, cushy booths, and world-class photo collection of the "old juke joint easy goin' South." Continuously named by various surveys as one of the top ten restaurants in Atlanta, the restaurant has been growing its way into the hearts of Southerners. Kudzu Cafe's clever contemporary Southern cuisine includes favorites such as cheese grits and fried green tomatoes, an assortment of fish and pasta dishes, and a great selection of salads. Kudzu Cafe is also well known for its good wine list and desserts.

Nightlife

The place to watch love in full bloom (maybe even getting out of control as so many plants do in the hothouse environment of Atlanta) is at the entertainment emporiums in Buckhead. Join thousands of romantic couples who marvel at Atlanta's dueling pianos at **Jellyrolls** (295 East Paces Ferry Road; 404–233–1133), enjoy silvery martinis while nibbling on caviar at **Beluga** (3115 Piedmont Road; 404–869–1090), or rock the night away at the **Celebrity Rock Cafe** (56 East Andrews Drive; 404–262–ROCK).

DAY TWO: MORNING

Breakfast

Maybe you're morning glories and maybe you're not, but when the time seems right, rise and shine, then dig into a delicious full breakfast at the inn. Eggs to order, bacon, sausage, pancakes, French toast, and waffles will satisfy any appetite. Prepare for a day of unsurpassed beauty.

Lose yourselves in the intoxicating atmosphere at the **Japanese Garden at the Carter Center** (Freedom Parkway; 404–331–0296), a perfect little gem downtown. Situated in a thirty-five-acre park, the center's spectacular grounds are conducive to romance. The serene Japanese Garden, designed by Japanese Master Gardener Kinsaku Nakane, flourishes with river birch, golden raintree, Japanese maples, camellias, azaleas, and rhododendron—all assuring year-round color. Designed to elicit a feeling of mountains and valleys, the garden features two waterfalls cascading over rocks into two small pools below. In addition, the grounds include a native oak forest, formal gardens, wildflower meadow, and a cherry orchard. The rose garden features four hundred plants and eighty varieties—including the coral Rosalynn Carter rose. Truly a peaceful haven, the gardens also afford one of the best views of the dramatic skyline. (The gardens are open from dawn to dusk and are free of charge.)

From the Carter Center, you and your rosebud will transplant yourselves to Buckhead and the variety of gardens at the **Atlanta History Center** (130 West Paces Ferry Road; 404–814–1000; admission $7–$10/$5–$8 for seniors). A magnanimous gift of hope and beauty, the thirty-three acres of gardens afford plenty of stolen moments that lovers can treasure. Who knows? Romance can bloom in the Garden for Peace with its sculpture, *The Peach Tree*, a gift of the Republic of Georgia; on the Swan Woods Trail; in the Mary Howard Gilbert Memorial Quarry Garden, filled with native plants and wildflowers; or in the Frank A. Smith Rhododendron Garden, featuring hundreds of rhododendron and azalea varieties. The Cherry-Sims Asian-American Garden showcases southeastern United States species and their Asian counterparts as well as Japanese maples, which are particularly breathtaking in the fall when their leaves turn a vivid red. The Tullie Smith farm gardens illustrate a typical house garden of the mid-1800s, in addition to a roadside bed, vegetable garden, and cotton patch. In contrast, the elegant Swan House gardens display grand lawns, formal boxwoods, fountains, and classical statuary. The woodlands areas, which depict the evolution of a Piedmont forest from grassland to mature hardwood forest, have native flora and rare plants punctuated by granite outcroppings. Entrance to the gardens is included in the price of admission to the history center. For the really serious gardener, the history center's Cherokee Garden Library houses more than three thousand unusual books and periodicals that contain historical and current information on all aspects of gardening.

Harvest Moon Stroll at the   Atlanta Botanical Garden

See the garden in a different light—moonlight that is. The annual October nighttime event makes a terrific first date or a romantic assignation for long-time lovers. See the trees and flowers bathed by the glow of the full moon against the backdrop of twinkling city lights and more than a thousand luminaries lining the paths. Visit the Moon Garden, where white and silver flowers and foliage gleam in the moonlight. Search for the moonflowers, angel trumpets, prayer plants (which fold their leaves in prayerlike position at night), and night-flowering and night fragrance plants. Every year, a theme is expressed in music, decorations, and refreshments. Free for garden members, $10 for nonmembers. Call (404) 876–5859.

A perfect way to end the day before you head for home is to have afternoon tea in the **Grand Hyatt's Japanese Garden** off the lobby ($16). Completely surrounded by the hotel, the secret garden is totally invisible from the street. A seductive waterfall, traditional Japanese plantings, and artistically placed rock formations create a harmonious oasis and a perfect hideaway for lovers.

FOR MORE ROMANCE

If you have time, visit **Fernbank Forest** at the **Fernbank Science Center** (156 Heaton Park Drive, N.E.; 404–378–4311; free) and the **Robert L. Staton Rose Garden** at the **Fernbank Museum of Natural History** (767 Clifton Road; 404–378–0127; free). At sixty-five acres, the forest is one of the largest virgin woodlands remaining in the Southeast. Self-guided tours along the 1½-mile, hard-surfaced trails permit lovers to view undisturbed examples of the area's original vegetation. Seasonal guide sheets identify the native flora and fauna. An "easy-effort trail" allows those with physical impairments to enjoy the forest. Located adjacent to Fernbank Museum of Natural History, the rose garden is named for the man who first established a rose garden at Fernbank in 1983, and it serves as an official test garden of the All-America Rose Selections (AARS) and the American Rose Society (ARS). The garden is one of only three in the country that has roses from both societies, and it includes entries from throughout the nation. View 1,300 roses, including miniature test plants. (The rose garden is open daily free of charge.)

For a complete change of pace, visit **Christine Sibley's Urban Nirvana** (15 Waddell Street, N.E., Cabbagetown; 404–688–3329; free) in historic Inman Park, where magical menageries of fauna and art featuring beautiful planters as well as garden art handcrafted on site by Sibley are for sale. Work of other local and regional artists is displayed and sold as well.

Challenge yourselves to search for and find your own little private world in Atlanta's secret parks and gardens, such as **Renaissance Park** next to the Civic Center and SciTrek; **Hardy Ivy Park** at the juncture of Peachtree and West Peachtree; **Georgia International Plaza,** an attractive front door for the Georgia World Congress Center and Georgia Dome campus; or corporate campus gardens, such as the one located adjacent to the **IBM building.**

Get an early taste of spring and revel in the beauty of nature in all its glory at Atlanta's best floral display, the **Southeast Flower Show** (404–888–5638) held during the third week **of** February. Water gardening has become increasingly popular as gardening in general has evolved into one of America's leading pastimes. In response, the **Annual Tour of Ponds in Atlanta** sponsored by the National Pond Society, the largest water gardening event in the country, attracts the serious ponderer as well as the curious weekend gardener. The self-guided, early summer weekend tour features approximately thirty ponds in the metro area. The $5 ticket price includes a map to the sites. For more information, call 770–859–9292 or visit the society's Web site at www.pondscapes.com.

Or check the "Beverly Hills Southeast" and "Adding Sparkle to Your Life" itineraries for other nightlife suggestions if you are confirmed night bloomers.

ITINERARY 25
Three days and two nights

ROOTS

ATLANTA'S AFRICAN-AMERICAN HERITAGE

$\mathcal{V}$isiting sights of personal significance with someone you love is always a turn on, and Atlanta is rich in couple-friendly attractions especially meaningful to African Americans (not to mention others as well). Martin Luther King Jr., catalyst of the Civil Rights movement of the 1960s, was born in Atlanta and preached here. The city accepted the inevitable changes that the Civil Rights movement brought more easily than most Southern cities and took as its motto the claim by a white mayor that Atlanta was a "city too busy to hate." The city has long had an affluent class of African Americans and has supported several renowned predominantly Black universities. Today Atlanta has a large population of both middle- and upper-class Blacks who have worked with others of all races to preserve the city's important African-American past. During this meaningful weekend, you and your loved one will visit several culturally significant sites, dine at traditional ethnic favorites, and shop for Afrocentric mementos of your visit.

Practical Notes: Public transportation is available to many of the attractions described here, but it is more convenient and you would probably be more comfortable taking your own car. You might want to time your visit to coincide with two major African-American festivals.

Black History Month, Atlanta's month-long February celebration, is one of the biggest and most active in the country. Daily activities honor the varied, colorful lives of African Americans through plays, gospel singing, poetry readings, lectures, and a jazz series. The **National Black Arts Festival,** a two-week July celebration, features the best in African-American art forms. Dozens of activities, ranging from an art show in Piedmont Park to musical performances at various venues, are ongoing.

Romance at a Glance

♥ *Pay homage to a giant in American history at the Martin Luther King Jr. National Historic Site.*

♥ *Celebrate African-American heritage at the APEX Museum.*

♥ *Marvel at the fruits of an early African-American success story at the Alonzo F. Herndon House.*

♥ *Admire examples of African-American culture at the Hammonds House.*

DAY ONE: AFTERNOON

Lunch

Although **Thelma's** (768 Marietta Street; 404–688–5855; inexpensive), an Atlanta meat-and-three-vegetables institution, was forced to move across downtown due to construction for the 1996 Centennial Olympic Games, the popular eatery still retains a loyal following of just plain folks from laborers to community leaders. They specialize in plain old "Down home cookin.'" Their entree menu typically includes pork roast, BBQ, fried chicken and catfish, meat loaf, and macaroni and cheese with sides of okra, collard greens, spinach, creamed corn, rutabaga, sweet potato soufflé, cornbread, and at least one kind of cobbler or pie.

Begin your mutual exploration of Atlanta's modern African-American history where it all began—**Auburn Avenue**. As a result of Jim Crow segregation laws, post–Civil War Blacks developed their own businesses and many of them were quite successful. In its heyday, which stretched from the 1890s to the 1940s, Auburn Avenue was known as Sweet Auburn because there were so many prosperous Black-owned businesses along it—stores, restaurants, nightclubs, and service enterprises. After the end of segregation, the lively inner-city neighbor-hood deteriorated as residents moved away from downtown or shopped elsewhere. Eventually, most of the establishments closed. Sweet Auburn was certainly sweet no longer—in fact, it became a district to be avoided rather than the bustling thoroughfare it once was. The Southern Christian Leadership Conference and the *Atlanta Daily World* remained, however, and Ebenezer Baptist Church has always had an active congregation, so the neighborhood was never completely abandoned. In recent years, the astounding success of the Martin Luther King Jr. National Historic Site has resulted in an exciting rejuvenation of the entire district, including Auburn Avenue. You and your sweetheart will see fine old Victorian homes now restored near King's birthplace and new Victorian-style homes blending in, all of which have drawn middle-class Blacks back to the neighborhood. Where folks live, businesses soon follow, so Auburn Avenue once again has a sweet future.

Pay tribute to all the brave, dedicated folks who conceived the Civil Rights movement and put their lives on the line for equality. Start at the **Kunta Kinte statue,** which represents the passing on of cultural heritage from one generation to another. Stop for a moment to contemplate what the two of you will want to pass on to other generations. From the statue, step into the visitors center of the **Martin Luther King Jr. National Historic Site** (Auburn Avenue; 404–331–5190; free) to pay homage to the dream. The third most visited attraction in Atlanta, the extensive Auburn Avenue site, which is the only official national or international memorial dedicated to the civil rights leader, has more than 3 million visitors annually. In addition to the new visitors center and a historic neighborhood fire station, the historic site includes tours of King's birthplace and boyhood home. (Tickets for the birthplace tour are available at the fire station.)

The MLK historic district, which is bounded by Boulevard and Courtland Streets and Edgewood and Auburn Avenues, encompasses a ten-block area surrounding the national historic site and includes the church where King, his father, and his grandfather preached; the civil rights leader's tomb set in a reflecting pool; and the **Center for Nonviolent Social Change** (449 Auburn Avenue; 404–524–1956; free). Trace King's dream from his birth to the flowering of the Civil Rights movements to his death to the rebirth of the area. Both of you will be inspired by photographs and memorabilia from Dr. King's public and private life, such as his clergy robes and his Nobel Peace Prize. In addition, the center contains the largest collection anywhere of material pertaining to the Civil Rights movement. A sight familiar around the world is the slain leader's tomb. Lit by an eternal flame and set amid a five-tiered reflecting pool, the tomb is one of the most-photographed spots in Atlanta. (The tomb is accessible twenty-four hours a day and is particularly photogenic at night.)

One-hundred-year-old **Ebenezer Baptist Church** (407 Auburn Avenue; 404–688–7263) is the spiritual center of the Civil Rights movement and has always had an active congregation. You may hear rousing gospel tunes wafting down Auburn Avenue and, of course, visitors are welcome to attend services.

Just five blocks from Auburn Avenue is the **Atlanta Marriott Marquis** (265 Peachtree Center Avenue; 404–521–0000; expensive $175–$350), your romantic hideaway for the weekend. This modern downtown high-rise (forty-seven floors) hotel with many amenities is a far cry from the limited accommodations early civil rights leaders had available to them. Enjoy the health club's indoor/outdoor pool, skyway connector to the shops in Peachtree Center, and a staff dedicated to serving your every need. Drop in to the Sports Bar, which honors many Black athletes. Ironically, these stars couldn't have gotten a room in any downtown hotel forty years ago.

DAY ONE: EVENING

Dinner

Heat up the evening with some authentic Caribbean cuisine at (appropriately enough) the **Caribbean Restaurant** (180 Auburn Avenue; 404–658–9829; inexpensive). Menu items range from curry goat or sheep to red snapper to jerk chicken. Let the hot island spices add some zest to your relationship.

Nightlife

Take a trip outside the historic district by driving to Midtown where young upwardly mobile African Americans gather on Friday evenings at the **Martini Club** (1140 Crescent Avenue, N.E.; 404–873–0794), a trendy cigar and martini bar with live jazz located in a historic home in Midtown. Although there are cushy overstuffed sofas and chairs, the lively crowds are more likely to stand and mingle so they can see and be seen. In fact, the crowds can be so thick, you can hardly stir them with a spoon.

DAY TWO: MORNING

Breakfast

Stoke up on energy food for the day from the generous breakfast buffet at **Paschal's** (830 Martin Luther King Jr. Drive; 404–577–3150; inexpensive). The legendary civil rights eatin', meetin', and greetin' place in a former motor hotel is still serving soul food and is where the power of Atlanta often eats. The story is told that many a struggling civil rights leader of the past was stood for a meal or two when a little short of cash.

Just because you spent time in and around the Martin Luther King Jr. National Historic Site yesterday afternoon doesn't mean you've seen everything there is to see on Auburn Avenue. You and your honey can learn more about the history of African Americans in general and the African-American community in Atlanta in particular at the **APEX (African-American Panoramic Experience) Museum** (135 Auburn Avenue; 404–521–APEX; $3), which offers an overview of the entire historic district. The walk-through exhibit details

African-American history from early Africa through present-day America using historical and artistic displays. A fifteen-minute audiovisual presentation shown in the vintage Trolley Theater describes the evolution of the Sweet Auburn district, and one of the museum's displays is a model of Georgia's first black-owned drug store.

DAY TWO: AFTERNOON

Lunch

Aleck's Barbecue (783 Martin Luther King Jr. Drive, east of Ashby Street; 404–525–2062) opened in 1951 and was a popular eating establishment for participants in the Civil Rights movement. It's still a popular hangout for Atlanta's Black community, and you're likely to see such luminaries as Marvin Arrington or Andrew Young. Pig out on Southern barbecue, a big serving of ribs, or Brunswick stew accompanied by cornbread and cool drinks, while you keep an eye peeled for some of Atlanta's current leaders. Don't expect much in the way of decor, this is a simple neighborhood eatery.

After lunch, you will visit Atlanta's **West End** neighborhood. This grouping of significant African-American attractions includes the **Atlanta University Complex.** Atlanta University is actually a collection of six predominantly African-American universities—the largest consortium of African-American institutions of higher learning in the country: Spelman, Morehouse, Morehouse School of Medicine, Clark Atlanta, Morris Brown, and Inter-denominational Theological Center Universities. Many great African-American leaders of the past and present received their higher education at one of these schools.

Known as the Atlanta University Collection of Afro-American Art, 300 works from annual art competitions held by Clark Atlanta University from 1942 to 1970 as a national forum for Black artists are on permanent display at the **Clark Atlanta University Art**

Gallery in Trevor Arnett Hall (James P. Brawley Drive at Fair Street, S.W.; 404–880–8671; $2). Among the works are pieces by Charles White, Jacob Lawrence, Henry Ossawa Tanner, Romare Bearden, Elizabeth Catlett, and Lois Mailou Jones.

Nearby the **Alonzo F. Herndon House** (587 University Place, near the grounds of the Atlanta University Center; 404–581–9813; $3) is a monument to an early African-American success story. Herndon was born a slave in 1858, but by 1895 he was the wealthiest African-American in Atlanta. In fact, he was Atlanta's first African-American millionaire. Although he started his business empire with a small barber shop, his fortune was realized from the Atlanta Life Insurance Company, which he founded. It became the largest African-American owned insurance company in America and is still in business. He designed an opulent mansion, which was completed in 1910 by African-American craftspeople, then set about to acquire lavish furnishings and important pieces of art, such as collections of Venetian and Roman glass dating to 200 B.C.

Now a house museum, listed on the National Register of Historic Places, its contents are mostly original to it. Herndon's success is a lesson to those of all races in how to overcome adversity.

You'll also want to make time to visit the **Hammonds House Galleries and Resource Center of African-American Art** (503 Peeples Street, S.W.; 404–752–8730; $2), Georgia's only museum dedicated exclusively to African-American art. The collection is housed in the 1857 Eastlake-style Victorian home of Dr. Otis T. Hammonds, who was a noted physician and art patron. The fourteen-room house is believed to be one of the three oldest homes in the West End. Among the items in the permanent collection are numerous Haitian pieces, works of Romare Bearden, and those of more than two hundred other artists. In addition to the permanent collection, several traveling shows are featured each year. Also be sure to note the chandeliers, brass and handblown lighting fixtures, and the seven fireplaces—all original to the house.

DAY TWO: EVENING

Dinner

Return once more to Auburn Avenue for a pleasant evening of dinner and entertainment. Enjoy Eretrian (East African) cuisine at the **Masswa Restaurant** (186½ Auburn Avenue; 404–880–0745, moderate), which specializes in goat, lamb, beef, and East African vegetables. The restaurant carries its East African theme into the decor.

Nightlife

After dinner, simply go upstairs to the **Royal Peacock Lounge** (186½ Auburn Avenue; 404–880–0745). Atlanta's Apollo Theater of the 1950s and 1960s, the Royal Peacock was where you went during that period to hear Black artists. Now visitors dance to a reggae band or music played by a DJ.

DAY THREE: MORNING

Breakfast

Sleep in after your late night at the Royal Peacock Lounge and get in a little snuggle time with your darling or attend services at Ebenezer Baptist Church. After recharging your romantic spiritual batteries, check out of the hotel and drive over to one of Atlanta's newest downtown eateries, **Sylvia's** (241 Central Avenue, at Trinity Avenue; 404–529–9692, moderate) for a Gospel Brunch. This fixed-price, all-you-can-eat soul food extravaganza features five to six different meat dishes, yams, greens, macaroni, "sassy rice," as well as all the other soul food regulars for only $16.95. A la carte menu entrees start at $13.95 and include two side dishes. The decor is straight out of twenties Harlem.

Spend the afternoon shopping for Afrocentric items with which to decorate your home or to give as gifts. Just a few shops include **African Connections** (1107 Euclid Avenue; 404–589–1834), which offers exquisite, affordable Afrocentric art; **African Interiors** (250 Auburn Avenue; 404–523–9458), which features masks, stools, jewelry, textiles, baskets, and sculpture; **African Pride** (88 Lower Alabama Street, Underground Atlanta; 404–523–6520), which carries authentic, one-of-a-kind African artifacts made from indigenous materials: embroideries, wax prints, dashikis, sculpture, carvings, paintings, baskets, and more; **Atlanta International Market** at Woodruff Park (56 Peachtree Street; 404–521–3389), which imports authentic African merchandise (not open on Sunday); **Diaspora Arts** (232 Auburn Avenue, N.E.; 404–525–7900), which shows African-American and Caribbean art, artifacts, and accessories (closed Sunday and Monday); **LaNIK Gallery and Fine Arts** (2298 Cascade Road; 404–758–5040), which has paintings, sculptures, masks, wood carvings; **Gallery Abayoni** (186-B Auburn Avenue; 404–581–1003), which shows the works of African, African-American, Haitian, and Caribbean artists, including paintings, jewelry, textiles, and books; also has an espresso bar; and the **Truth Bookstore** (56 Marietta Street, N.W.; 404–523–3240), which has Georgia's largest collection of African-American, Caribbean, and African books, videos, audios, games, and

Kwanzaa items (closed Sunday). Some other places to browse are **Afrimec Fine Arts** (40 Marietta Street, Suite 110; 404–523–4940); **Afrocentric Network** (576-A Lee Street, S.W.; 404–756–0200); **Greenbriar Mall** (2841 Greenbriar Parkway S.W., at I–285; 404–344–6611), which has a unique collection of Afrocentric shops; **South DeKalb Mall** (2801 Candler Road, Decatur; 404–241–2431), which features several Afrocentric specialty shops and restaurants as does **Underground Atlanta** (50 Upper Alabama Street; 404–523–2311).

FOR MORE ROMANCE

Instead of striking out on your own, you might prefer to take a guided tour of the Civil Rights District. **SCLC/W.O.M.E.N., Inc.** (328 Auburn Avenue; 404–584–0303) offers African-American civil rights tours that last from three hours to two days. The three-hour Heritage Tour of Atlanta encompasses most of the sights listed in this itinerary. If you have more time and are interested in civil rights sites beyond Atlanta, there are two more inclusive tours. The one-day tour includes Atlanta and Birmingham, while the two-day tour includes sights in Atlanta, Birmingham, Montgomery, and Selma.

The **High Museum of Art** (1280 Peachtree Street, N.E.; 404–733–4400; admission $6/$4 for seniors) has an outstanding permanent collection of Afrocentric art works. The **Omenala-Griot Afrocentric Teaching Museum** (337 Dargan Place, S.W.; 404–755–8403) in the West End offers visitors a "hands-on," product-oriented approach to the African-American experience. Br'er Rabbit and his pals and enemies live on at the **Wren's Nest** (1050 Ralph David Abernathy Boulevard, S.W.; 404–753–7735; admission $6/$4 for seniors), the former home of journalist and author Joel Chandler Harris, who chronicled the Uncle Remus tales he heard as a small boy from former slaves. **Zoo Atlanta** (800 Cherokee Avenue, S.E., in Grant Park; 404–624–5678; admission $9/$6.50 for seniors) transports you to an African Rain Forest and the Masai Mara, exhibits that simulate East African terrain. (For much more detailed information about the zoo, check out "Indulge the Kid in You.")

ITINERARY 26
Two days and one night

FOREIGN AFFAIRS

AN INTERNATIONAL TOUR OF ATLANTA

*P*hineas Fogg may have needed every transportation vehicle available in the late-nineteenth century—from an elephant to a hot-air balloon to a stage coach to a railroad hand car—to complete his record-shattering trip around the world in eighty days, but fortunately, all you world travelers need is your car to make a weekend global journey around Atlanta's internationally inspired hotels, restaurants, nightspots, and shops. This exotic getaway concentrates on intriguing foreign cuisines and shopping for international antiques.

Practical Notes: Be forewarned: This romantic holiday is not for the fainthearted—there's a lot to do in a very short time. You'll also be sampling international cuisines, so if you're not used to exotic dishes packing some antacid might be prudent. The hotel is located directly across the street from the Buckhead MARTA rapid rail station, which gives you easy access to many parts of the city. You'll need your car, however, to reach many of the destinations on your itinerary.

DAY ONE: AFTERNOON

What better place to find a luxurious, cosmopolitan, international hideaway than by "journeying" to Switzerland? Your destination, the sleekly European **Swissôtel** (3391 Peachtree Road, N.E.; 404–365–0065; rooms $180–$245, suites $210–$295; presidential suite $1,700), is on the right just before you get to Lenox Square Mall. Ensconce yourselves at the classically elegant hostelry, where you sophisticated travelers will find the renowned efficient and precise Swiss service coupled with traditional Southern hospitality. The marriage of these attributes earned the upscale lodging a place on the *Condé Nast* Gold List of 500 Best Places to Stay in the World and the Hotel of the Year award among the Swissôtel four-continent chain of hotels. The four-diamond deluxe hotel has breathtaking architecture reminiscent of Atlanta's High Museum of Art and an expressionist art collection in Atlanta second only to that of the museum. Guest rooms and suites are luxurious, oversized, and furnished with the spare modernism of contemporary Biedermeier-style pieces. Other standard amenities include a marble bathroom, refreshment center, and coffeemaker. We suggest that for this special weekend away, you go for a room or suite on the "Swiss Butler Executive Level"—actually three floors where accommodations feature finer detail in the furnishings, and guests are treated to extra amenities such as evening hors d'oeuvres, fruit baskets, mineral water, and continental breakfast.

Romance at a Glance

♥ *Try a black and tan at fado Irish Pub.*

♥ *Be waited on hand and foot in a tatami room at Kamogawa.*

♥ *Tango, cha-cha, or rumba the night away at The Sanctuary.*

♥ *Shop for European antiques at The Red Baron.*

♥ *Take a magic carpet ride to dinner at The Imperial Fez.*

If you would like to surprise your sweetheart with some of his/her favorite things take advantage of the Swissôtel's "Customized Rooms" service, a special concept that allows guests to personalize their accommodations in advance of their arrival with everything from their favorite beer to their favorite music to specialty pillows. Swissôtel's commitment to providing the "little things" for their guests allows prospective lodgers to choose from a list of more than thirty items to choose from at the time the reservation is made. Most amenities are complimentary, although a few, such as personal shoppers, are at a nominal fee. In addition, the hotel offers a variety of extraordinary weekend packages, which change depending on the time of year. Perhaps one of these will strike your fancy. The Romance package ($369 for suite, $249 for Club Level) includes champagne, Swiss (what other kind could there be?) chocolates, continental breakfast, and free self-parking. For the same price, the Shoppers package substitutes a gift certificate in place of the champagne and chocolates. The Spa package ($289 Club Level, $439 suite) includes an hour of spa services.

Located in the hotel is **Claiborne's Day Spa and Salon** (404–239–9191), rated one of the Southeast's top ten salons by a group of national magazines. Try to arrive for your "overseas" journey in time to take advantage of some of its health, beauty, and fitness services or devise some other time in your schedule to luxuriate in the full-service hair salon, indoor lap pool, steambath, his-and-hers sauna, outdoor sundeck, massage service, facials, body treatments, manicures and pedicures, fitness training, aerobics, weight rooms, personal trainers, and nutritionists—all of which would be the envy of any Swiss, German, or French spa.

In the late afternoon or early evening, after you're thoroughly pampered and spoiled, head for drinks and rare *ould* good times at **fado Irish Pub** (3035 Peachtree Road; 404–814–0066), voted Best Irish Pub in Atlanta by *Creative Loafing*. The name of the pub (pronounced fuh-DOE) in Gaelic Irish means long ago and was used by *seanchai* (storytellers) to begin old stories or fables in the manner of "once upon a time." In that tradition, fado is dedicated to bringing to life the story of Ireland's rich and celebrated pub culture. The artfully designed interior, which was crafted in Ireland, uses natural stone, exposed wooden ceiling beams, tile and wood floors, and Irish antiques to create an authentic feeling of the

Ould Sod. A wickedly clever, warrenlike layout of rooms further subdivided by wooden partitions guarantees privacy for billing and cooing. To enhance your Irish experience, choose from the large selection of dark Irish beers, ciders, and teas. Better yet, order a black and tan—a two-tone combo of golden Harp lager on the bottom and rich, dark Guinness stout on top. (You can try this at home—to pour a perfect one, simply draw the stout over a spoon to keep it from mixing with the lager.) If you want a small appetizer, the pub serves Irish food *boxtys* (potato pancakes) with a choice of fillings, but because we've scheduled you to eat dinner on a different continent, the shepherd's pie, Irish stew, salmon, seafood, pork, and beef entrees will have to wait for another visit. In keeping with the easy-going pub camaraderie, fado offers sing-along entertainment and dancing, so join in the fun.

DAY ONE: EVENING

Dinner

Reluctantly leave Ireland and the boisterous atmosphere of fado behind and journey to the mysterious Far East for a traditional Japanese dinner at serene, refined **Kamogawa** (Grand Hyatt Atlanta, 3300 Peachtree Road; 404–841–0314; expensive), an elegant Japanese restaurant. Using ancient skills, the entire restaurant was hand crafted by artisans in Kyoto to ensure authenticity, then shipped in pieces to Atlanta and reassembled. If you're brave enough, begin your Eastern experience by sampling from the sushi/sashimi bar—considered the best in town. Then retire to a tatami room for a unique experience and exceptional privacy. Take off your shoes and step into the reed-covered room highlighted with just the right spare accents. (Don't worry, eating at the low table won't be uncomfortable. A well under the table allows you to stretch your legs and stiff-backed cushions support you comfortably.) An oh-so-respectful, kimono-clad waiter or waitress takes your order (we recommend the eight-course Kaiseki dinner; $75 per person) and serves you unobtrusively throughout the evening. Incredibly romantic, a tatami room is an ideal place to pop any important question or to present your loved one with a very special gift. Reservations are essential for a tatami room and recommended for dinner in the main dining room.

Despite your feeling of well-being, it's time to continent hop again, this time to South America for Latin music and dancing. **The Sanctuary** (128 East Andrews Drive; 404–262–1377), you can pour yourselves into the Argentine tango, meringue, rumba, samba, cha-cha, and other Latin dances. You'll appreciate the spacious dance floor, which so many Atlanta clubs lack, and the outdoor patio, where you can go for a refreshing drink when you need to cool off. (Open Wednesday, Friday and Saturday nights until "whenever." They'll stay open until the patrons finally leave.)

When your personal "whenever" comes, return to your Swiss hideaway and dream of the two of you sharing a mountain glen in the Alps.

DAY TWO: MORNING

Breakfast

Early risers can use some of the spa or health club facilities after breakfast in the Executive Level lounge; late risers will just have to be satisfied with breakfast.

Today you globetrotters will continue your trip around the world, but now with an added dimension—traveling back in time, visiting a series of international antiques emporiums. Set out on the trail of exceptional antiques with which to accent your home by traveling to Chamblee, a cute little town inside the I–285 perimeter highway. Begin your search by poking through the shops of **Antique Row of Chamblee** (3350 Broad Street; 770–458–6316). Surrounding the corner of Broad Street and New Peachtree Road, this is reputed to be Georgia's largest antiques shopping area. With about two hundred dealers in shops ranging from cozy to immense spilling out of twenty buildings, why argue? A vast array of quality antiques and collectibles from around the world are just waiting for you to find them in shops like **Rust 'n' Dust** (770–458–1614), which specializes in toys, glass, and kitchen utensils, and the **Moosebreath Trading Company** (770–458–7210), which claims to have the largest and most unusual selection of collectibles in the world. (As an added bonus, Moosebreath offers custom neon for those lovers who want to see their names up in lights.)

Don't get too carried away digging around in all these stores, however, because you need to save plenty of time to explore the Big-Three purveyors of primarily European architectural antiques and other large indoor and outdoor decorative arts. **Great Gatsby's Architectural Antiques** (5070 Peachtree-Industrial Boulevard; 770–457–1903 or 800–GATSBYS) covers ten acres, and the staff has done its very best to bring Western Europe to you and your sweetheart. A marketer of a drop-dead collection of antique cars, Gatsby's also offers palatial-size chandeliers, fountains, saloon bars, entire paneled Gothic rooms, carved furniture, eighteenth- and nineteenth-century American and European oil paintings, garden statues, and much more. This is an antique hound's dream. The staff tells us they've recently sold Romeo and Juliet statuary from Verona, Italy, a statue called *Young Lovers*, and an original *Gone With the Wind* script, so you're certain to find a romantic or erotic piece to take home as a remembrance of your international tour of Atlanta. Perhaps you can time your trip to coincide with one of Gatsby's periodic auctions.

DAY TWO: Afternoon

Lunch

For a light lunch, you travel-wise connoisseurs will remain in historical Western Europe, this time in World War I-era France, so when you're hungry for more than antiques, take Clairmont Road south and watch for signs to the **57th Fighter Group**

How to say the three most important words wherever in the world you happen to be (taken from the book I Love You, *BRG Publishing).*

China: Wo ai ni *(woll-eye-knee)*

Finland: Mina rakastan sinua *(min-neh rock-ah-stah sin-you-ah)*

France: Je t'aime *(zheh tehm)*

Germany: Ich liebe dich *(eeek leebah deek)*

Italy: Ti amo *(tee ah-moe)*

Norway: Jeg elsker deg *(yie elsker die)*

Poland: Kocham cie *(cock-em chell)*

Spain: Te amo *(tay ah-moe)*

(3829 Clairmont Road; 770–457–7757; moderate), a long-time favorite with locals. Located just off the runways at Peachtree-DeKalb Airport, the restaurant is built to resemble a wartime farmhouse, which might have been commandeered for an Allied squadron headquarters. An ambulance and other period military vehicles litter the yard. Inside parts of the walls are protected by sandbags. World War I songs play in the background, and newspaper clippings keep patrons abreast of the war's progress. The dining room isn't open on Saturday, but the bar is. You don't need a big meal after last night anyway, so enjoy excellent bar food while you watch small planes take off and land. In good weather, sit outside on the patio, just off of which nostalgic vintage biplane flights are offered. We'd recommend that you take one, complete with World War I aviator's helmet, goggles, and streaming scarf, but how romantic is it if both of you can't go together?

Perhaps, instead you could coax someone to take your picture by the plane. The pilot might even lend you the accessories for your portrait.

Don't stay too long—many more antiques are waiting for you to find them. The second of the Big Three, **Red Baron Antiques** (6450 Roswell Road; 404–252–3770), takes up several buildings on both sides of the road. Just to say that this huge antiques emporium specializes in eighteenth- and nineteenth-century furniture, architectural antiques, collectibles, pop culture memorabilia, classic cars, and decorative arts is to vastly understate what goes on there. In addition to the Louis XIV armoires, Italian marble, Irish pub bars, Tiffany clocks, and saloon doors, Bob Brown—the Red Baron himself—has acquired and sold Benito Mussolini's mantel, a life-size figure of Ronald McDonald, a model of E.T. used in filming live action sequences, and celebrity-owned items, John Lennon's Rolls Royce, Elton John's grand piano, Elvis's first guitar, Arnold Schwarzenegger's pool table, and Jimmy Carter's hand-carved chess set. Brown readily admits that nothing he carries is anything people need, but he caters to the nouveau riche's craving for an instant personal history. To that end, Brown, his wife, and five buyers comb the world for massive architectural elements, such as a wall from London's Victoria Station, street lamps from Paris's Musée du Petit Palais, and even entire rooms from European castles and country homes—easily having $10 million in treasures on hand at any time. Periodic invitation-only auctions attract hundreds of millionaires from around the country clad in everything from long sequined evening gowns to cowboy boots, hats, and jeans to attend a lavish party with a bountiful buffet and free-flowing booze. Just in case you're not on the invitation list, drop by the showrooms to feast your eyes on all the far-out items. Who knows what romantic treasures you might find?

Don't let your energy flag now. The last of the Big Three on the antiques trail, **The Wrecking Bar** (292 Moreland Avenue, N.E.; 404–525–0468), also specializes in architectural masterpieces. This emporium is situated in the handsome 1900 Victor Kriegshabar House in Little Five Points. An elaborate and pretentious Beaux Arts Classical Revival, the mansion is listed on the National Register of Historic Places. Among the notable exterior architectural accents on the creamy yellow brick edifice are a semicircular portico with Ionic columns that support a conical slate roof, wraparound porch, and port cochere with smaller Ionic columns. Inside stained-glass transoms top doors and lintels are crowned with deep double shells emerging from curving stylized wave elements.

It's finally time for you two jetsetters to end your travels in time and return to the present, so that you have plenty of time to get ready for a magical evening. After a day of world travels, you lovers will want to take some private time for yourselves, but drop in at the Executive Level lounge for some drinks and hors d'oeuvres before you return to your room for some snuggle time.

DAY TWO: EVENING

Dinner

Dinner tonight is an event. You worldly wise travelers will take a magic carpet ride to Fez, the first imperial capital of the exotic North African country of Morocco, for an exotic dinner and traditional entertainment. Named the "Best Restaurant for a Sexy, Seductive Date" by *Atlanta* magazine, the **Imperial Fez** (2285 Peachtree Road, Suite 102; 404–351–0870; expensive) is an experience you mustn't miss. Cross the threshold of the "Casbah of Buckhead" to a world of enticing aromas, fragrant spices, and opulent decor. Decorated to resemble a silky tent, that effect is achieved with billowing fabric walls and ceiling. Leave your shoes at the door and your inhibitions at home. Sink into the deep pillows by a low table in this rug-covered paradise and prepare yourselves for Moroccan food, musical performers, and erotic veiled belly dancers. Traditionally dressed staff cater to your every wish, as if you were royalty. For starters, they'll pour warm water over your hands to cleanse them, then serve you a seven-course prix fixe dinner that includes soup, a choice from six salads, appetizer, entree, couscous tea, and dessert. Vegetarian dinners and an a la carte menu are also available. (Reservations for this special event are required.)

After such a sensual experience, you're bound to have some erotic ideas, so return to the privacy of your own Shangri-la to write your own thousand-and-one-nights love story.

DAY THREE: MORNING

All this international travel and all the time zones you've crossed may have left you jet lagged or with a few kinks that need working out, so check into the spa for a Swedish massage (you'll have made reservations when you checked in) before you reluctantly leave your love nest and head for one more country for brunch.

Brunch

Dress in anything from nice casual to business attire to very dressy and prepare to dine on a dreamy brunch in modern-day France. What could be more conducive to romance than to complete your world travels in the country synonymous with love for a champagne brunch at a quaint restaurant named for the saint of love? Named not only for its English translation, but also because it is the name of a popular vineyard in Beaujolais, **Le Saint Amour** (1620 Piedmont Avenue, N.E.; 404–881–0300; expensive) is a cozy restaurant in a former residence. Contemporary French cuisine is served in traditional home style with an atmosphere reminiscent of the French countryside. Each of the six quirky dining rooms is filled with unique furnishings, fabrics, and table settings. Many of the tables are one-of-a-kind pieces hand painted and/or stenciled by the partners, and each table has its own dinnerware, flatware, hand-painted glassware, and place mats. Because the restaurant has so many small rooms, there are innumerable private corners where lovers can devote their attentions to each other in near privacy. On a particularly nice day, you may prefer to dine on the deck. A cozy library with a comfy sofa and chairs beckons smokers, before- or after-dinner drinkers, or those intent on conversation. Look for additional whimsical touches, such as the little boy's and little girl's outfits tacked to the doors to identify the men's and ladies' rooms and the check presented in a gift box.

All three owners have devoted their attention to creating a distinctive menu and milieu where diners can enjoy a relaxing, indulgent meal. Chef Jean-Marc Carelle has worked in Paris and the West Indies as well as on the *Orient Express* and the *QEII*. For brunch, he creates an array of enticing items, including *croquant de chèvre chaud* (hot goat cheese in a crisp shell on a bed of salad with walnut dressing), *oeuf cocotte du marché* (poached eggs with fresh cream and vegetables), *mousseline de poisson sauce homard* (fish mousse with lobster or bell pepper sauce), or classic *crêpes*. Among the sumptuous desserts, you might want to try the made-to-order *soufflé au chocolat* or *soufflé au Grand Marnier*. As you'd expect, the wine list emphasizes French wines, but also features selections from Chile, Spain, and the United States.

Unfortunately, it's time to end your world tour and return to your own time and place with a trunk full of dreams that you can cherish until your next visit to Atlanta's international community.

FOR MORE ROMANCE

If you're still hungry for the romance of international travel, head for Buford Highway north of Clairmont Road where Latin America and the Pacific Rim beckon you. In recent years, scores of immigrants from south of the border and from Far Eastern countries such as Japan, China, Korea, Viet Nam, Thailand, and Indonesia have settled along the Buford Highway corridor. Such a large concentration of like-minded new residents resulted in a boom of exotic restaurants, grocery stores, and shops catering to them, so spend time poking into these pleasant little cubby holes. In addition to exotic foodstuffs to take home, you might find some exceptional bargains in jewelry. If you can stay over another day, the **Atlanta International Museum of Arts and Design** (Peachtree Center, Marquis Two, 285 Peachtree Center Avenue; 404–688–2467; $3), the city's only exclusively international museum, seeks through changing exhibits to promote international understanding.

RECOMMENDED ANNUAL EVENTS

January

Atlanta Boat Show
Atlanta Garden and Patio Show
Chick-fil-A Peach Bowl and Parade
Martin Luther King Jr. Week
Super Bowl (2000)

February

Love Among the Orchids, Atlanta Botanical
  Garden
Love in the Zoo
Southeastern Flower Show

March

Atlanta Home Show
High Museum of Art Wine Auction
St. Patrick's Day Parade, Buckhead

April

Atlanta Dogwood Festival, Piedmont Park
Atlanta Steeplechase
Atlanta Symphony Associates Decorators' Show
  House

Earthweek, Zoo Atlanta
Inman Park Spring Festival and Tour of Homes
Sweet Auburn Festival, Auburn Avenue
Taste of Marietta

May

Atlanta Caribbean Folk Festival
Atlanta Jazz Festival
Black Expo Atlanta
Decatur Arts Festival and Tour of Homes
Gardens for Connoisseurs Tour
Music Midtown Festival
Springfest and Taste of the South, Stone
  Mountain Park

June

Arts Festival of Atlanta, Centennial Olympic
  Park
Virginia-Highland Summer Fest
Willie B.'s Birthday, Zoo Atlanta

July

Fantastic Fourth Celebration, Stone Mountain
  Park

Peachtree 10K Road Race

Salute 2 America Independence Day Parade

Star-Spangled Night Independence Day
Celebration, Lenox Square

August

Montreaux Atlanta Music Festival, Piedmont
Park

Street of Dreams Festival

September

Atlanta Greek Festival

Sweet Auburn Heritage Festival

Yellow Daisy Arts and Crafts Fair, Stone
Mountain Park

October

Fall Georgia Renaissance Festival

Great Halloween Caper

Scottish Festival and Highland Games, Stone
Mountain Park

Tour of Southern Ghosts, Stone Mountain Park

November

Lighting of Rich's Great Tree, Underground
Atlanta

December

Atlanta Ballet's *Nutcracker*

Candlelight Tours, Atlanta History Center

Christmas at Callanwolde

Christmas in Roswell Historic District

Country Christmas, Atlanta Botanical Garden

Egleston Children's Christmas Parade

Festival of Lights, adjacent to Centennial
Olympic Park

Festival of Lights, Georgia World Congress
Center

First Night Atlanta, Midtown

Holidays Around the World, Zoo Atlanta

Marietta Pilgrimage Home Tour

New Year's Eve Peach Drop, Underground
Atlanta

Multimonth Activities

Atlanta Ballet Spring Season (March–May)

Six Flags Over Georgia (March–August)

Atlanta Braves Baseball (April–October)

Atlanta Opera (April–June,
September–October)

Spring Georgia Renaissance Festival
(April–June)

Lasershow, Stone Mountain Park
(May–September)

Fox Summer Film Festival (June–August)

Georgia Shakespeare Festival (June–August)

Atlanta Falcons Football (August–December)

Atlanta Symphony Orchestra (September–May)

Alliance Theater Co. Season (September–May)

Atlanta Hawks Basketball (October–March)

Holiday Celebration, Stone Mountain Park
(November–December)

Legacy of Lights Celebration, Georgia
International Horse Park
(November–December)

Lighting of the Chateau, Chateau Elan
(November–December)

Magical Nights of Lights, Lake Lanier Islands
(November–December)

GENERAL INDEX

ROMANTIC RESTAURANTS

All restaurants are listed; particularly romantic ones are starred (keeping in mind that "romantic" is in the eye of the beholder).

American

★Alon's on the Terrace ($$$), 659 Peachtree Street, 9

★Beehive Restaurant ($$$), 1090 Alpharetta Highway, 181

Breezes ($$$), PineIsle Resort, Lake Lanier Islands, 215

Buckhead Bread Company and Corner Cafe ($$), 3070 Piedmont Road, 110

Buckhead Diner ($$$$), 3073 Piedmont Road, 68

Cafe at the Ritz-Carlton Buckhead, The ($$$$), 3434 Peachtree Road, 106

Cafe at the Ritz-Carlton Downtown, The ($$$), 210 Peachtree Street N.W., 33

★Canoe ($$$), 4199 Paces Ferry Road, 48

Churchill Grounds ($$), 660 Peachtree Street N.E., 67

Copenhill Cafe ($), One Copenhill, 441 Freedom Parkway, 34

Corner Bakery ($), Fourteenth and Peachtree Streets, 96

Crocker's Place ($$$), 3050 Big Creek Road, Buford, 211

Dave & Buster's ($$$), 2215 Dave and Buster's Drive, 246

Depot Chicken Restaurant ($), Stone Mountain Park, U.S. 78, Stone Mountain, 201

★Einstein's ($$$), 1077 Juniper Street N.E., 161

Euclid Avenue Yacht Club ($$), 1136 Euclid Avenue N.E., 116

Flying Biscuit Cafe ($-$$), 1655 McLendon Avenue N.E., 222–23

Gondola Grill ($), Stone Mountain Park, U.S. 78, Stone Mountain, 204

Gotham City Eatery ($), 7561 Six Flags Parkway Georgia, 228

Hamilton's ($$$), 500 Powder Springs Street, Marietta, 169

Hard Rock Cafe ($$-$$$), 215 Peachtree Street, 222

Hemingway's ($$-$$$), 29 West Park Square, Marietta, 172

Huey's ($$), 1816 Peachtree Road, 45

★Mansion, The ($$$$), 179 Ponce de Leon Avenue, 36

Max Lager's American Grill Brewery ($$$), 320 Peachtree Street, 24

Mittie's Tea Room ($$), 952 Canton Street, Roswell, 181, 244

Munchies Beach Cafe ($), Lake Lanier Islands, 214

★Murphy's ($$$), 997 Virginia Avenue, 124

Papa Coots Beachside Cafe ($), Lake Lanier Islands, 214

★Pleasant Peasant Restaurant ($$$), 555 Peachtree Street N.E., 34

★Public House ($$$), 605 South Atlanta Street, Roswell, 178

Red Lantern Inn ($$), Brown's Bridge Road, Buford, 212

★Shillings on the Square ($$$-$$$$), 19 North Park Square, Marietta, 170

★Sun Dial ($$$$), 210 Peachtree Street N.W., 32

Tasty Town Grill ($$), 67 Forsyth Street, 227

Varsity, The ($), 61 North Avenue at Spring Street, 224

Vortex Bar and Grill ($-$$), 438 Moreland Avenue, 54, 115

ROMANTIC LODGINGS

NIGHTLIFE

ABOUT THE AUTHORS

Carol and Dan Thalimer have lived in Atlanta for more than twenty years, during which time they have taken every possible opportunity to explore the city's many romantic places. Formerly the travel editors for Atlanta's *Daily News,* they have written many articles on things to do in and around Atlanta, including a weekly "Lost Weekend" column. They are also the authors of Globe Pequot's *Quick Escapes from Atlanta* and *Fun with the Family in Georgia* and several other guidebooks about the South.